MORE THAN MERELY EYES CAN SEE

Susan Carey

LAUREN SIMONE

PUBLISHING

GET PUBLISHED TODAY!   EST. 2017

Misty Blue
Words and Music by Bob Montgomery
Copyright © 1965 Dimensional Songs of The Knoll and Talmont Music
Copyright Renewed
All Rights Administered Worldwide by Reservoir Media Management, Inc.
Used by Permission. All Rights Reserved.
Reprinted by Permission of Hal Leonard LLC

The Hill We Climb: An Inaugural Poem for the Country
Poem by Amanda Gorman
Copyright 2021 Viking
Used by Permission. All Rights Reserved.

The Scripture quotations contained herein are from the New Revised Standard Version Bible, copyright 1989, by the Division of Christian Education of the National Council of Churches of Christ in the USA. Used by permission. All rights reserved.

Library of Congress Cataloging-in-Publication Data
Carey, Susan L.
More Than Merely Eyes Can See
p. cm.
ISBN 978-1-948071-76-5 (paperback)
I. Title.
1. Community Service 2. Hartford History 3. Hospitality
2024907033

Cover and book design by Aadil Khan
Photographs by Bernie Michel
Edited by Leslie R. Kriesel
Proofreading by Tamira Butler-Likely, PhD

www.laurensimonepubs.com
info@laurensimonepubs.com
@laurensimonepubs

Special Praise for

More Than Merely Eyes Can See

Written with the belief that listening to the stories of others is a powerful tool for building empathy... Susan Carey's humane community memoir *More Than Merely Eyes Can See* celebrates the power of shared storytelling...Arguing that storytelling and listening are acts of discovery and empathy, this is a text that celebrates individuality and that eschews labels and judgment...[H]istorical data and references to the work of experts are used to reinforce such notions of empathy building as crucial to healthy communities...A hope-filled, community-centered memoir that suggests that authentic service to others can have a positive impact on one's own relationships, More Than Merely Eyes Can See allows one church's dinner guests to tell their stories in their own voices.

- Clarion Foreward Reviews (May 16, 2024), starred review

More Than Merely Eyes Can See portrays the stark, real, and often heartbreaking humanity present in the unseen lives around us, lives that are small yet somehow bigger than we can ever imagine. The individual portraits presented show the world as it is and lives that are undeniably beautiful, frustrating, tragic, and, at times, funny. They open the mind and the heart to the simple idea that a meal, a conversation, and a radical acceptance of a human being, with all their individual strengths and flaws, can build community in ways more powerful than politics or slogans. *More Than Merely Eyes Can See,* and the individual stories therein, is a reminder that fiction is often a poor facsimile for real life.

-Marc Fitch, novelist and investigative reporter for CT Inside Investigator

Table of Contents

Author's Note

Diners and Their Stories

Most of these stories are based on interviews that were conducted between 2019 and 2022, and were preceded by casual conversations that stretch back to 2011. A few stories were composed after a diner had passed or moved away. Occasionally I reached out to diners' friends and families, looked up newspaper articles, or referenced other printed materials. Some diners responded to questions by text messaging and email. Some dialogue has been edited for the sake of clarity and readability.

During interviews, I took notes but did not record our conversations. Storytelling requires trust, and the process of compiling these stories depended on it. I describe the collaborative effort between the storytellers and me more fully in chapter 4.

I use the words "neighbor" and "neighborhood" loosely. Most diners live within walking distance of Grace Lutheran Church. Some live in the Asylum Hill neighborhood where Grace is located or in nearby neighborhoods, and some live in the suburbs. All are embraced as neighbors, and everyone attending the Friday Gathering is referred to as a diner, including the volunteers.

Some names have been changed to protect privacy.

Colorblind or Black and White

We know from science that identifying people by race is artificial and contrived. It is debatable whether we can be colorblind toward one another because declaring ourselves colorblind reinforces racism by silencing its effects. I aspire to live in a society where all people are treated equitably without regard to race, but we aren't there yet.

I deferred to the authors and antiracist activists Ibram X. Kendi and Drew G.

I. Hart about whether to mention a diner's racial identity. Kendi makes the point that race influences not only how we see others but also how we see ourselves. He says it's ironic that to be antiracist, we must call out racial identity in order to identify privileges and grievances, writing that "Our societies, our policies, our ideas, our histories, and our cultures have rendered race and made it matter."[1]

Hart points to the discomfort that many white people experience when discussing racism, writing, "Colorblind rhetoric prevents people from evaluating the majority of their social relationships, the places they feel they either belong or do not belong, and the kinds of cultural, intellectual, and artistic influences that are worthy of engagement."[2]

When I asked diners to describe their identities, most simply answered Black or white. A few objected, and their perspectives on race are included in their stories. I'm grateful to them because their thoughts personalize how painful it is to racialize identity.

Each neighbor is introduced with a brief visual description, the year of their birth, their gender expression, and their racial or ethnic identity. By standardizing this description, I aimed to satisfy our natural curiosity about visual appearances and confront some of the stereotyped assumptions.

Chapter Photographs

The portraits presented in each chapter were chosen at random and do not correlate with the people whose stories are told.

Diners by Chapter

The chapters below identify where each diner's primary story is told. The diner may play a part in another diner's story, so this reference to their primary narrative may be helpful.

Chapter 2   Darrell and Nancy, Lenny

Chapter 3   Louisa, Hilda, Bernie

Chapter 4   Lynn, Tommy

Chapter 5   Harry, Robert, Sonny, Roy, Edison

Chapter 6   James, Vicki, Albert

Chapter 7   Addison, Janet

Chapter 8   Lee, Setsuko

Chapter 9   Barb, Eddie, Papa Charles, Lily, Paul, Claudia

Chapter 10   Lamont, Arnell, Woody, Richie, Lorraine

Chapter 11   Todd, Alfred, Kenny, Nicky

Chapter 12   Gladys, Louis, Cheryl and Sharon

Chapter 13   Samantha

Chapter 14   Carmelita

Chapter 15   Rich

Chapter 16   Edith

Introduction

There is no greater agony than bearing an untold story inside you.

— Zora Neale Hurston, *Dust Tracks on a Road*

Most Fridays since 2013, Harry, a sixty-five-year-old white man, walks from his apartment to the Friday Gathering—about three-quarters of a mile—to where Grace Lutheran Church serves a free weekly supper. He lives in Hartford, Connecticut, a midsize city, and his apartment is located on a large, beautifully landscaped campus that serves adults with disabilities and seniors.

The complex is gated and set back from the busy street that serves as a major artery to the nearby interstate highway, whose entrance and exit ramps border one side of Harry's complex. The street is lined with a mix of nineteenth-century Queen Anne-style homes and mid-twentieth century three-story brick apartment buildings, symbolic of the changes this section of the city has experienced over the last century. A few of the houses are run-down and need new roofs and paint. Some operate small bodegas on the ground floor and Harry worries because a few of them are boarded up. Mature trees, towering over the roofs, line the street and are evidence, too, of the age of the neighborhood.

In the summertime, the leafy canopy shades the sidewalk. It offers relief from the heat for pedestrians and residents escaping their hot apartments. As Harry heads to Grace, he passes people who linger along the way. They don't acknowledge him and he keeps his head down. At the corner, Harry knows a couple who live by the Subway sandwich shop. If he notices them, he says hello and continues on his way. Most people keep to themselves. They are city people, dressed for the weather and for being on foot. Many are Black or Latino, a reflection of the city's demographics.

Harry turns the corner onto Farmington Avenue, a busy east–west corridor that connects Hartford with the suburbs. At this corner, both sides of the street are filled with fast-food and small restaurants, a gas station, and strip malls. In 2016, a streetscape improvement project added decorative lighting, new brick sidewalks, traffic islands, and landscaping. Bus stops are located here and they draw tenants from apartment buildings that are tucked away on adjacent side streets. The small businesses on Farmington Avenue give way to a row of three-story brick buildings. A few blocks later, Harry passes a sprawling lawn that was once Mark Twain's home, now converted into a museum. On Tuesdays in the summertime, a farmer's market sets up near the large parking lot that's reserved for museum tourists.

At this hour of the afternoon when Harry walks to Grace, suburban commuters—employees of the nearby insurance companies and medical center—fill the streets, their cars jockeying for position with city buses as they head for the highway and out of Hartford. During the week, their morning influx and afternoon exodus ebb and flow like the tide. City people fill the sidewalks and buses while suburban commuters, safe inside their automobiles, fill the streets.

Although they are in close proximity to each other, the gulf that separates city and suburban residents is vast. City people are mostly Black and brown while suburbanites are predominately white. Hartford is one of the poorest cities in the state whereas the surrounding communities are well off.[3] The absence of meaningful relationships between these neighbors allows negative stereotypes to persist about people of color and people who are poor. Many city people absorb these characterizations of themselves too. The separation and isolation between them fuel mistrust and disrupt the capacity to form healthy social bonds.

Meaningful social connections are essential to our survival and ability to thrive. They are the remedy for loneliness, which has been called an epidemic that reaches across all levels of society: rich and poor; young and old; and rural and urban. Jacob Sweet, an associate editor for *Harvard Magazine,* wrote about the findings of social psychologists who study loneliness, stating that it is defined "as the gap between the social connections you would like to have and those you feel you experience."[4]

John Cacioppo, founder of the Center for Cognitive and Social Neuroscience at the University of Chicago, studied the impact that loneliness takes on health and well-being, writing that it interferes with our ability to cope with even the normal frustrations of day-to-day living.[5] His research showed that "Loneliness not only alters behavior but shows up in measurements of stress hormones, immune function, and cardiovascular function ... that may be hastening millions of people to an early grave."[6]

Expanding on these findings, Vivek Murthy, MD, the nineteenth US Surgeon General, said that loneliness magnifies the pain of dealing with addiction, violence, anxiety, and depression. Murthy focused on the benefit of social connections, stating: "While loneliness has the potential to kill, connection has even more potential to heal. ... It's in our relationships that we find the emotional sustenance and power we need in order to thrive."[7]

When I interviewed Harry and asked him why he returned every week to the Friday Gathering, he said he comes because Pastor Eva invited him. Even though she has been gone many years, the power of that first invitation hasn't faded. Harry said that at the Friday Gathering, he doesn't feel as lonely as before he arrived. The Friday Gathering is where people say his name when they greet him, acknowledge his contributions, and understand his desire to matter to the friends he made there. Harry said that he often feels invisible and lost, even though he's lived in Hartford and in the same apartment complex for decades. The isolation is so intense, that Harry blurted out, "When people say hi to me, I know I'm alive."

Recognizing our own need for meaningful connections makes it possible for us to imagine others' need for it. Dr. Murthy stated: "We all have a deep and abiding need to be seen for who we are—as fully dimensional, complex, and vulnerable human beings. We all need to know that we matter and that we are loved."[8]

In 2010, the congregation of Grace Lutheran Church was facing some of the same obstacles as Harry. Although it is located in the heart of the city, Grace was isolated from the neighborhood. Most members lived in the suburbs and commuted into Hartford for worship services. Their relationships with neighbors had dissolved a decade earlier. Neighbors who cut through the church parking lot and members of the congregation were strangers to each other. The congregation's isolation had allowed an incomplete image to form of the people they saw on the street.

The members of Grace found themselves struggling to be relevant. They asked, "Why has God put us in this place? If Grace ceased to exist, would anyone care or notice?" The congregation confronted the gap between the commandment to love thy neighbor and how they practiced it. They resolved to rebuild relationships and integrate back into the neighborhood. They started with hosting the Friday Gathering, a free community supper.

To the casual observer, the Friday Gathering may look like a soup kitchen. But from the beginning, the Gathering was about building community, and at the heart of community is relationships. Many organizations, not just churches, want to be perceived as warm and welcoming. But the hospitality we are used to practicing is rooted in our culture with prescribed roles for the host and guest. It creates a hierarchical structure that can be a barrier to building deep, enriching relationships. This book takes a fresh look at what it means to practice hospitality and the competing interests of hosts and guests.

For faith-based people, we are called to love our neighbor and that begins with knowing them. We may think we know a person because we know their family, grew up with them, work with them, or know the neighborhood where they live. Yet, to genuinely know our neighbor, we must become listeners to their stories and comprehend the conditions that bear down upon them.

We develop our sense of self—and make sense of who we are and our place in the world—through the stories we tell. Our stories convey how we connect the seemingly random events of our lives and derive meaning from them. They are the vehicle for sharing our experiences and how we learn to understand one another. Stories make it possible to imagine what it is like to walk in another's shoes.

When I moved to Hartford, I was ready to embrace city living. My suburban friends urged me to be careful, to not walk alone, and to carry protection. They were projecting what they thought they knew about the people who live in Hartford. I was eager to experience different cultures and make new friends, and instead, grounded my perceptions in what I experienced firsthand.

I joined Grace and was part of the committee that formed the Friday Gathering. For thirteen years, between seventy-five and a hundred of us have gathered around the dinner table every week to share life. We became the keepers of each other's stories. More than forty neighbors agreed to share their stories in this book and trusted me to tell them, that we might know each other more fully.

The people I met, many who are poor or people of color, are funny, hardworking, intelligent, and loving. Their stories push back at the stereotypes and stigma that sensationalize the headlines and keep us from widening our circle of relationships. Census data and crime statistics frame a single story about the people who live here, which includes me. We need more stories, more than data, to know our neighbor. Even the wealthiest communities have poor and disenfranchised members, and if we only pay attention to the stereotypes, we all suffer. It is in affirming our differences and honoring our humanity that we become whole. This is how even the wealthiest, most educated, and most socially connected of us find belonging, in relationships where we can be our whole selves. Belonging is the antidote to loneliness and our souls long for it.

Although it is Grace Lutheran Church that hosts the Friday Gathering, this book is intended for a wide audience, including people who do not identify with a faith tradition. The lessons we learned about offering hospitality are useful for any group that strives to be warm and welcoming. Many for-profit and nonprofit organizations claim that their mission is to build community, and this book centers that discussion on relationships. Many folks want to be involved in charitable work; they want to give back and create a more equitable society. This book examines how charity maintains the status quo and it considers who bears the cost of giving.

Know thy neighbor begins with know thyself, and that is where this story begins. Understand the conditions that bear down on the congregation and the neighborhood. Out of the desire to know one another—to see more than what merely eyes can see—we found community and belonging to one another.

1

What They Thought They Knew

We have opportunities to be in relationship with one another—people who wouldn't ever otherwise encounter each other, or wouldn't engage a conversation. Our stories can be a really powerful way in, in a way that argument isn't.

— Lennon Flowers, in "Cultivating Brave Space," On Being with Krista Tippett, original broadcast October 17, 2019, onbeing.org

On Christmas Eve 2010, Grace Lutheran Church, a Christian congregation in Hartford, Connecticut, opened its doors just after sunset. It was Friday, and the usual bottleneck of commuters exiting the capital city was over early. The buses were running but empty, and most of the small shops closed early. It was hardly 5 p.m. and already the city was dark and unusually quiet.

The lights were on at Grace, where the neighborhood was invited to dinner. The congregation had never hosted a Christmas Eve dinner, at least not that anyone remembered. I wondered: *Who would come? Would anyone come?* The relationships that once existed between Grace and its neighbors had dissolved in recent years. The most tangible connection was the church parking lot, where neighbors took a shortcut as they walked back and forth between home, the business district on Farmington Avenue, and the soup kitchen at Immanuel Congregational Church at the end of the block.

Grace has a long history in Hartford, stretching back to 1894 when German immigrants came together to establish a Lutheran congregation. A culture of creating a home for immigrants took hold and has been expressed anew with each generation. Following World War II, Grace welcomed refugees from Estonia, Latvia, Yugoslavia, Germany, and Austria. The next generation cared for refugees from Vietnam and Laos. More recently, Grace embraced refugees from Myanmar and their desire to form a new congregation. They as well as the First Calvary Baptist Church hold weekly services at Grace. Grace is a "home away from home" for Christians studying nearby at the Hartford International University for Religion and Peace (formerly Hartford Seminary). Students from Ethiopia, Tanzania, Botswana, Zimbabwe, Côte d'Ivoire, Rwanda, Ghana, Indonesia, and Germany have worshipped at Grace. Donated in the 1960s, two ornamental cherry trees adorn the front lawn: one honors the congregation's relationship with a student from Japan, and the other recognizes Grace's support of the Japan International Christian University. Folks from Jamaica, other Caribbean nations, Guyana, and India have made Grace their home.[9]

After relocating to Hartford in 2006, I started searching for a church home that was rooted in the community and reflected Hartford's makeup. At Grace, I found that diversity was manifested in more ways than just ethnically. The congregation was led by a woman pastor, parishioners using braille hymnals sat up front, adults with intellectual disabilities sat up front too, and members were fluent in German, French, and Spanish. I noticed that while the pews were lightly filled on Sunday mornings, the liveliness of the congregation filled the space. Like good Lutherans, they sang their hearts out. I had grown up in the Lutheran church, and Grace's friendliness, the service's familiarity, and the mix of people won me over.

When I joined Grace, the congregation was in the process of reexamining its calling. Like at many mainstream churches, the congregation was aging and attendance had been receding for years.[10] Some members had grown up at Grace and remembered when the pews were filled for two Sunday services. They fondly recalled the days of Sunday school and summer youth programs, and they missed the youths' energy and vitality. By 2008, weekly attendance hovered around forty.

I eventually learned that most members of Grace lived in the suburbs and commuted into the city to attend church, including members who were African American or had immigrated from the Caribbean, Africa, or Europe. Like me, a few white middle-class members lived in Hartford but not in the immediate neighborhood. One young Black woman, who grew up in Africa, lived a few blocks away and walked to church with her young children.

Although Grace had a tradition of embracing immigrants from around the globe, the congregation had not treasured as fully the diverse peoples living in the vicinity of the church. Grace was disconnected from the neighborhood, including the families whose children attended the elementary school down the street. We asked ourselves, "If Grace ceased to exist, would anyone in the neighborhood care or notice?" The congregation confronted the idea that Grace likely mattered most to those who did not live nearby. Grace was not the neighborhood church I had first imagined it to be.

A small group of us formed a "listening" committee to begin exploring how Grace could rebuild relationships with the neighborhood. We started by listening to and surveying the congregation. I called church members and asked: "What do you like about the community? What concerns do you have for the community? How do those concerns affect you personally?" I did not define "community" and let members interpret it for themselves. I was still relatively new to the area and eager to learn about Hartford from people who had roots here. I recorded their responses in a spreadsheet.

Members' statements about what they appreciated were straightforward and similar.[11] They enjoyed Hartford's cultural riches, including "the opportunities for entertainment, theater, music, and art," and how these resources made their lives "fuller and vibrant." They valued that the city was ethnically diverse, "a wonderful cross section of the world." They appreciated the access to hospitals and social services and that the church "is located near one of the best bus routes in the city." One member said that Grace has a good reputation and spoke about the tradition of inviting neighbors to breakfast on Easter Sunday. However, they said neighbors were not invited "last year," and no one from the community came.

Members were more specific about their concerns for the city, focusing on the poverty and violence they heard about in the news or attributed to people they observed on the street. It impacted them personally because they did not know how to respond to problems that seemed overwhelming, and it made them afraid. One woman said, "Crime scares me. During church services, I hear sirens and think there must be a crime happening." Her thoughts surprised me because the St. Francis Medical Center is two blocks from the church, and ambulances arrive there from all over the region.

Another person said, "You see people pushing carts, but you don't know what's in them." And another, "The people who live in the neighborhood are working class and not church literate. They are not churchgoing. It's depressing. We've had bad experiences with this neighborhood. When they want money, they come." A different member said, "This is where they kill people. It's beyond scary." Another member seemed to link the economic downturn and drug addiction, saying, "I noticed in recent years that more people are approaching me for money. They are drug addicts. It's happening more now with more people out of work." Another said, "Many of us come from the suburbs," adding that "the problems of this neighborhood are not my problems."

Some expressed anxiety about whether Grace could survive. One member said, "I'm concerned that we could lose our spirit and faith." Another remarked, "Blight has driven people from the community. People who might have been interested in Grace have moved away." Another person echoed the sentiment, adding, "All the troubles that go with a city—homelessness, violence—can affect which church people will want to join." While one person lamented the lack of response to a church brochure mailed to neighborhood residents, another commented that not enough effort had been put into engaging with people living in the nearby apartment, condominium, and senior housing buildings.

Others expressed compassion, a desire to help families, to "get people off the streets when it's cold," and a general concern for the welfare of residents. One member said, "Although Grace used to be much more connected to the neighborhood, we have gotten away from it." Another member said, "I don't feel connected to the community, and I don't know much about it. It's as if Grace is an island."

The congregation's perceptions aligned with those expressed by suburban dwellers who, in the absence of personal relationships with city residents, relied on stereotypes about the people they supposed live in Hartford. Pulitzer Prize–winning journalist and author Susan Campbell noticed the disparity too. In the introduction to her book about Hartford's Frog Hollow neighborhood, published in 2019, she said:

> But Hartford was so much more than gangs and crime and troubled schools. I know because I was there, and when I was occasionally asked to give speeches in suburban libraries or small-

town schools, invariably someone would raise a hand to ask if I went into the big, scary city every day. … The suburbanites whose main contact with Hartford was to drive in for a concert or play, or to commute to work and then rush home at 5 p.m., were only responding to *what they thought they knew* [emphasis added]. Too often, stories of the schools doing incredible things with limited resources or of trailblazers making the capital city awesome got lost, along with the history and context that might have helped explain Hartford.[12]

I presented the responses from the survey to the congregation at a meeting one Sunday. We talked about the disparity within the community and between the community and the congregation and how that affected members' ability to connect with people in the neighborhood. As members revisited their longing to care for the children and families who lived nearby, we confronted how fear interfered with our self-image of being warm, welcoming, inclusive, and in the most basic of biblical callings, a good neighbor.

That meeting was a reckoning for us: taking stock of the moment, acknowledging the enormity of the impact of poverty, and conceding how isolated Grace had become. All of this was discussed in the context of what it means to be "the people of God." When the conversation shifted to answering, "Why has God put us in this place?" I sensed a softening in outlook; members were excited and optimistic about Grace's future in the community. They expressed a new commitment to being a good neighbor.

All of this mattered deeply to me. I sympathized with elderly members who were facing their own physical frailties. At the same time, I was disappointed. I chided myself for presuming that I had found an inner-city church that was integrated. Although the congregation was diverse in several ways, in economic and geographical terms Grace manifested a white, suburban, middle-class temperament.

Over the next year, the listening committee met regularly and reflected on what we were learning. I represented Grace at monthly neighborhood meetings, got involved with the local education committee, began meeting neighbors, and absorbed details about the community's resources and the struggles people faced. These were worthwhile efforts but nevertheless missed the mark. At street level, we were still mostly strangers in the neighborhood.

After months of soul searching, Gail, a member of the listening committee, announced that she would organize a dinner on Christmas Eve and invite the neighborhood. Christmas Eve—when messages about being "home" for the holidays are heavy laden and imagery about "no room at the inn" is not a romantic story but a modern-day reality for many—was an occasion to throw open the doors and gather church members and the community around the dinner table. Christmas—when coffee shops and the library are closed and city bus routes shrink for a holiday schedule—leaves those who are poor, unsheltered, alone, or struggling in other ways to fend for themselves. Even in a small congregation like Grace, some members would pass the holiday alone. Sharing a meal offered common ground for gathering together.

Throughout December, flyers announcing the dinner were printed and handed out on street corners, posted at the nearby soup kitchen, shared with local churches, and announced at the monthly neighborhood meeting. On Christmas Eve, turkey, roasted potatoes, glazed carrots, macaroni and cheese, and other side dishes were prepared for hundreds of people. Church members brought homemade cookies and cakes. Gail and other church members decorated the tables with faux tea candles and holiday centerpieces. Two artificial trees glowed with holiday lights and Christmas ornaments. Tables were set up with activities for children. A family made Christmas cards and gave them out as guests arrived. One member played the violin, another played the guitar, and people joined in singing familiar Christmas carols. The atmosphere was mixed with anticipation and good cheer.

We met people at the door and showed them the way to the dining hall. "Welcome! We're so glad you came!" I introduced myself and wished I were more confident about initiating a conversation. *Would my efforts at being friendly seem arrogant or intrusive?* As one of the hosts, I felt responsible for putting people at ease.

Many of us volunteers had some experience working at soup kitchens, and we wanted this dinner to be different. Tables overflowing with food separate the servers and the served. Serving tables camouflage the power differential between those with abundance who are giving and those with needs who are receiving. The table separates those who have a service to perform and therefore a purpose and those whose purpose is to be grateful. It separates those who have a key and access to the building from those who line up and wait for the doors to open. On Christmas Eve, church members—the hosts—were encouraged to take turns serving and welcoming neighbors, and to also spend time on the *other* side of the table, having servers fill their plates and sitting with guests to share the meal and conversation. Some members ate with neighbors, while others shared the meal with their families and church friends.

At the dinner table, the host and guest were initially strangers to each other. But in the act of sharing the meal, they were also becoming acquainted. Offering simple hospitality seemed straightforward: Greet all who come, provide a delicious meal and homemade pastries, and celebrate the season. Later, offering unconditional hospitality would be more difficult and have to begin with surrendering presumptions and judgments about the neighborhood and the people who live there.

The front page of the Christmas morning *Hartford Courant* newspaper featured a story about the dinner. They reported that food was prepared for 400 people, although church records noted that about 150 attended. "About two-thirds were not members of the church," the *Courant* said. One man told the reporter he had planned to spend the evening at an all-night

Alcoholics Anonymous meeting, adding, "Christmas is an emotionally difficult time … I think it is for a lot of people." He continued, "When the whole world is telling you it should be the most wonderful time of the year, but you're not feeling joyful, it makes you feel twice as bad." Another said that if his friend hadn't invited him to the dinner, he would have spent the night alone. One man sat with friends from the neighborhood and said he liked the Christmas carols, and the home cooking was so good it was like "fine dining." Another man said he was out of food and would not have eaten if he hadn't seen the flyer.[13]

As dinner wound down, a hush descended over the room; all the goals for the meal had been fulfilled. From upstairs, the sound of Christmas carols played on the church organ drifted down to the dining hall, replacing the hum of conversation that had filled it earlier. Members invited neighbors to come upstairs for the Christmas Eve service. Some folks bundled up and headed out into the chilly night while others hesitated and eventually chose to stay.

The experience of eating together, of being served from the same pot, knit us together in a nonhierarchical way where the status of host and guest was irrelevant and different from dinners where hosts do not share in the meal with diners. Stories of family, childhood memories, and Christmases past were retold while new stories about this Christmas were stored away for telling another day. The seeds of belonging had been planted.

The time spent together at dinner brought us physically nearer to each other. For us church members, the intimacy of the dinner table created an opening where we could begin to confront our perceptions about our neighbors, what Susan Campbell called "what they thought they knew." The authentic relationships we hoped for would depend on trust, and building trust takes time. For Grace, fitting back into the neighborhood would take time, and time would take commitment.

2

Delving into Our Neighborhood and Challenging Perceptions

Know thy neighbor as thyself. That is, comprehend his hardships and understand his position, deal with his faults as gently as with your own. Do not judge him where you do not judge yourself…this is the meaning of the word love.

—Pearl S. Buck, *Pavilion of Women*

By many measures, the Christmas Eve dinner was a success, but by itself, it could not fulfill the aspiration to "know thy neighbor." Many circumstances influence the paths our lives take, and delving into our neighborhood and the conditions that bear down on it is necessary to gain context for such understanding.

Hartford is relatively small, just eighteen square miles. For thousands of years, Native peoples inhabited this land and called it Saukiog. In the 1630s, Dutch and English colonizers arrived and named the area Hartford. Over the years, the settlers flourished. By the mid-1800s, Hartford was one of the

United States' richest cities. Here, entrepreneur Samuel Colt built his gun manufacturing facilities on the banks of the Connecticut River and traveled the globe to promote his business. More manufacturing followed: bicycles, sewing machines, typewriters, tools, screws, and machine shops to support the rapid expansion of the new industrialists. Waves of immigrants—Irish, German, Italian, Polish—supported the burgeoning manufacturing base. Many settled within walking distance of the factories, organized churches, and built new neighborhoods.[14]

Giants in the insurance industry—the Hartford Financial Services Group, Inc. and Aetna, Inc.—built their headquarters in the city's Asylum Hill neighborhood, which they have occupied for a century. Grace Lutheran Church is here, too. The neighborhood name pays tribute to The American Asylum at Hartford for the Education and Instruction of the Deaf, the first school of its kind in the United States, which opened in 1817.[15]

In 1945, when Grace purchased property on Woodland Street to construct a new building for its growing congregation—following the merger of two Lutheran churches from the Charter Oak and Frog Hollow neighborhoods—the street was an elegant thoroughfare of spacious mansions and wooded lots, emblematic of upper-middle-class society.[16] Immediately south of the church is the 1895 Louis R. Cheney House, a Georgian-style mansion. Next to it is the 1895 Theodore Lyman House, which in 1925 became the Town & County Club, Hartford's first private club for women. At the end of the block is the 1899 Immanuel Congregational Church, whose structure is an amalgam of Roman, Byzantine, and Colonial Revival styles. Across Farmington Avenue from Immanuel is the 1874 home of Samuel Clemens, known today as The Mark Twain House and Museum.[17]

On the other side of Woodland Street, across from Grace, is the 1861 Gothic Revival villa built for Charles Perkins, Mark Twain's lawyer, and a Tudor Revival–style home built in 1908 for Melancthon W. Jacobus, dean of the Hartford Seminary. Two blocks north stood Hartford's finest home, the

1871 Goodwin Castle built by Rev. Francis Goodwin for his father. Constructed of gray granite block with a tower patterned after the Law Courts in London, it rivaled the Newport, Rhode Island, "cottages" in size and elegance. However, when the pull of commerce came to this corner of Asylum Hill, the house was torn down in 1940.[18] By the time Grace's church was built, the site was the home office of Industrial Risk Insurers, with the National Fire Insurance Company across the street. Today, the site fits within the sprawling campus of Saint Francis Hospital and Medical Center, the largest Catholic hospital in New England.

The 1945 architectural plans for Grace's new building called for a gray stone Gothic edifice with a "clerestory effect" in the interior.[19] It was a grand plan that suited the character of the street. But in 1948, when projected building costs escalated, the congregation adopted a more modest plan, and the church was built in the colonial style, reminiscent of a typical New England church, the kind you see on a village green.[20] Today, with a mix of 1960s-era high-rise apartment buildings nestled between the historic homes, Grace fits modestly among its neighbors.

Following World War II, on side streets near the posh Woodland, private homes were torn down. The Asylum Hill Neighborhood Association chronicled this transformation, noting that historic single-family homes were "replaced by apartment houses constructed in a utilitarian, cost-effective way" to house employees of the growing insurance industry.[21] When those workers relocated to the suburbs, "many of the apartments aged in place and decreased in value."[22] In a report to the churches in the Asylum Hill neighborhood, reflecting on this period of transition, the Rev. Sarah McLean stated that by the end of the 1960s, "Asylum Hill was no longer fashionable or exclusive."[23]

Members of Grace felt the changes descending upon them and the neighborhood. In 1969 Grace celebrated its seventy-fifth anniversary, nearly twenty years after relocating to Asylum Hill. In commemorating the occasion, a member wrote with prescience:

> The growing jungle of apartment buildings that surround Grace
> signal one of the greatest challenges for the future that we could
> face. They speak of the radical change in family and community
> with which we must work. Neighborhood doesn't mean the same
> now as it did when the '60s started. It doesn't matter if we're
> talking about an apartment like the Woodland House or the
> newest subdivision of a Hartford suburb. The person next door
> may be your best friend or twenty years a stranger. … How to
> move across the barriers that separate us from those around us is
> THE REAL CHALLENGE of the future.[24] [emphasis in
> original]

Now, more than fifty years later, revitalization efforts led by the
Northside Institutions Neighborhood Alliance have helped preserve the
character of the neighborhood, including its remaining Victorian-era
homes.[25] Nevertheless, most neighbors live in tight quarters. The history of
Asylum Hill, as told by the neighborhood association, noted that "More
than 90 percent of the occupied housing units are in multi-unit housing
buildings, mainly one-bedroom units."[26]

Housing is one factor that impacts a community's vitality, and it explains
some of the circumstances our neighbors cope with. Comprising
approximately one square mile, Asylum Hill is one of the most densely
populated neighborhoods in Hartford: about 10,300 people per square mile
compared to 6,965 citywide.[27] Approximately 13 percent of residents own
their homes, compared to 26 percent citywide and 66 percent statewide.[28] In
2022, the neighborhood's new ten-year strategic plan documented that "In
Asylum Hill, 51% of residents are cost-burdened households, paying more
than 30% of their income toward housing costs."[29] The plan also states,
"According to the City of Hartford's 2019 Affordable Housing Study, 25%
of Asylum Hill's rentals are subsidized units."[30] The underlying economic
circumstances of so many of our neighbors limit their access to housing
that is affordable, not to mention safe and satisfying.

Other factors contributed to the divergence with suburban neighbors. Between 1960 and 1990, 70 percent of manufacturing jobs were lost.[31] New jobs were created in the insurance and financial sectors, but these were white-collar positions that many city residents were not qualified to fill.[32] The failure of the Hartford public school system reached a critical point in 1989 with the filing of the Sheff v. O'Neill lawsuit. The complaint argued that racial segregation and poverty denied Black, Latino, and white Hartford public school students an education equal to that of their suburban neighbors. Sheff v. O'Neill and subsequent rulings affirmed the inequities between Hartford and suburban schools. This dynamic persists for half of the city's school-age children.[33]

By the 1980s, Hartford's ethnic makeup had shifted radically. The city had become primarily Black in the north and Puerto Rican in the south and remains so. The Asylum Hill neighborhood straddles the northern and southern parts of the city, manifesting both cultures, along with residents from Jamaica and the West Indies, Peru, and other Latin American countries.[34] Asylum Hill is also a receiving place for refugees and has welcomed settlers from Myanmar, Somalia, Syria, and Afghanistan.[35]

The prosperity that had characterized Hartford since the late 1800s shifted, following World War II, to the suburbs. Opportunities for gainful employment, a top-notch education, and homeownership were available to suburbanites while becoming out of reach to many city residents. As Hartford and the Asylum Hill neighborhood changed with the times, the congregation at Grace endured. But there were growing pains. Members relocated to the suburbs, and their relationships with city neighbors—people they would not encounter in the suburbs—were tested. It is not documented when the congregation officially became more suburban than urban. The transformation was most likely complete by the 1980s when Rev. Sarah McLean commented: "There is tension built into churches which own buildings in complex inner city neighborhoods but whose members almost all live in the suburbs."[36]

Census data provide one measure of the contrast that persists between Grace's city neighbors and its suburban church members (see table 1).

- The Median household income in Hartford is well below the state and national averages. Income disparity exists within the city, too. The median household income in Asylum Hill is $28,498, compared to $86,343 in the adjacent "downtown" neighborhood.[37]

- Twenty-eight percent of city residents live in poverty, more than double the state and national averages.

- Forty-three percent of residents speak a language other than English at home, twice the state and national averages.

- Nearly 12 percent of Hartford residents under age sixty-five have a disability—making it difficult to bathe, dress, and run errands—higher than the state and national averages.

- Twenty-six percent of Hartford residents aged twenty-five and older did not complete high school, double the state and national averages.

Table 1: Demographic Data for Hartford, Connecticut, and the United States[38]

	Hartford	Connecticut	U.S.
Median household income in $	37,477	83,572	69,021
Poverty rate	28.4%	10.1%	11.6%
Speak a language other than English	43.5%	22.3%	21.7%
Percent under age 65 with a disability	11.9%	7.8%	8.7%
High school graduate, age 25+	73.9%	91.1%	88.9%

Source: United States Census QuickFacts: Hartford, Connecticut, United States, 2017-2021 American Community Survey

There is a prevailing stereotype, particularly in urban settings, that areas with deep poverty overlap with areas of high crime, as if poverty and crime are inextricably linked. This oversimplification stigmatizes people who are living in poverty and entire neighborhoods. Research has shown that "hot spots" as small as an intersection, a single city block, or a narrow social network account for a disproportionately high percentage of crime.[39] Yet crime data is reported by census tract, and whole communities experience the stigma. They are labeled as unsafe places to live and too dangerous to visit for sports, arts, dining, and other recreational activities.[40] *Does that make them too dangerous to visit, especially in the evening, to attend church programs?* I ask. Grace's congregation faced these perceptions when they considered their place in the neighborhood.

Perceptions matter, and how we perceive others is reflected in how we treat them. Bernard Weiner, a social psychologist at UCLA, studied how people explain the causes of poverty and how their explanations inform their responses to people who are poor. When the causes of poverty are attributed to circumstances perceived to be beyond a person's control—illness, old age, or disability—responses tend to be sympathetic and helpful. When poverty is attributed to circumstances perceived to be within a person's control, such as laziness, bad habits, or poor choices, responses tend to be reproachful and unaccommodating. The more it is believed that a person has a choice about their situation and deliberately chooses not to improve it, the more likely they are to be scorned and stigmatized.[41] It is easier to treat people with contempt when we believe the mess they are in is all their fault.

Facing the unrelenting need for basic services such as food, shelter, and safety can take a toll on both people who are chronically poor and those who care for them. Bearing the guilt of not being able to do enough can lead to self-defense tactics like feelings of contempt and indifference. Matthew Desmond, the Pulitzer Prize–winning sociologist and author of *Evicted: Poverty and Profit in the American City,* writes about a single mother struggling to provide for her children: "But when they wanted more than she could give, she had ways, some subtle, others not, of telling them they didn't deserve it."[42]

It is not just people who are living in poverty who may use contempt as a shield. Wealthier, more "comfortable" people may resort to it when they feel overwhelmed by the crushing circumstances that living in deep poverty imposes and are unable to help. Desmond imagined the internal dialogue of the mother who was poor, which could also be imagined for a volunteer who is overwhelmed. Desmond wrote, "You could only say 'I'm sorry, I can't' so many times before you began to feel worthless, edging closer to a breaking point. So you protected yourself, in a reflexive way, by finding ways to say 'No, I won't.' I cannot help you. So, I will find you unworthy of help."[43]

Census data tells one important story about a community. But it is far from the whole story, as novelist and storyteller Chimamanda Ngozi Adichie explained in a TED Talk: "The single story creates stereotypes, and the problem with stereotypes is not that they are untrue, but that they are incomplete. They make one story become the only story."[44] We must remember this when census data are used to describe the Asylum Hill neighborhood or any other population.

American culture is grounded in stories of self-reliance, dogged determination, and an attitude of pluck and rugged bootstrap perseverance when the going gets tough. The idea that hard work and sacrifice can help anyone achieve success is a cornerstone of the American Dream. This mindset also makes it easy to judge people who are poor. It presumes they didn't try hard enough or didn't care enough to improve their lives. When our relationships with a community are weak, we risk relying on negative stereotypes to inform our perceptions. The single, incomplete story restricts our capacity to engage and connect with one another.

As arrangements for the 2010 Christmas Eve dinner took shape, Darrell (a retired Lutheran pastor and participant in the listening committee) and his wife, Nancy—members of Grace who identify as Euro-American—

announced plans to organize a weekly supper and invite the neighborhood. Gathering a congregation and its neighbors around the table was how they had made friends years earlier when they moved across the country to accept a pastoral call at a church in Brooklyn, New York. There, they created a practice of sharing life together, and from it flowed relationship building and a spirit of belonging.

The weekly community supper idea allowed Grace to respond to a mix of expectations. There were members of the congregation who had lost their jobs in the 2007 recession and were still struggling. Additionally, the congregation had a history of serving the hungry. Members collected nonperishable food items and delivered them weekly to the elementary school three blocks from the church. In the early 1980s, Grace was one of the founders of the Loaves & Fishes soup kitchen that continues to serve and is housed at the Immanuel Congregational Church nearby. The sustained level of poverty in the neighborhood suggested that more food assistance would be welcomed. Dinner was a way to reach out to the congregation and the neighborhood without prioritizing one over the other.

More importantly, sharing a meal is a social experience. It creates the kind of intimacy where who you sit next to is as important as what is served. Eating together opens up space for conversation and for sharing information and stories. Sitting down together slows the pace of living; it puts a pause in the day. It lets you catch your breath. Spending time together is how we make connections and how we build trust. The meal nurtures our relationships and our bodies.[45]

When Darrell, Nancy, and the listening committee set a date for the next dinner after Christmas Eve, they committed Grace to a year of weekly Friday Gatherings. Although there was no budget and the dinners would be led by volunteers, it was the idea of showing up every week, no matter who came or did not, that was most ambitious. There would be no other goal or measure of success. The commitment made Grace accountable to the neighborhood; success would not be contingent on the neighborhood's response.

As the Friday evenings proceeded, stereotypes about the neighborhood were challenged. The vacuum created by the lack of meaningful relationships with neighbors created a space where biases and negative stereotypes could persist. Those perceptions would be tested. Deliberately choosing to withhold judgment became an act of unconditional hospitality.

***

One summer afternoon, I was walking in the park when Lenny called out to say hello. He was a tall, slender, middle-aged white man. One of the men from the Friday Gathering had introduced us a year earlier. Lenny didn't come to Grace for dinner, but when I saw him in the park, I often stopped to talk with him. When I mentioned to his friends that I had seen Lenny, they would shake their heads and comment on his alcoholism.

That summer—the first summer of the COVID-19 pandemic—I saw Lenny often. He would casually mention that he had slept in the park the night before or had spent a few nights on a friend's couch. One day, I noticed he was limping barefoot.

"Gout," Lenny said. "It's worse than usual." He didn't stop to chat and continued hobbling across the park.

A week or so later, I saw Lenny sitting with a friend. I noticed he was wearing shoes, and he said the gout had passed. Then he asked, "Can you loan me some money? If I could get to the laundromat and into clean clothes, I could get a job."

"What kind of job?" I asked.

"Painting," he answered right away. "I paint houses. Inside or out. It doesn't matter."

A few of the diners at the Friday Gathering are house painters. They hire their friends and share the work, so house painting sounded reasonable. I hemmed and hawed, changed the subject, and hung around. I thought about the people who had gone out on a limb for me and the difference it had made in my life. I could afford to take a chance on Lenny and handed him twenty dollars.

He accepted the cash, and I gave him two thumbs up.

Before I could finish saying, "You can do it," my heart sank. I saw Lenny's friend nudge him in the side. The two men looked at each other and grinned. I was embarrassed. The money was a way to clear my conscience. I felt foolish for thinking that twenty dollars could solve Lenny's homelessness. He didn't ask me for money again, and we still chatted whenever our paths crossed.

A few weeks later, Lenny was in the park talking with a city police officer. Lenny said hello and resumed grumbling to the officer: he had no money, he needed a clean shirt to get a job, he was tired of the sandwiches the soup kitchens served, and he'd had a hard time the night before because it rained. I had heard it all before. I pushed myself to listen without judging, or trying to fix his problems, or running away.

When Lenny left to meet a friend, the officer looked at me and said, "We can't all be remarkable." He paused, then continued: "We don't all have what it takes to be resilient in every situation."

Following his train of thought, I added, "We don't all start from the same place—a stable home, a good school, someone who cares about you." The officer and I went back and forth, naming the things that are easy to take for granted when you have them: a clean shirt, a hot meal, a safe place to rest. *Someone who cares about you.* These advantages help build resiliency.

***

In 1988, Rev. Sarah McLean wrote to the Asylum Hill Christian Community:

> There is tension in trying to respond to the spiritual needs of people who chronically need food, clothing, shelter, and medical care. There is tension in trying to minister to a population which includes both the victims and perpetrators of street crime, those who oppose drugs and those who are addicted to them, those who suffer from substandard housing, and those who own it. In some cases, it is clear where justice lies; in others, it is not.[46]

3

Sharing Meals, Sharing Gifts, and Sharing Stories

No one has ever become poor by giving.

—Anne Frank, *Tales from the Secret Annexe*

Although it's the rough side of Hartford that often makes the headlines, there is a soft, compassionate side, too, especially when it comes to feeding the hungry. Search the internet for soup kitchens and you'll find more than a dozen listed. Visit a soup kitchen and its diners will refer you to even more meal sites and food pantries that are spread across the city. Some serve breakfast, lunch, or both every weekday, or dinner in the late afternoon. Others operate on weekends. There are groups who serve in the parks. One site offers sandwiches and a beverage daily at 4 p.m., including holidays. Each has a distinctive neighborhood vibe. Many of their diners are regulars and have been coming for years; they know each other. The abundance of locations is a blessing for people who would have to give something up to afford the time and bus fare to travel to another part of the city. A neighborhood soup kitchen means that people do not have to go too far on foot, an advantage for those with disabilities or those who care for infants and children, and it is especially appreciated in winter.

The need for food, shelter, and other services is relentless, and no organization can satisfy all the demand. Newcomers seeking assistance arrive with regularity. Not just city residents rely on services: people who are struggling migrate to the city to find the help they need. The migration creates tension between the city and the suburbs, where the city struggles to satisfy needs and the suburbs struggle to protect their standard of living.

Since its launch in January 2011, the Friday Gathering has been a magnet for generosity, endowed with an assortment of gifts that create a shelter of hospitality in the neighborhood. Churches and nonprofits rely on volunteers to prepare and distribute meals, wash the pots and pans, set up tables and chairs, and keep the facility clean. They rely on contributions of food and cash to purchase what is not donated. A kitchen that offers one meal a week can serve hundreds of people a month.

The first Friday dinner in January 2011 was like Christmas Eve all over again. *Will anyone come? Will there be enough food?* We printed flyers, posted them at the nearby soup kitchen and laundromat, and announced it at neighborhood meetings. At first, attendance on Friday nights was slim. About a dozen people came from the neighborhood and about the same from the congregation. Grace wanted to build relationships with the neighborhood; growing them would take time.

The listening committee talked about getting out into the community. Louisa—a new member who had joined the committee—did it. She walked the neighborhood regularly, and people began to recognize her. "I remember walking down Farmington Avenue when Richie and Jesus leaned out of their second-floor apartment window, above the Green Apple convenience store," she said. "They called out my name, waved, and shouted hello to me." Louisa invited them to dinner. "You'll see me there. I'll be at the door," she said.

***

Louisa was born in 1953 in Canada and grew up there. She is a strong white woman with long hair. The seeds for doing the work of social justice were planted in her youth. "My dad had his principles. They involved co-ops and credit unions. He said that if you can get by without a job, then leave it for someone else who needs it. At that time, there were a lot of people who were unemployed. He meant, 'Don't take more than you need.' I was a Brownie Girl Scout, and I took the motto to 'lend a hand' seriously."

Louisa was thirty-one when her husband died in a workplace accident, and she was left to raise three children. With a settlement from the insurance company, she moved her family across Canada, from British Columbia to New Brunswick, and enrolled in the fine arts program at Mount Allison University. She painted, made sculptures, and worked at the university art gallery on weekends.

"I met my second husband when he came to Mount Allison as a visiting artist. He used his art to stir things up and draw attention to the causes he cared about," Louisa said. He became ill and died from AIDS in 1996.

"In the early 2000s, I became aware of an effort to award a private for-profit corporation a multimillion-dollar contract to manage the water system in Moncton, where I lived. There were a lot of problems with the water company's proposal. We discovered that in other regions where the company had done these projects, city leaders had gone to jail for accepting bribes. The promises of efficiency and cost savings hadn't panned out, and rates went up. It was especially disturbing to me that people could be cut off if they were unable to pay their water bill. I believe that access to water is a fundamental human right.

"I got involved with campaigning against the project. Catholic and Protestant Christians were united and opposed the project, too. I met Christians who were faith-driven in their support for social justice issues—matters that affected people's lives, such as caring for the planet, restorative justice, affordable housing, and homelessness. I began to explore Christianity. It took two years to stop the privatization of the water system, but we did it. And from these new relationships, I became a baptized Christian when I was fifty-three."

In 2008, a friend invited Louisa to Connecticut. She heard about Grace and the congregation's aspiration to integrate back into the neighborhood. She met Pastor Eva, a white woman, who led Grace at the time. Pastor Eva paved the way for Louisa to apply for a US visa as a religious worker and welcomed her participation in Grace's efforts to reconnect with the neighborhood.

Louisa said, "The culmination of my childhood experiences and adult social responsibilities gives me the ability to connect with the City of Hartford at its most basic, person-to-person level. I know what it is like to be an immigrant, to be transient, to be alone and overwhelmed, and to be invisible. The efforts I have helped to lead at Grace minister to Hartford's many disenfranchised residents at this basic level of need."

It mattered that Louisa ventured out to where neighbors lived. She was friendly and curious about the city. She converted the passive posting of flyers into action. She made the invitation to dinner personal. "Be my guest! I'll be happy to see you!" After Louisa crossed paths with Hilda for the third time, attendance at the Friday dinners began to grow.

***

Hilda is a community connector. She is an authority figure within her social network, offering people information about how to access resources. An endorsement from Hilda is relayed through her matrix of relationships. In early 2011, Grace was not strategic enough to search for community connectors; meeting Hilda was a gift.

Like Louisa, Hilda is an immigrant. She was born in 1947 in Guyana. Hilda and the Guyanese people are culturally affiliated with the West Indies. Like other countries in the region, Guyana was a British colony until independence was granted in 1966. Hilda identifies with the Afro-Guyanese, the descendants of enslaved people from Africa. She grew up the youngest of four daughters with an absent father and witnessed her mother's struggles.

"I observed the frivolous choices that my older sisters made," Hilda said, "and made different choices for myself. My sisters spent all their loose change on candy and other treats while I saved my money. When I was a teenager, I was able to purchase the land that my mother's house sat on." At the time, Guyanese could own their homes, but they paid rent for the land the homes sat on until the country moved toward independence and land ownership opened up. "Everyone was shocked when they broke open my savings bank and saw that I had saved enough money to purchase it. I was the only family member with savings."

Hilda pursued an education with the same determination, choosing advanced courses instead of easier, basic classes. She built a career in government service. Hilda said, "I planned it so that if I was left to fend for myself, I would be able to care for my family.

"This is my philosophy: You have to find a way to save from the little that you have. Someday, it may be beneficial to you. Save for the rainy days that are sure to come." She compared her outlook to how beavers work. "Little by little, that's how they build a dam. Every day, you carry a little bit. Eventually, you'll make a whole block."

Like Louisa, Hilda's husband died suddenly in an accident. She was widowed with two small children to raise. She worked first in the office of Guyana's president and later in the customs office. When political power shifted in the mid-1990s from the minority Afro-Guyanese to the majority Indo-Guyanese, Hilda came to New York. In 2006, she moved to Hartford. She settled in an apartment complex a few blocks from Grace. She advocated for residents' rights and pushed back against negligent landlords. She connected neighbors with the Loaves & Fishes soup kitchen, the weekly Foodshare mobile pantry, and other neighborhood resources.

***

One late-spring afternoon in 2011, when the Friday Gathering was still in its early stages, Louisa saw Hilda walking home from Loaves & Fishes. The two strong women came face to face on the sidewalk by Grace. When Louisa invited Hilda to the Friday dinner, Hilda brushed her off and said, "This is the third time you've handed me your flyer. I can get a pasta meal at any of the churches."

It was an intense exchange. Ten years later, both women still remember it and burst out laughing. Hilda challenged Louisa and it was just the opening Louisa needed.

"It's not a pasta dinner. Come and see," she said.

Bread, pasta, and rice are among the affordable staples for many kitchens and food pantries. Pasta, particularly, is a go-to. It mixes well with different foods, and many kitchens depend on it to stretch serving sizes and budgets. The trouble with staples like pasta, though, is that they dominate the diet. Instead of a side dish to accompany a meal, it becomes the main course. Hilda's protest helped us see one soup kitchen meal in the context of a steady diet of soup kitchen meals.

Louisa had another perspective on soup kitchens. "They make pasta because they don't think out of the box—pun intended. People want a little variety in what they eat. You don't serve pasta just because people are poor."

What is on the menu at Grace is an expression of hospitality. Providing nutritious and balanced meals serves a community already at risk for diabetes and other chronic diseases. Good diets help build resiliency. In addition, we honor customs and cultures when we serve food that reminds people of home. What is on the menu at Grace is as much about serving dignity as it is about serving food.

Virginia Woolf wrote, "One cannot think well, love well, sleep well, if one has not dined well."[47] At Grace, dining well means that menus emphasize protein and lots of fresh fruits and vegetables. Hartford has been labeled a "food desert" because of the scarcity of major grocery stores and residents' reliance on processed foods from small neighborhood markets. In contrast, fresh produce on the menu at Grace reflects the rhythm of the seasons and balanced nutrition that promotes well-being.

The menu aside, however, the Friday Gathering is about building community. Soup kitchens serve meals; the Friday Gathering serves relationships. "Relationships build community, and community creates belonging," Darrell—who hosted the Gatherings through 2016—said.

"Authentic community is earthy," he continued. "It's laughing and crying, singing and sharing, hugging and holding hands. It's not a chore. It's fun!"

Darrell's words, "It's not a chore," grabbed my attention. *When does offering hospitality become a chore? If I approach the Friday Gathering as a chore, how does that affect my relationships with diners and volunteers?* Having fun, I realized, put relationships first.

"This is the place where you want to belong," Darrell repeated week after week when he welcomed diners. He invited them to join the planning committee and participate in running the Friday Gathering. "Volunteer to prepare dinner. Pitch in to serve or clean up. Tell your neighbors and invite them to dinner. You are the host. This is your community. Welcome each other. Share information and help one another."

Grace is a small congregation, and members have fretted over income and expenses for years. There is a tension for spirit-led people between being fiscally responsible and having faith that all our physical needs will be met. When Darrell said, "This is the place where you want to belong," he was thinking more broadly than neighbors who needed dinner. Volunteers, food suppliers, musicians, and others also found belonging, and in the process, the Gathering's needs were met.

As the Friday Gathering moved into its sixth month, Foodshare—Hartford's regional foodbank—invited Grace to be *their* partner. Foodshare partners receive fresh fruits and vegetables at no cost. They are eligible to purchase meat, cheese, and other foods for 8.5 cents per pound. Grace can serve a healthy, plentiful dinner to a hundred people for about $10 because of food banks like Foodshare.[48]

There were additional benefits. Foodshare required staff to be trained in safe food handling, funded an outreach worker for a year, and covered the costs of a new dishwasher, freezer, and refrigerators. They expanded Grace's network of food providers to include Stop & Shop, Target, Panera Bread, Aetna's corporate kitchen, and Trader Joe's. Local farmers donate from their harvests, too.

A range of services arrived as gifts. Lucia and Pat gave free haircuts and shaves. Pastor Pam and her friend Donna offered reiki massages, a touchless form of meditative relaxation. Urban Alliance posted volunteer positions on their website. They and World Vision donated socks, t-shirts, gloves, and personal hygiene products—not just a few of each, but enough for every diner. Agencies sent representatives to help diners apply for social services. Each September, a spokesperson talked about mammogram screenings and appealed to the men to encourage their wives, mothers, sisters, and daughters to take care of themselves.

Gifts arrived from suburban congregations: two chefs, kitchen volunteers, a hairdresser, and Sylvia, who knitted scarves and went table-to-table to visit with diners. St. Matthew in Avon, Christ the King in Windsor, Our Savior's in Newington, and St. Andrew's in Ridgefield donated to Foodshare, made cash contributions, brought casseroles to assist the chefs, filled in when the host was away, and funded a new stove, ovens, and a dishwasher after the first ones wore out. Their partnerships are how they practice "we are in this together, we are one."

Gifts of music and dance appeared, too. For years, the local Christian rock band, Oasis, brought amps and guitars and played for the Gathering. The Casey Family, five sisters with perfect pitch and harmony, cut their teeth on giving live public performances at Grace. Maxine, a Hartford native and

New York City performer, played her tenor saxophone. Between Christmas and New Year's, ballerinas from a Russian troupe performed excerpts from *The Nutcracker* to a standing-room-only crowd.

A week after Hilda declared she didn't need another pasta dinner, she came to the Friday Gathering. The next week, she was back with her neighbor, Albert. When word spread that Hilda was cooking at Grace, her neighbors came, and they returned again with their friends.

Jocelyn, Gladys, Louis, and Emma joined Nancy and Louisa as chefs. Lamont and Woody took to heart the invitation to get involved. They joined the congregation and served on the church council. They volunteered to be the kitchen and dining room stewards. Lamont became the church's paid sexton when the former sexton retired. Mary proudly called herself the Salad Lady and frequently thanked Darrell for giving her a job. Jesus, Arnell, Vaughn, Victoria, Ruth, Greg, Wilson, Chris, Carlos, David, Nina, Lou, Cephus, Giovani, Laura, Luz, Quincy, Lee, Barb, Ivy, Setsuko, Naomi, Samantha, Leah, A'Niya, and Rachelle and her daughter Cassandra, became volunteers and contributed to building community.

Just as the day has a rhythm, the Friday Gathering has a rhythm, too. Before COVID-19, the doors opened at 4:30. Diners helped themselves to platters of fresh vegetables with dips, fresh fruits, cheese, crackers, olives, pickles, and other hors d'oeuvres. At one table, a foursome played dominos, at another, a game of cards. A children's corner was stocked with puzzles, building blocks, and books. Neighbors shared the latest news. Some diners sat alone, watching videos on their phone, reading, or napping.

At 5:45, the host welcomed diners, announcing, "This is not a feeding program. We are building community here." The host asked about birthdays, anniversaries, and other milestones. Diners sang "Happy Birthday" in unison and off-key. The evening's menu was announced. The chefs are known for their specialties: Louis's barbeque, Evelyn's fish, Gladys's collards, Nancy's shepherd's pie, Louisa's roasted lamb, and Hilda's curried dishes. Mouths salivated, and the crowd shouted and clapped their appreciation. The host moved around the room, recognizing and naming volunteers, musicians, barbers, and special guests. The backslapping and laughter continued when diners lined up to fill their plates, fertilizing conversations and sparking new relationships.

Volunteers come from the neighborhood and the suburbs. They are the servers and the served. They and the diners pollinate each other with their stories and their caring. They rub off on each other and carry it home. Stereotypes and stigmas are challenged.

"Our resident photographer, Bernie, is in the house," Pastor Rick calls out. "Resident photographer" expresses the pastor's esteem for the neighbor whose gift of hundreds of 8" x 10" portraits fill the walls of the dining hall. "He took all of these wonderful photos. If you want your picture added, see Bernie," Pastor Rick announces. The diners give Bernie and one another a round of applause.

***

Bernie was born in 1946 and grew up in Akron, Ohio. He's a white man, lean like a long-distance runner, and soft-spoken. In college he studied philosophy and considered joining the priesthood in the Roman Catholic Church. Instead, he settled on a career in sales. He took a position that brought him to Hartford, where he married and settled in the Asylum Hill neighborhood. In the early 1990s, at a time when people—those who could afford it—were once again leaving Hartford and moving to the suburbs, Bernie and his wife decided to stay. They bought an old Victorian house and committed to making a difference in the city.

Bernie became a part-time community organizer. He joined the Asylum Hill Problem Solving Committee. He stayed on when it evolved into the Asylum Hill Neighborhood Association, serving in leadership roles until he retired in 2022. He brought residents together with city and state officials as needed to solve neighborhood problems. They tackled broken streetlights, renovating the elementary school, relocating the public library, creating affordable housing, building an accessible children's playscape in the local park, and reducing the impact of the interstate highway that cuts through the neighborhood. Bernie's affection for the community was expressed in articles he wrote for the monthly *Asylum Hill News & Views* about the volunteer of the month, neighborhood clean-ups, block parties, pollinator gardens, farmers' markets, mural projects, community performances, and youth programs. He celebrated everyday acts of kindness and illustrated his stories with his photographs, shaping how the neighborhood functions and sees itself.

In 2013, Bernie attended his first Friday Gathering. He was curious about the program and the opportunity to get to know more of his neighbors. The next week, he returned with his camera. He took informal photos of diners at their tables. Some people were reluctant to have their picture taken, but Bernie was discreet and stayed on the edges of the room.

The diners' hesitation was not about vanity. There is a surrendering of identity when another person controls your image. Holding on to their anonymity gave diners a measure of protection in a community where trust is tentative. I had taken photographs too, trying to capture the essence of the Friday Gathering. People protested if I got too close. They turned their backs or walked away or simply said, "Don't take my picture."

Bernie experimented with camera angles and candid close-ups. At home, he selected his favorite shots, made 8" x 10" prints, and brought them back to the Gathering. He showed the prints to the diners who were featured and offered them copies to keep. Diners gathered around the photographs, pointing to the pictures and each other. They laughed and admired themselves and one another.

"As I began accumulating a small collection of interesting prints, the subjects began to enjoy and even looked forward to being surprised with what I brought in," Bernie said. Respect for Bernie and his skill with the camera increased. He proposed displaying the portraits on a dining hall wall, but the idea was turned down. It would take time for the congregation to be comfortable with the new relationships that were forming. At that time, some members said Pastor Eva cared more about the neighborhood than the members, which was not true.

Meanwhile, in a corner of the dining hall near the kitchen, 2" x 2" photographs of members of the congregation hung on the wall. The portraits were humorously called "mug shots." Members brought a coffee mug from home, wrote their name on the bottom, hung it on a hook where their picture was displayed, and used it at the fellowship hour. It was a kind of status symbol to have your mug shot displayed, signaling who was a member of Grace and who, by default, was not. By 2013, the mug shots had outlived their purpose. A new way of belonging was emerging.

Bernie continued to photograph on Friday nights. In 2014, Pastor Rick, a white man, was installed at Grace after Pastor Eva took a new pastoral call. When Bernie showed him the collection of portraits, Pastor Rick said, "These should be hanging up so everyone can see them." Pastor Rick invited Bernie to visit on Sunday mornings and photograph the congregation. Bernie came, and a new wall of portraits replaced the old mug shots. The wall knit together diners with members of the congregation.

As the display of photographs expanded, Bernie's practice shifted from casual poses to closeup portraits. From his attic he retrieved a tripod for the camera, an umbrella flash, and a canvas backdrop and set them up on Friday nights. The ability to control the lighting and background and to print in black and white added to the professional quality of the portraits. The uniformity of the images, detached from symbols of power or poverty, compelled the viewer to confront each person's humanity.

Diners' enthusiasm for seeing themselves on the walls increased. "There were, of course, the usual jokes about breaking the camera, but mostly people were pleased with the results," Bernie said. "One person was moved enough by his photo that he asked for a digital copy—and finally joined Facebook, something his friends were trying to get him to do—so he could use it as his profile picture."

The weekly rhythm of photographing neighbors had a transformative effect on Bernie. He said, "As for me, I began this process believing that I was a practicing Devotee of Sathya Sai Baba, a guru whose teachings emphasize service as an integral part of sincere spiritual seeking." As his immersion in the Friday Gathering grew, more and more he disassociated the souls of the individuals from "the qualities that make us useful to society," he said. Stripped of those qualities, Bernie came to appreciate that he had "been given this privilege … to look deeply into their faces and into their eyes and see more than what eyes can merely see."[49]

The effect is startling. The dining hall walls reflect who you meet on the street. As a metaphor, the walls speak about who is welcomed in, not about who is kept out. The photographs make the walls porous.

On Friday nights, I ask newcomers how they learned about the Gathering and who invited them. It is important to thank diners for extending hospitality to each other and appreciate how networking sustains the community. I want to celebrate when I see people show their portraits to their friends because their energy feels healthy and strong.

When I ask diners what brings them back, some will raise their arm in a giant sweep of the room and say, "The photos. The faces. I fit in here."

***

Pastor Eva arrived at Grace in 2005. Her drive to reconnect the congregation with its neighbors led to the formation of the listening committee, which in turn inspired the Christmas Eve dinner and the Friday Gathering. Pastor Eva reflected on that early period and described it as a *kairos* moment. *Kairos* is an ancient Greek word that can be translated as the "right time," different from chronological time. Paul Tillich, a German American Lutheran pastor and philosopher, described *kairos* as "God's time." It is the moment when events come together—at the right place at the right time—and we "receive the breakthrough of the manifestation of God."[50] Pastor Eva explained:

The birth of the Gathering was clearly a *kairos* moment. *Kairos* is not a clock time, but a time when people and circumstances build up—sometimes over a long period—and converge in such a way that something important can seem to happen suddenly, quickly, and with great clarity. The time is right, in other words. *Kairos* is primarily the work of the Holy Spirit.

I learned to trust the Holy Spirit. Maybe a bigger change was that the congregation became proactive. Over time it became part of the personality of the congregation for more and more people just to step up and do what they thought needed doing. By default, maybe, we never had much of a committee structure, and that worked just fine for Grace. Janet's establishing her [free clothes] closet is a good example. There was the woman who gave haircuts. Somebody else came and did touchless massages. [Cloth] napkins kept showing up. Jim brought chicken soup. The first time Hilda came, serving was not going smoothly, so she came around the table and started dishing up. One older man, who never said a word to anyone, made it his mission to get enough tables outdoors in the summer. A brightly painted archway was built at the gate from the parking lot to the rear door. The doors were painted blue! A men's group formed. A Bible study bubbled up at 10 Marshall Street. The backyard became a riotous display of vegetables and flowers.

Another thing I learned about the Holy Spirit was that evangelism is the Spirit's job. We made it a practice not to pressure people to come back on Sunday mornings. Building the Sunday morning attendance was never the goal of the Friday Gathering. But they came. I think they saw a group of Christians who were creative and generous and welcoming, and they wanted to be part of that. At the end of one of the first gatherings, Woody came up to me and said, "I like this church. I'm coming back on Sunday. I'm going to join." And he did.[51]

4

Building Trust

Relationships move at the speed of trust.

—The People's Supper

One evening when we were talking about the photos, Bernie said, "It gives people a different way of seeing themselves when they see their portrait up on the wall."

It wasn't just about how people saw themselves. The photos gave us a new way to see each other. That "still" quality of the portrait gave us time to linger on a face, make eye contact, and take in the person in front of us, without turning away as if self-conscious for being caught looking too long or too deeply. Gradually, out of that lingering came a yearning for knowing, the kind of knowing that Pearl Buck meant when she wrote, "Know thy neighbor as thyself."

That yearning stirred in Pastor Rick. He said, "There should be stories to go with the pictures." It was easy to agree with him. We were beginning to forget the names of people we had not seen for a while. A few diners had passed away, and we mourned more than their absence. We grieved the moments that would never be and the opportunity to know them more wholly.

One Friday a woman arrived at the Gathering, searching for her brother. She had lost touch with him and was frantic to know that he was alive. She had heard about our walls of portraits. If we could find his photo, there would be evidence that he had been here. But we could not connect his name with a photo. Later, as we walked around the room trying to name the diners in the portraits, we discovered more whose names we could not recall. It was unsettling. *How could we be together week after week but only know one another in such shallow ways? Didn't we have a responsibility to know something about the people whose faces were displayed on the walls? The people we shared dinner with each Friday?*

The Friday Gathering had begun as a way to build relationships, but it had stalled. William Mather Lewis, a former president of Lafayette College in Pennsylvania, said: "The tragedy in life is not that it ends so soon, but that we begin it so late."[52] In that spirit and before another diner was lost to us, Louisa began looking for volunteers to record stories. Lynn, a white woman and neighbor who lived in the same building as Louisa, answered the call. Lynn was a champion for pollinator and urban gardens, and her activism made her well-known in the community. She was diagnosed with multiple sclerosis decades ago and used a wheelchair.

Lynn came to the Friday Gathering and documented eight stories, including that of Robert, who died a year later, and Tommy, a quiet eight-year-old boy who sat and played at the children's table. Lynn's story about Tommy began with his words, "I like sharing food with everyone."

> Tommy was born in 2008 in Hartford to a family that came from
> Puerto Rico. His grandmother lives in Florida, and Tommy loves

to go there where it is warm and he can swim. Richie is his father, his mother is Diana, and his uncle is Chino. They and Tommy's siblings, Joshua, Manny, and Athena, often come to the weekly Supper Gatherings. Tommy is in second grade at Parkville Community School. He has some difficulty with math, so a volunteer from Grace, Miss Lou, has been helping him. He loves playing with his Avenger models and doing puzzles while he sings "Jesus Loves Me." Tommy likes to stay for the prayers that Pastor Rick leads at the end of the Friday Gatherings. He is a gentle and thoughtful boy.[53]

When Lynn couldn't continue recording stories, Louisa asked me to turn my conversations with diners into short articles, but I had reservations. Diners were reluctant to talk about their lives. Some said their story was "too bad" to tell; they didn't explain what that meant. Some were skeptical. How would the information be used? Who would profit from it? One woman said she'd been through "this kind of therapy" before and wouldn't do it again. Others said, "It's nobody's business." Opening up invites the risk that we will be judged, misunderstood, or treated with indifference.

The invitation to share a story angered one man. He yelled, "You have no right to do this!" I wanted to understand what it meant to him, but he only shouted, "You have no right," over and over until I walked away.

I didn't brush off his words. I wrestled with whether a white, middle-class woman could be a legitimate storywriter for our neighbors. *Is it possible to tell another's story with dignity and empathy when the experiences that formed us arose from such different circumstances?*

Essayist Leslie Jamison wrote in *The Empathy Exams,* "Empathy isn't just something that happens to us … it's a choice we make: to pay attention, to extend ourselves. It's made of exertion."[54] The idea that we have to have lived the same experience in order to relate to each other is a barrier to empathy. Empathy is an action that allows us to get "inside another person's state of heart or mind."[55] We can work at empathy; it's like a muscle that grows stronger the more it's used.

Malcolm Gladwell, a journalist and *New York Times* bestselling author, focused on another aspect of empathy: suspending judgment. He made the case that to be empathetic, judgment must be suspended and set aside. Like Jamison, Gladwell concluded that this takes effort. In an interview posted on YouTube, he said:

> Withholding judgment about people is what permits you to be empathetic. So the thing about empathy is that the desire to look at something through someone else's eyes only works if it's universal. It doesn't work if I'm selective, and I say, oh, I kind of like you, and so that encourages me to look at things through your eyes. That's not empathy. Empathy is where I confer that benefit on absolutely everyone regardless of whatever negative impression I might have of them. That's what it is. And the only way you can get there is if you withhold judgment in cases where you desperately want to reject someone or be negative toward them or hate them. Before you can do any of those things, you have to stop and affirmatively grant the universal gift of empathy. I would like to think it's helped to make me a better person to do that.[56] [edited for clarity]

When I began recording stories, I settled on a format to guide our conversations. It took the mystery out of what we might talk about. I asked, "Where were you born? What brought you to Hartford? Would you share a memory from your childhood? Do you have a message for the community?" Then the storyteller steered their narrative.

Later, I drafted the story and reviewed it with the storyteller. They could edit the draft and often did, adding more details. Occasionally they accepted it as it was. One time the story was ripped up and discarded. When the storyteller was satisfied, they signed a printed copy and kept one for themselves.

If we don't tell our stories, we relinquish the meaning-making of our experiences to others. The African proverb, "Until the lion has his or her own storyteller, the hunter will always have the best part of the story," expresses the relationship between the storyteller and power.[57] I felt an urgency to know our neighbors in their own voices, not through someone else's lens. Who we are—our identity—is grounded in memories of where we come from and the experiences we have lived. We can imagine that others' memories of us will live on through these stories. To be remembered is a way of cherishing one another, and being remembered by the Friday Gathering signified belonging to the community.

A diner put it in perspective for me one night. He said he'd made copies of his finished story and mailed it to his daughters with the instruction that it be read as his eulogy at his funeral. His death wasn't imminent, he assured me, but he regretted that he and his daughters weren't closer. "I want them to know who their father is," he said.

The process of sharing stories tested our relationships: the bonds between diners as well as the bonds between diners and me. Trust is one way to measure the strength of relationships. Despite the years that we had spent in each other's company—showing up week after week, the hundreds of photos on the walls, and the neighbors who shaped and ran the Friday Gathering and its offshoots—trust remained tenuous. One diner said, "I don't trust anybody." She explained that she'd been let down too many times. "People are just in it for themselves; I'm nobody's fool," she said. I wondered: *Is trust a luxury only the privileged can afford?*

After a few stories were completed, I mulled over how to share them with the Friday Gathering. There wasn't enough space to put copies on the walls the way the photographs were displayed; besides, some diners cannot read or cannot read in English. On a whim one Friday, I asked Harry if I could read his story aloud to the Gathering, and he agreed. His story didn't sugarcoat that he'd had trials and torments and didn't dwell on them either. There were details about his childhood that surprised us. He described what gave him pleasure and what gave meaning to his life. Harry said that people caring about each other makes the Gathering special to him. Diners nodded while they listened, and at the end, they enthusiastically applauded for him.

Each Friday, I invited a different diner to share their story. Neighbors paused their conversations and listened closely. When the reading was finished, the hall erupted with handclapping, whistles, and shouts of appreciation for the storyteller.

Sharing stories made the invisible visible, more than what merely eyes can see.

As I continued collecting stories, I tried to be the proverbial "fly on the wall," an impartial observer, curious and interested, while keeping neutral and emotionally detached. I didn't want to encourage embellishment or avoidance of details or affirmation or disapproval. But then, there was the moment when Chris told me about his eighteen-month-old brother, who died when he stuck a fork in a toaster and was electrocuted. He talked about how it devastated his mother in such a bland tone of voice that I couldn't reconcile the depth of the tragedy with his aloofness. And Jack's story about how he'd spent his entire adulthood raging at the world because he was nearly grown when he discovered by accident that he was adopted, and how betrayed he felt when his grown daughter contacted his birth mother without telling him first. I needed to stop and be in the moment with the storyteller. I needed to put our relationship first; it mattered more than recording stories. I couldn't be sterile and antiseptic to their lives. The process of telling and receiving stories was how we were building connections and making community.

As the recorder of stories, I confronted: What is truth? Every story has its facts: where you were born, awards and diplomas received, and dates of military service, for example. Other details are interpretative and describe how people make meaning of their experiences. Who your parents, brothers, and sisters are isn't always clear-cut or straightforward. There are blood ties and legal ties, and then there are the people who raised you and the people you grew up with, or didn't. There is family lore, too; the stories that are told in coded language.

Naming disabilities and making clinical diagnoses are subject to interpretation, too. There are inconclusive test results, misdiagnoses, new research data, and conditions for which there is no consensus. Truth can be elusive and fickle.

A diner told me that he had served jail time for a crime he didn't commit; the testimony was falsified, his innocence was eventually established, and after serving twenty years, he was released from prison early. Regardless of what fact-checking might reveal, his reality was that he'd been to prison, faced charges that he disputed, and now was here. He wanted to talk about the terror and death he witnessed in jail; how he never experienced love, even as a child; how he had made peace and was now facing surgery for cancer. This was his truth.

Stories inevitably require editing. Who decides which details are cut and which ones remain? Tammy Erickson, writing for the *Harvard Business Review,* said, "No account represents an absolute truth."[58] All reporting includes some whittling down of the story, a culling of details that are somehow deemed irrelevant, and all reporting has a point of view. The stories told here blend points of view, the storyteller's and mine. I aimed to preserve the storyteller's perspective and voice while adding observations to provide context.

When the stories were first recorded, the audience was the diners at the Gathering. The story-hearers were our community and acquainted well enough with each other. The process of recording stories for a wider audience led to the storytellers and me spending more time together, often twenty hours or more, listening and feeling and putting the meaning they made of their lives into words. Their collective voices captured the essence of the neighborhood: caring for family and friends, celebrating and mourning, and dreaming and struggling. These stories are not captured in media headlines and census statistics.

Just as important as sharing the tragedies has been sharing joy and successes: performing at your graduation ceremony, being in the delivery room when your child was born, having your book about golf published, and moving into your own apartment. There is acknowledgment, too, of how much work it takes to survive: being evicted from your apartment while being hospitalized; leaving the Friday Gathering before dinner is served because it takes two city buses to get to the shelter, and if you aren't there by the 6 p.m. curfew then you do not get a bed; losing your teeth because unemployment doesn't cover dental insurance; asking for menstrual supplies because food stamps do not pay for them.

One Friday before dinner, I read a draft of Sparky's story to him.

"I like it," he said. "You did good. Real good."

I asked him to tell me more, to describe what he liked about it.

"You told my story without judging it," he said.

***

"We are called to love others as Jesus loves us," Pastor Rick reflected in a note to me. He continued:

> We are all saints and sinners at the same time. We are clearly imperfect. No one is better than anyone else. We all carry with us the stains of our lives, along with the glory of seeing what God leads us to see and, importantly, to do.
>
> The stories herein call out to us, saying, "We are here, see us. The world is broken; we have near the worst of it." At the same time, these very same people teach us to care, to love, to laugh, to dance, to rethink, and to understand anew.
>
> They watch us and how we behave with each other. They sense when something is wrong. They ask, "Why?" or "Where is

so and so? We miss her/him," just as we, knowingly and lovingly say, "Why?" or "Where is so and so? We miss her/him." All of us have hurts, and sickness, and we die. We care if someone goes missing.

Our humanity is built into us, but sometimes locked in out of fear, loneliness or need. This isn't because God created us to be that way. It's because our wounded world teaches us all the wrong responses. If that is to change and be different, we must gather to do the Lord's work, by seeing what he has put before us and discerning what it is we are to do with it. Even though we think we've got all the answers, it is our God who has us embraced, empowered, energized, and wondering. We just need to see it, hear it, feel it, and do something about it.[59]

***

The stories call us to see beyond poverty, color, disability, gender, education, and all the ways we divide ourselves. They call us to know one another. In the telling and receiving of stories, we create a shelter where we belong to one another.

5

Our Truest Dignity

This is our truest dignity, to be alive, and to have a story to tell.

—Pádraig Ó Tuama, *In the Shelter: Finding a Home in the World*

Treating others as if they matter is a recognition of their inherent dignity. We feel whole, satisfied, and even joyful when others take us seriously. The stories that follow—of Harry, Robert, Sonny, and Roy—get at how these men make sense of the relationships that matter most to them. Affirming their dignity and becoming their story-listener knitted us together.

***

Harry was born in 1958 in Queens, New York. His father worked for the Chevron oil company and was transferred to Belgium when Harry was twelve years old. "They moved the whole family. It was really hard," Harry said.

Harry's younger siblings stayed with their parents in Belgium while Harry attended a boarding school in England, "because there was a language barrier," he said. He didn't talk about his experience at the school, except to say that he was bullied. After one semester, Harry asked his parents not to send him back. Besides, he missed his family "very, very much."

Harry's parents enrolled him in a school in Germany where English was spoken. "That's where I learned to fix lawnmowers!" he said. "We worked on small motors. I liked taking things apart and figuring out what was wrong. I liked getting my hands dirty. There's no use fixing the wheels or anything else on a lawnmower if the motor won't run. You have to see the big picture before you start fixing things. Besides, the teacher said I was good with my hands. I loved all of it." Then Harry repeated, "I missed my family very much."

After five years, Harry's family moved back to the States and settled in Stamford, Connecticut. "I went through a miserable time," Harry said. He had no friends at the high school, and the principal couldn't relate to him. "I didn't tell my parents and I didn't know to ask for help," he said. Harry supposed that a teacher who was aware of his struggles eventually talked to his parents, and they arranged for a guidance counselor to work with him. "I was happy that somebody wanted to help. I wasn't ready to graduate and I needed the extra support. We worked on math and social studies, and he caught me up on all the subjects. That counselor stuck with me. It took two extra years and I got my GED. I wanted it bad."

A few years later, Harry came to Hartford because there was a program that offered supportive housing for people with disabilities. For nearly fifteen years he rented a room in a house. Lois was his landlady.

"Lois was a perfect person," Harry said. "She was really sweet. She got along with my parents. She taught me to say, 'How do you do?' when I meet someone new. When she went out to eat or out to the movies, she invited me to go with her. We went to Hometown Buffet. I like that place a lot."

called Reverend Bell. He attended the Friday Gatherings and became a member of Grace in 2011.

Harry continued: "A couple of months before he died, Rev. Bell was driving his car. He saw me walking and pulled over. He just wanted to ask me how I was doing. We talked for forty-five minutes, as if he had nothing else to do. That's the way Rev. Bell was, taking an interest in people. He really touched my heart."

When I asked Harry what the Friday Gathering meant to him, he said, "It's people caring about each other. When people say hi to me, I know I'm alive."

***

Robert, a Black man, was born in 1958 in Bridgeport, Connecticut, and lived there until he moved to Hartford in the mid-1990s. I grew up in the area and had worked in Bridgeport for nearly thirty years before moving to Hartford. The idea that Robert and I shared geography—that we knew the same streets, landmarks, and neighborhoods—drew me to him. When I felt out of place in Hartford, I could sit with Robert and reminisce about the city of our youths.

When Robert discovered the Friday Gathering, he was hooked and came every week. He sat at the same table toward the back of the hall and teased the people who passed by. He purposely and persistently mixed up people's names and events. "Hi, Linda," he'd call to me, or "Hi, Bob," he'd shout to Roy. "Merry Christmas!" he announced at Halloween. It was his way of horsing around and getting attention. The responses were predictable. "I'm not Bob; it's not Christmas!" Sometimes it was impossible to have a conversation with him. He could be relentless, keeping up the guise, and occasionally I walked away exasperated.

Walking was not something Robert could take for granted. He used a cane, and sometimes two, one in each hand. Robert was wiry and stick-figure-thin, just like his canes. When he walked, he looked like a novice learning to use stilts. He lurched forward, then jerked to the side, and then lurched forward again. He cut a ragged, zig-zag path from one end of the room to the other. Sometimes it seemed he took running steps and depended on the forward momentum to hold him up until he reached a table and pivoted into a chair. He said the bones in his legs had deteriorated but didn't explain why. Sometimes when I watched Robert walk, I realized I was holding my breath, afraid that he would fall.

Occasionally, I overheard a diner ask Robert why he didn't use a motorized wheelchair. It was more a statement than a question. Robert would ignore the diner or change the subject. He didn't entertain the thought, at least not in public. Robert was a man who walked.

Diners laughed at his jokes, even though they were repetitive. They accompanied him to the serving table and carried his plate while he picked out his favorite foods, or they told him what was on the menu and filled a plate with his preferences.

Robert attended the Sunday worship services at Grace and came to know members of the congregation. He tenaciously called a few of us for rides to church and scolded us if we were late; punctuality mattered to him. Robert sat up front with other members who helped him navigate two hymnals and a bulletin to get through the service. He stayed after church for the fellowship hour, chatting and playing his pranks. Parishioners filled a plate with snacks and brought him coffee and a napkin. Then one of us gave him a ride home.

Reliability was a quality Robert brought to the Chrysalis Center. He volunteered as a greeter and often mentioned it on Friday nights. He planned his time around the shifts he was assigned and told me that the work gave him purpose. People expected him, depended on him. He helped those who were new and encouraged them to stick with the program. He invited them to dinner at Grace. It was how he gave back to the center. Robert said, "Without the Chrysalis Center, I wouldn't have a reason to get up in the morning."

One Friday night, Robert said he would be away for a few weeks. He was taking the bus to Bridgeport to visit his two sisters. One was having surgery, and Robert wanted to be there for her. He was gone a short while and then was back at dinner again. I asked him how the visit went. He said his sister was fine, and there wasn't much he could do to help. He ended the conversation there.

Robert seldom talked about his youth. He said he was one of nine children, and his family struggled with health problems, including diabetes and addiction. Three siblings and his parents died of these diseases. By the age of sixteen, he was addicted to alcohol and drugs and stealing to support his habit. He was in and out of jail and rehabilitation programs for years. In 1995, Robert arrived in Hartford. He came, he said, "to clean up my life. Even so," he added, "I didn't reach out for help until 1999." In 2016, Robert quietly told a few of us at the Friday Gathering, "I've been clean and sober and living in my own apartment for a year."

"Discovering Jesus changed my life," Robert said. Some Fridays, his playfulness disappeared, and he was quiet and withdrawn. In a whisper, Robert asked me, "What does salvation mean? What is redemption?" He sporadically asked these questions as if we had never discussed them before.

The first time Robert brought them up, I wanted to say, "Let's ask Pastor Rick." But I didn't want to abandon Robert at the dinner table, and I trusted that he knew Pastor Rick would welcome talking with him. Robert mumbled regrets about his life and said he was trying to be "his best self," a statement he frequently used when talking about being a greeter at the Chrysalis Center.

I believe we live suspended between knowing that we fall short of perfection and knowing we are made perfect through God's grace. It's a paradox. How can we be both? I tried to reassure Robert that he was, with all his imperfections, part of God's beloved creation. I was sure God could handle Robert and loved him, even in his worst moments.

Robert lived alone on the ground floor of an apartment building about a half mile from Grace. He didn't like his living situation and said the landlord was giving him trouble. He talked about drug dealers who banged on his windows and wouldn't leave him alone. He complained that residents left the main door to the building open, and people who didn't live there wandered in and out. Robert didn't feel safe and began looking for a new apartment.

The search took about a year, and then Robert moved to the South End of Hartford, miles away from Grace. The number of bus transfers required to get back and forth to the church was an obstacle. His presence at the Friday Gathering and on Sunday mornings soon faded.

I drove Robert home a few times to the South End, but he never let me take him all the way. He would say, "Stop here and let me out." He ceased giving directions, and I had no choice but to drop him off where he asked. On a dark street in a residential neighborhood, Robert stood alone on the sidewalk, juggling his canes, and waited for me to drive away. I didn't want to leave him there, but he insisted on it. Robert soon stopped calling for rides. Pastor Rick tried to keep in touch with him, but Robert didn't return his calls.

We lost track of Robert until we heard that he had died of a drug overdose on New Year's Eve in 2018. On a cold Friday night in January, when neighbors had gathered and settled down for dinner, Pastor Rick said a prayer in Robert's honor. People stood, took off their hats, and bowed their heads while he spoke. Pastor Rick thanked God for Robert and told us that we were fortunate Robert had spent time among us where we could care for him. I silently added my thanks for all the times Robert chose me to laugh with him.

I never saw Robert inebriated or high, which made it easy to see his vision of his best self. I like to think that we reciprocated and gave him our best selves, too.

***

Sonny was born in 1962 in South Islip, Long Island, and identifies as white. He's of average height and weight. "My eyebrows are my trademark," he said, referring to their thick, bushy, unibrow shape. "Everybody has a trademark. Sinatra had the voice. Elvis had the hips. I have my eyebrows!"

For more than a year, Sonny and I talked about his life. Then one late summer afternoon, he arrived at Grace and said he had written his autobiography, three hundred pages in longhand. With his permission, the following dialogue synthesizes notes from our conversations and excerpts from his manuscript.

"I grew up in a real Italian family," Sonny said. "My grandmother Rose, on my mother's side, was born in Catania, Italy. I don't know where my grandfather Vito was born. My father's father came from Sardinia. On Sundays, my mother made her pasta. She made that every Sunday, and the table was always full of food. We always had a jug of wine on the table, too, and before the day was over, that jug would be empty. My mother always listened to a radio station that played Italian music from ten in the morning until two in the afternoon.

"I had a rocky childhood," Sonny continued. "My parents divorced when I was two or three years old, a year after my brother was born. I would hear them arguing and fighting, and it would make me scream and cry. We lived in Florida then, and my father cheated on her. My mother left him and Florida and took my brother and me back to New York and her family. The thought of not seeing my father really hit me hard.

"My mother got a job to support us, and that's how she met Tony. He was divorced and had two sons a little older than my brother and me. They married around the time I started kindergarten.

"Tony had his good side and his bad side. He drove a Pontiac convertible, and he took us four boys everywhere. Places like the drive-in movies, where we saw *Planet of the Apes;* to drive-in hamburger places that served root beer floats in frosted glasses. He even took us to the circus once, and he put a snow cone in my face because I was scared the tiger was going to come and bite me, so I screamed. He did it to my stepbrother, smashing a snow cone in his face, too."

Turning to his memories of school, Sonny began, "I was not the best of students. My first couple of years were good, but the third grade was when my problems started. I did two tours of the third grade. Math wasn't one of my best subjects. My favorites were English and social studies, but Tony wanted me to do good in math. Like I said, I was never the best of students. I was a teacher's pest.

"By grade six, classes were tough, and some of my grades were not too good. Every quarter I would get these unsatisfactory reports. My mother was mad every time I got one of those papers. Tony got wind of one of them, and he got angry about it. He wanted every grade to be perfect, and he got mad at me for not bringing home good grades. I couldn't do it, no matter how hard I tried." It was a pattern that continued through high school, but there were no more second tours or repeated grades.

Sonny was drawn to television sitcoms like *The Lucy Show, The Beverly Hillbillies, and Bewitched.* He watched *The Ed Sullivan Show* and admired pop singers like Bobby Vinton, Elvis Presley, Frankie Valli, and Tom Jones. Most of all, he idolized the Italian Americans, Frank Sinatra and Dean Martin.

In ninth grade, the choir teacher told Sonny, "You have a fine voice for a guy so young."

"When he asked me how I got my singing voice," Sonny said, "I told him, 'Too many Dean Martin records.' He laughed at that.

"I was always a dreamer," Sonny said. "Everybody has dreams, and mine was to be the best baseball player ever." Sonny wanted to play for the New York Mets. If he couldn't watch a game on TV, he listened to it on the radio, even when Tony took his privileges away because of his grades in school. Sonny tried out for the school teams but didn't make them. "No matter how hard I tried, no matter how hard I worked, I could not get on the baseball team." Still, the dream persisted. "I wanted to hit baseballs over walls, make great catches, win a Gold Glove, a few World Series rings, maybe an MVP.

"I wrote letters to major league baseball teams requesting a tryout, and in the spring of 1984, I got a letter in the mail. It was the New York Mets sending me an invitation to try out for them. My mother had a fit. She didn't want me to do it. She told me I was going to make a fool of myself.

"I'm going to do it anyway," Sonny told her. "I wanted to make my dream of playing major league baseball a reality. I worked my butt off getting a new glove, new shoes, bat, you name it. I even worked to get my body in shape. I tried out for the Mets and didn't make the team."

Sonny had another dream. "I wanted to be Batman; still do," he said. "Batman is just a regular guy. His superpowers come from battling his weaknesses and building up his body and his mind. That and his determination to fight for justice.

"I always dressed up as Batman for Halloween, and I drove my mother crazy with it. Every time I saw something with Batman on it I would ask my mother to get it for me, and she would tell me not to get selfish about it." Sonny collected a Batman kite, PJs, watch, posters, and comic books.

As he grew up, Sonny's dreams and his performance in school didn't fit with his stepfather's expectations. "Sometimes Tony could be easy to get along with, but when he was in one of his moods, you had better watch out," Sonny said.

He recalled one episode. "Tony hit me so hard I had a fat lip and a few bumps and bruises, and again, I was sore for days. Tony said he was like that because his father was like that with him. Tony's father ruled his house with an iron hand, and that's the way Tony ran his house."

Two months before high school graduation, Sonny withdrew from school. He went to work for a family-owned print shop and silkscreened t-shirts, hats, jackets, sweatshirts, and more. "They liked me as a worker and gave me a raise after only a month of being there," Sonny said. He stayed over ten years, until the husband-and-wife owners became ill and closed the business in 1993.

"She came down with lung cancer, and he ended up with cancer of the liver. He was a drinker, and she was a smoker," Sonny said. They passed away within a year of each other.

In 1994, Sonny couldn't find work. He moved back home, and his mother was diagnosed with pancreatic cancer. She died in early November. He barely got through the holidays with Tony.

"Tony said it was my fault that my mother died. He said I drove her crazy all her life, that I was the reason she got worse instead of better, that I was the reason she's not here anymore. That's when I started calling him step-monster," Sonny said. In January 1995, after the holidays, Tony kicked Sonny out of the house.

In his autobiography, Sonny described the next twenty years of living on the streets, sometimes sleeping in a neighbor's van, being in and out of shelters, and being placed in—then expelled from—residential treatment programs. "I wasn't there for drugs or alcohol," Sonny explained. "I was there for anger management."

He was mugged, beaten up, and had a toe amputated to prevent gangrene from taking the rest of his foot. He was diagnosed with diabetes. He described catnapping in public libraries and having the police called to remove him.

"On my forty-sixth birthday, I was diagnosed with bipolar depression. They said I'd had it since I was a kid." In 2009 he was told to leave Turning Point, a recovery program, because he was uncooperative. A bed was arranged for him at a shelter in Hartford.

Sonny got to know people in the city. He met them at the shelter, soup kitchens, and the library. Edison, Ray, Jeff, and Justin became his friends. "But mostly, I would keep to myself. I went to Bushnell Park on a nice day and sat on a bench and read a book. Every now and then, somebody would come around and bring me lunch. They were nice people and looked out for me," he said.

When a new educational program was launched to engage the homeless community, Sonny was asked to join. It was run by the Charter Oak Cultural Center, a nonprofit committed to the work of social justice. Charter Oak called the new program the BOTS Center for Creative Learning. The center sponsored the *Beat of the Street*—BOTS—newspaper, a monthly paper featuring articles written by people experiencing homelessness, dealing with addiction and recovery, or coping with heartbreaking misfortune.

When he was invited, Sonny said, "Why not? It was free of charge, no homework, no exams, and they served free breakfast. They said you had to complete at least twelve of the fifteen courses, and in May you would graduate. They were all good classes, and I went to every one of them. I met people who were really good to me."

Sonny was a member of the first graduating class and sang "The Rose" at the ceremony. "I had to get a haircut. I wore a nice shirt, nice dress pants, and good dress shoes—my friend Justin loaned them to me. I was able to shave, shower, and get really nice for it. I sounded like Sinatra with a little Bobby Darin mixed in. The people loved it, and they gave me a standing ovation. Now I know what it feels like to be in the spotlight." He received special privileges that evening and was allowed to return to the shelter after curfew.

One of the BOTS classes was taught by a journalist who wrote for the *Hartford Courant*. "She became like a mother to me," Sonny said. In 2015, when agencies across Connecticut launched the 100-Day Challenge to End Homelessness, the journalist and staff at Journey Home, a nonprofit addressing the needs of chronically homeless people, worked with the Chrysalis Center on Sonny's behalf. They succeeded in helping Sonny move into his own apartment in Hartford's West End.

Journey Home, which manages a warehouse for donated furniture and household items, helped furnish Sonny's apartment. They gave him a voucher for Walmart and took him shopping. "The first thing I saw were these cool Batman bedsheets and pillowcase set, so I got them," Sonny said.

"Being in my own place has really made a difference. I'm able to come and go as I please, stay up late, and wake up when I want. I don't have to look over my shoulder to see who's behind me wanting to beat me up or stab me or whatever."

Sonny joined the Methodist church and their choir, went to a Mets game in New York, and signed up for the Faces of Homelessness Speakers Bureau. He worked two temporary part-time jobs. He submitted applications for other jobs and has yet to be hired.

The Speakers Bureau brought him to schools and churches, and he was interviewed on Connecticut Public Radio. "I even spoke at the Legislative Office Building and at the Capitol Building, but it's the schools that I like speaking to the most," he said.

"I like going to the schools because the kids listen and ask questions. They especially like it when I wear my Batman jacket. The kids say I tell an inspiring story and some of them have tears in their eyes, and the thank you cards they send me are really cool. They draw pictures with the Batman logo or they paste pictures of Batman on them.

"So, my life has completely turned around. Since coming off the streets and moving into my own apartment, I'm able to do things I couldn't do when I was out there."

On Fridays at the Gathering, Sonny wears his Batman baseball cap, a Batman t-shirt, and a short black cape draped over his shoulders. "I like it when people call me Batman," he said.

***

Roy was born in 1954 in Hartford. We sat on the steps in front of his apartment and talked for hours, getting his thoughts down on paper. He was a tall, large Black man with a strong, charismatic voice. When people remarked that he should be in radio—and they often did—he wholeheartedly agreed, saying, "I'm the prettiest voice in radio."

Roy was the second-born child of five and the first of his siblings born in Hartford after his parents emigrated from Jamaica, a British colony at the time. "My mother went to nursing school in England," before she emigrated, Roy said. "My father came to work in the fields. He picked tobacco, potatoes, and apples." They were part of a wave of West Indian immigrants who settled in Hartford.[63]

His parents were hardworking and purchased a large two-family home on Sterling Street, built in the Queen Anne/Colonial Revival style. "They were blockbusters," Roy laughed, "moving into a neighborhood that was mostly Italian and Irish." His mother made a career in nursing, and his father got into the construction business. "He worked concrete on big projects, at Pratt & Whitney—an aircraft engine manufacturer—and other industrial plants. It was a rough trade. There were some unsavory characters in the business."

Roy attended a series of schools and ticked them off. "Northwest-Jones Junior High, Weaver High, and the Cathedral of St. Joseph. I took piano and drum lessons at the Hartford Conservatory. They sent me to Mount Saint John Academy in Deep River for a while, because they said I was incorrectable—make sure you spell that just like I said it," and he laughed. "I was expelled from all of them. Put that in there, too.

"Dad was a strict disciplinarian. He said his daughters needed protection," Roy recalled, referring to his two younger sisters. "If someone said something or looked at them the wrong way at school, it was up to me to defend them. I could get into a fight at school, or I could get it from my father when he got home. He said I had a high tolerance for pain. After so many fights at school, you get expelled. At the cathedral, I got caught sneaking wine, and then I got expelled.

"Teachers said I wasn't living up to my potential," he added.

"In 1971, my dad said I had a choice: I could go back to school or work for him. I'd had enough of school and wanted nothing to do with concrete. I saw what it did to his hands—how beat-up and swollen they were—and I didn't want to work for him, either. Over both of my parents' protests, I enlisted in the army and went to Vietnam.

"They each had their own reasons," Roy said about their objections to his enlistment. "My dad saw all the Black kids assigned to combat troops and said it was wrong. My mother took it personally; she knew what it was like to lose a child. My older brother, David, died in the service; he served in Jamaica." Roy signed up anyway. He didn't need his parents' consent or a high school diploma.

"I went to boot camp at Fort Dix," in New Jersey. "I had advanced infantry and helicopter familiarization training. I served in the Second Battalion; started in the Charlie Company and got moved to the Alpha Company." He spent five months in Vietnam.

"I was high the day they lined us up and asked for volunteers to reenlist. I didn't know what I was doing when I said 'yes.' There was a cease-fire in Vietnam, so we were assigned to Cambodia. All those bullets and rockets firing. I was scared shitless. I cried like a baby.

"I look back now and see that God's grace and mercy protected me. God was answering my mother's prayers, not mine. I didn't know yet what it was like to lose a child. Or what it was like to be hit by a bullet.

"I was honorably discharged on July 1, 1975, which included eight extra days to make up for the times I went AWOL and once for stealing C-rations. I made Buck Sergeant …" He paused before adding, "and was disrespected when I got home. People spit in my face. They called me a baby killer. And I came home addicted to opium."

In Hartford, Roy fathered two daughters. He wanted to "act responsibly," he said, "and support them." He went to Nashville, Tennessee, to attend radio broadcasting school.

Roy became an "air personality." He wrote the scripts for the shows he hosted and was controversial. "I went after the local politicians. I called them out, demanded they take responsibility, exposed their shady associations. They threatened the radio station with lawsuits for slander, and the stations let me go. I moved from station to station across the South. After eight or nine years, I'd had enough and moved on."

Roy found work cleaning up petroleum and chemical spills and traveled to sites scattered from Florida to Arizona. He moved to Baltimore, where his sisters were living. He worked in construction and at the horse track. In 1988 his third daughter, Mooshie, was born there.

In Baltimore, he was shot and robbed, which made his left arm permanently disfigured and disabled and left a deep scar across his backside. "For the first time, I knew what bullets tasted like and what I was spared in Cambodia," Roy said. "I had always believed in God, but now, it was personal. God was my shield."

"The deaths of my first two daughters in the '90s brought me back to Hartford. They were killed a few months apart. One was hit by a truck while she waited for the school bus. The truck slid out of control, going downhill on an icy road. The other died in a car accident when a car hit them." Roy lived with his father in his childhood home and stayed after his father passed away in 1996. "Coming back to Hartford brought me back to drugs, too."

Meanwhile, Baltimore was becoming more dangerous. "There were shootings and innocent kids were getting killed. It got so bad, they started naming squares after little girls that were shot, like Tiffany Square.[64] Mooshie's mother wanted to get her out of there, so Mooshie came to live with me in Hartford. That's when I got acquainted with the House of Bread."

The House of Bread serves nearly two thousand people a day in the North End of Hartford. More than a soup kitchen, they offer housing, a day shelter, and educational programs for men, women, and children.[65] "They saved me," Roy said.

"I couldn't provide enough for Mooshie, and they gave me bags of food to take home. It wasn't enough, though. DCF [the Department of Children and Families] got involved." After four and a half years, Mooshie went back to her mother in Baltimore.

"There are no words to describe losing a child. It's no use wondering what you could have done different. I loved all my daughters. I still talk to their mothers. Mooshie is following in my footsteps. I tell her to learn from my mistakes, but she isn't ready to hear it. I want to go to Baltimore to see her, but she disappears; then, no one can reach her."

Roy served two three-year sentences in jail on drug charges. During those years, his disability Social Security income was forfeited. Property taxes on his childhood home accumulated, then penalty and interest fees were added. It was too much to recover from. In 2013, the water and electric services were turned off. The house was condemned and boarded up.

Roy staked out three rooms and lived in the shuttered house with Rex, his pit bull. Roy's brother and his VA caseworker urged him to take advantage of veterans' benefits and move to "real" housing. Roy didn't think he'd be allowed to keep Rex, and he refused to move. He kept his valuables in a large suitcase with wheels. He took it everywhere—on the bus, to the library, soup kitchens, and VA appointments—because he couldn't be sure his belongings would still be at the house when he got home.

Roy volunteered at the House of Bread, Monday through Friday. He was out of the house before 6 a.m. and at the House of Bread by 6:30. He had special privileges and could take a shower without having to sign up for it. "You never notice me smelling bad," Roy said, and it was true.

He got the dining room ready to serve breakfast. More than a hundred people came. He volunteered there for more than twenty years and knew the regular diners. "I watch for the new ones and welcome them," he said. When breakfast service ended, he helped clean up and got the dining room ready for lunch. A few times, when Roy ended up on the wrong side of an argument, he was dismissed from his volunteer duties. He took it hard, Roy said, because "the House of Bread is part of my identity. They saved my life." Eventually, he would work his way back in and regain his volunteer status.

House of Bread ran a "ServSafe" food certification program. In 2015, three volunteer chefs from the Friday Gathering attended the program. One of them was Gladys, and she and Roy became friends. "She gave me and my suitcase a ride home when lunch service was finished. We sat in her car and talked, and that's how we got to know each other," Roy said.

"I read the Bible to her every morning. I call about 5 a.m. because I have to leave before 6:00 to get to the House of Bread on time. We start the day with the Book of Proverbs. On the first day of the month, we read chapter 1. On the second day, we read chapter 2. There are thirty-one chapters in Proverbs, one for each day of the month. When the next month starts, I go back to chapter 1.

"Proverbs puts me in the right frame of mind to deal with the personalities at the House of Bread. I'm a sinner like everybody else. I'm just trying to commit less than the day before. God will forgive you, but you've got to ask for it." Then Roy recited:

> Do not withhold good from those to whom it is due,
>> when it is in your power to do it.
> Do not say to your neighbor, "Go, and come again,
>> tomorrow I will give it"—when you have it with you.[66]

"I have some regrets, and one of them is that I withheld mercy when I could have made a difference in a man's life. The man who shot me had a chance to go to school, to better his life. I denied him that chance when his sentence was reviewed. It would have helped him get a job when he got out of jail instead of robbing. It might have turned his life around. Might have turned it around for his family."

Roy learned about the Friday Gathering from Gladys. "I came because she invited me. That and I wanted to taste her cooking. I was naturally curious. There were people at the House of Bread who said they went to Grace on Fridays, too."

Sonny's friend Edison was one of them. "Edison knows how much I like the New England Patriots," Roy said. "He found a Patriots jacket in the dumpster, size XXL, and gave it to me."

Edison said he was looking for bottles and cans with five-cent deposits when he found the jacket. "For several years, I had a route that I followed. I didn't need the money, but the nickel deposits covered about half of my monthly health insurance premium until I turned sixty-five and went on Medicare. I collected about $300 a month worth of nickel deposits. I got a kick out of the hunt, and I had the time to do it. Some of the things people throw away are valuable."

Edison wasn't a football fan, but he knew Roy was crazy about the Pats. "The jacket was rolled up in a ball inside a plastic bag. The snaps down the front didn't work, but other than that, the jacket was perfect. I took it home, laundered it, and gave it to Roy. I knew he wouldn't try to sell it for money."

When the weather turned cool in the fall, Roy pulled out the jacket. As temperatures dropped, he fit one sweater, and then two, underneath it. "It never bothered me that the snaps didn't work," he said.

When Roy arrived at the Friday Gathering—with his suitcase—he picked up a name tag and headed to the back of the room. He sat at a table next to the piano where he could stretch out his long legs and not be in the way. He pulled out his cell phone, propped it up on the table, and started a movie he'd downloaded from the library.

During supper, Roy put aside some of his dinner to take home to Rex. He wrapped the food in a paper napkin or a plastic container that he had saved. If Gladys was cooking, she set aside bones and wrapped them in foil.

Roy wasn't shy about sharing his dinner. "I'm saving this for Rex! Boy, is he gonna feast tonight!" Roy's deep voice boomed to no one in particular. Diners who didn't finish their meal offered Roy the leftovers, and if they had pork or beef ribs, Roy asked them to save the bones, too.

Between settling down at a table when he arrived and getting in line to be served, Roy often fell asleep. When it was time to bless the meal, Harry, who sat one table over, nudged Roy and told him to wake up. After dinner, if Roy fell asleep waiting for the prayer circle to start, Harry nudged him again. When Roy fell asleep during the prayers, Harry lightly shook him awake. When it was time to stand, Harry made a sweeping motion with his arms. "Get up, get up now," Harry told him. Roy never objected to Harry's instructions.

One evening after dinner, Harry was moving chairs into a prayer circle. He was unaware that Roy was right behind him. Harry swung a chair around in an arc and whacked Roy in the knee. Roy fell to the floor and howled in pain. Harry felt the collision, saw Roy on the floor, and howled, too. One of the volunteers rushed over and began yelling at Harry, accusing him of being clumsy.

Roy pulled himself up and shouted back, "It was an accident; he didn't mean any harm!" Roy repeated it over and over until the volunteer backed down. Roy didn't doze off that night during the prayers. He sat next to Harry, comforting him each time he said he was sorry for the accident.

One Friday, Roy arrived at the Gathering and said, "I've got something to show you. It's in the top pocket of my suitcase. Unzip it, and you'll see."

Inside was a wooden plaque with Roy's name engraved in gold lettering. It recognized his service to the Shiloh Baptist Church and honored him as their Usher of the Year. Roy called Pastor Rick over to show him and passed the plaque around to his friends. He invited me to church with him and explained the key role that ushers served in the Baptist church. As long as Roy continued to bring his suitcase to the Friday Gathering, he periodically took the plaque out so we could admire it together.

On Saturdays, Roy polished his best pair of shoes to get ready for Sunday. He set out a clean, pressed dress shirt. Sometimes he visited a dry cleaner where he was offered unclaimed clothing. Roy was the first to arrive at Shiloh on Sunday mornings and waited for the deacon to unlock the doors. His church friends told me that he was their spiritual ambassador; he made sure everyone knew they were welcomed. Like his volunteer role at the House of Bread, it was fitting; Roy made a point of knowing everybody. After the second service on Sundays, Roy stayed for lunch. "They always make a package for me to take home," he said.

In 2018, Roy's neighbors complained about Rex. "They say he barks when I'm not there. I have to leave Rex tied up. They tease him and call the animal control officer to complain. After too many complaints, they shot Rex and put him down."

Roy's brother and caseworker urged him again to move into an apartment. "I'm getting older, and my brother asked me how long do I think I can live this way? There's a program to help veterans get housing. I wouldn't miss being cold."

Roy moved to a second-floor walk-up in the Frog Hollow section of Hartford. The landlord wouldn't allow pets, and after a while, Roy stopped talking about wanting a service dog—a comfort animal. He still took his suitcase with him when he left the apartment. At the Friday Gathering, the most noticeable change was that Roy was better rested and he stopped sleeping through dinner and the prayers. "I'm glad God woke me up today," he bellowed, and a diner somewhere answered back, "Amen."

One Friday evening, Vicki, a middle-aged woman, sat at Roy's table and cried through dinner. She had been coming to the Gathering since the first Christmas Eve dinner and was well-known to many diners. After she lost custody of her daughter, Vicki didn't come as often. It wasn't unusual for her to cry, but this particular night was the first time Roy met her. He came to me and pleaded, "You have to help her." Roy listened to her story as she opened up to him. He invited her to join the prayer circle, and she did.

Another week, Roy called me over. "My next-door neighbor doesn't have a coat." It was early December. "She's taking care of her two granddaughters and gives everything to them. You have to get a coat for her." Then he stood up and described the woman so I would know what size to get. "There's snow in the forecast," he added. We found a coat at a Salvation Army store, and Roy gave it to her.

Six months after Roy moved into his apartment, he was at the House of Bread one morning when he collapsed. One of his friends suspected drugs. But the staff recognized other symptoms and called an ambulance. Roy suffered a stroke that weakened his left arm and leg and affected his speech. He spent two months in rehab. "The House of Bread saved my life," Roy said, and this time he meant it literally.

As soon as Roy got home, he was back to reading the Bible to Gladys at five in the morning and volunteering at the House of Bread. "I have to get up at 4 a.m. to be ready. Take my shower, read the Bible, and get to the bus stop before 6:00. It takes two buses from Frog Hollow to get to the House of Bread." When Roy got off the first bus, he phoned me while he waited for the second one. If Gladys hadn't answered when he called her at 5:00, he insisted that I find out if she was okay. This was how they looked after each other.

After the stroke, Roy used a walker and couldn't haul his suitcase around. He dragged the walker up twenty-two stairs to his apartment and back down again when he went out. Once, when we met at the library, I suggested we use the ramp. Roy said, "No need for that. I'm strong and can use the stairs. If I don't exercise, I won't be able to do anything." His brother and VA caseworker wanted him to move to an assisted living facility. Roy said, "No. I'm holding on to my independence for as long as I can."

In September 2020, Roy and I sat on the steps outside his apartment and talked. Because of the pandemic, the House of Bread had suspended indoor dining and served their meals to-go. They didn't need him to volunteer, and he was discouraged. This was a different side of Roy I had not seen before. "I feel worthless," he said, and that got us talking about dignity.

"In spite of all the troubles in my life, God keeps forgiving me. I learned to ask for forgiveness, and it taught me how to forgive. I've loved, and I've been loved back. I wrestled with the devil himself, and he hasn't gotten the best of me. I've tried to act responsibly, even though others can't always see that. I wish I could get to Baltimore. I wish my daughter would call."

A week and a half later, Roy's brother called me. He said he hadn't been able to reach Roy by phone and went to check on him. Roy had passed away at home.

Roy's brother and sisters, their spouses and extended family, the Shiloh Baptist Church, and his friends celebrated Roy's life. They told stories about him—his prettiest voice, the honor that Usher of the Year meant to him, his service in Vietnam, and his surviving daughter—with affection and humor and without minimizing his weaknesses. It was a fitting tribute. To diminish parts of his life would have diminished all of it. His brother cleaned up the apartment and distributed his belongings to neighbors in need. He brought bags of clothing to Grace. It was exactly what Roy would have wanted.

Sometimes Roy called me twice a day to talk. He was engaged with what was happening worldwide and in our community. He had an opinion about all of it, backed it up with news reports, and would tell anyone he could get to listen. He fought for the ideal of American freedom, and it bothered him to see it maligned or wasted.

At Grace, Pastor Rick shared his grief in a letter to the congregation:

> Roy was a presence to me from the very first time I met him. So much of our world and country now is twisted, confused, and separated. Roy always felt like solid ground to me. He accepted

his imperfection, just as he did the same for others. He cared about people's lives, even as he fell asleep exhausted during a Friday prayer circle. You see when you are up before sunrise, gather all your stuff, take care of your dog and kittens and start your trek to the House of Bread to volunteer, and then after working hard for hours that you made your way to another part of town to have a meal on a Friday, see some friends, and talk for a couple of hours, he'd be tired.

As we got to know each other I came to love his sense of humor, and his deeply felt and lived faith. He never missed our prayer circle and communion after dinner, and he actively participated in our joking about birthdays, anniversaries, and events going on in the community. He was an example of those who loved. He really cared about every single person.[67]

***

A single story couldn't define Roy any more than it can define any of us. Roy lived a series of chapters, each with a before and an after, none of them complete or whole on their own. It's the same for Harry, Robert, Sonny, and all of our neighbors.

The stories we tell are more than words. Just as Roy said that asking for forgiveness taught him how to forgive, telling our story teaches us how to listen to others' stories. We hear and then feel what it means to be alive. The connections we have—the relationships—begin with a shared story.

6

Honoring the Struggle

It's easy to judge others if you've never suffered an experience like that.

—Isabelle Allende, *Maya's Notebook,* trans. Anne McLean

Let's face it: We all know struggle. When we are dealing with a problem—paying a bill, holding onto a job, providing for a loved one, facing a health issue—the effort we put into it is our struggle. At the center of struggle is purpose. It is the fuel that drives our will to prevail, even when the odds seem stacked against us. When we lose our sense of purpose, the will to struggle fades. The pain, loss, and effort that we could bear because of our purpose turns to suffering when it is no longer connected to what gives our life meaning.

Sometimes, struggle is judged as failure, as if we didn't do our best or try hard enough. We should have "seen it coming" and been prepared. How many times has someone said, "You brought it on yourself," as if we could remove the obstacles or at least reduce their power over us? We live in a litigious culture that expects there is someone to blame, that someone is at fault, even if it's ourselves. I know that doing my "best" changes from day to day depending on whether I've had enough sleep, my children are okay, and other factors that affect my sense of well-being.

At the heart of the stories that follow, and of diners throughout the book, is the longing for connection that defines their struggles. They want to matter to the people who matter to them. They want to be significant because it gives meaning to their lives.

***

James is a tall Black man. He was born in 1959 in Jamaica and lived there until he came to Connecticut in 2016. In 2018, he started attending the Friday Gathering. James and I didn't begin to know each other until our paths crossed at a recycling center at the grocery store. My grandchildren and I were sorting cans and bottles to redeem the nickel deposits when James walked in.

"James, hello!" I called out. "Do you remember me, from the Friday Gathering? Come meet my grandchildren."

On Fridays at Grace, James usually arrived after 6 p.m., missing the announcements and blessing. His entrance was noticeable: he appeared as others were beginning to leave. I learned his name and that he rode a bike to Grace. He was courteous to the volunteers and efficiently settled in. He put his backpack and jacket on a chair at an empty table, filled his plate, and sat alone to eat. When he was finished, he brought his plate and utensils to the dishwashers, packed up a loaf of bread and leftovers, and went home.

James recognized me at the grocery store. We hugged each other hello, like old friends. I introduced him and my grandchildren, and then we turned our attention to recycling. I noticed that James was pushing a grocery cart piled high with large plastic bags full of cans and bottles.

"Did you drink all of this?" I asked, pointing to the bags of containers.

"Noooooo," he said, laughing. "I collect them. When I'm not at work, I go looking for them."

That short conversation was just the spark I needed to see James as more than a Friday Gathering diner. The following week, I sat down at the dinner table with him and he began to tell me about himself. He spoke in a soft, unhurried voice.

"My mother had nine children, and I was the second-born. As a child, I saw my mother struggle. There was no fooling around with her; she was a serious person. She had all those children younger than me to take care of, so my grandfather raised me. When I was nine years old, my mother sent me away to live with him. His name was James.

"He was a farmer," he continued, "and we lived off the land. As a child, I felt like we lived in the middle of the forest. My grandfather told me not to wander too far away because there were wild animals in the woods. I think he meant boars. He said if I got hurt, no one would find me. It was scary.

"In the morning, the wet dew on my feet made me cold and my feet cramped. There was no life in them. We didn't wear shoes; the clay soil and wet ground would have destroyed them. I remember those days. We lived far away from other people, too far away for me to go to school. If I heard a motor, like an automobile, I came running to the front of the house. We didn't have paved roads like here. It was unusual to have a visitor so the sound of a motor attracted attention. Living with my grandfather is how I learned to fend for myself. It was a lonely time.

"My grandfather was a good cook," James said, "and he taught me to cook. He said, 'Come here, boy, watch me,' and he was very strict. Things had to be done his way, and he didn't permit me to try it myself. I learned by watching and paying close attention to everything he did. He was particular about a lot of things and skeptical of people in general.

"I dreamed of being an airplane pilot," James said. "I saw planes fly overhead and I dreamed about where they were going. I wanted to go someplace too. I dreamed of Africa, the land of my ancestors. I wanted to see what the real Africa is like. I had a big imagination about life in faraway lands.

"When I came to Connecticut, it was my first time on a plane. Getting through the airports—so many people in one place. The chaos! When I was a child, I didn't know that planes crash and people die. I don't dream of being on an airplane anymore.

"I dreamed I'd have a hundred sons, and that they would spread my name around the world. I love children." To make his point, James laughed and said, "I love babies and babies love me."

"I'm serious," he insisted. "If a baby is crying or fussy, I hold that child in my arms and they settle down. It's so precious, to feel a baby relax into my arms. But I saw the poverty that so many babies put on my mother. God gave me three beautiful daughters and they have given me grandchildren. They make me very happy.

"I came to the United States to be closer to my middle daughter. I have a sister in Georgia, an auntie in New York, and my middle daughter in North Carolina. When she was about nine months old, I had to leave her and go to Kingston to get work. My daughter's mother moved to the United States to make a better life for us. We were supposed to join her here and get married, but she married an American man instead. My daughter stayed with her grandmother in Jamaica until she was twelve or thirteen years old. Her mother brought her to the United States and divided her against me. I haven't seen my daughter once since I got here. I want to know my daughter and my grandchildren and I want them to know me.

"When I arrived in Connecticut," James said, "I cried for three months straight. I was so far away from home. Nothing was familiar. I was so homesick.

"My daughter sponsored my immigration but when I got here, she wouldn't permit me to live with her. I had a friend from Jamaica in Hartford.

He put me up until I could afford to live on my own. That's how I came to be in Hartford.

"I registered for work with a temp agency and I took whatever jobs they offered me. In Jamaica, I had experience with plumbing, landscaping, and working with concrete.

"The temp agency got me a job as a maintenance worker at an apartment building for seniors in Newington. I took three buses and walked another half mile to get there. I've had lots of jobs. I worked at a warehouse. I packed barrels with dry goods—sardines, dry milk, rice, and flour—that families ship to their relatives in the West Indies or Africa. I filled in at the Mr. Sparkle car wash when their workers called out. The boss at the temp agency saw that I was good with my hands, that I could fix anything, and sent me on jobs no one else would do.

"I learned about Grace and the Friday Gathering at the House of Bread," James said. "I got to know a young woman who volunteered there. She handed out the forks and spoons wrapped in napkins. One Friday, I was riding my bike back from a job when I saw her walking. I stopped to say hello and asked her where she was going. She told me she was on her way to a church where they cook good food on Friday nights and send you home with bread and leftovers, if they have any. She was talking about Grace. See, the Lord has been watching out for me my whole life.

"I go to church as often as possible," he continued. "The Methodist Church on Sundays and King's Chapel on Wednesday evenings. God moves in mysterious ways." James recited Psalm 121 from memory and ended with, "The Lord will keep your going out and your coming in from this time on and forevermore."[68]

"I got my faith from my grandfather. He was a deacon in his church. Sometimes he took me to church and left me there by myself. I liked going on Sundays. It was the one day of the week I could wear long pants and shoes. I liked getting dressed up pretty."

In late December, two days after Christmas, James was riled up when he arrived at the Friday Gathering. He put his things down at a table and before he got his dinner, he confronted me. "Not one of my daughters called on Christmas Day. Not one Merry Christmas." He paced in a small circle and continued, "How can they not remember their father? No card, no phone call, no Merry Christmas. Is this how they honor their father?"

The next week James said, "I made copies of my story, the one you wrote, and mailed it to my sister and each of my daughters. They don't understand my life and this explains it. I want my grandchildren to know who their grandfather is. I told them that when I die, I want it read at my funeral. It's my eulogy."

A few weeks later, James was stirred up again when he arrived for dinner. In a high-pitched voice, he said, "She woke me up at six o'clock this morning! Who calls at that hour? Can you believe it? My daughter called to wish me happy birthday. Yes," he added, "today is my birthday. My daughter remembered me. She called before I left for work."

I asked him if he thought sharing his story had made a difference.

"Yes, maybe so," he said.

Months later, James said his daughter was inspired to write her story and shared it with him.

One afternoon when James arrived, Barb—a volunteer—and I noticed the Mr. Sparkle car wash logo on his shirt and cap. "Do you have a new job?" we asked him.

James smiled and nodded. "I'm the boss. I've been filling in at different Mr. Sparkle car washes when their employees call out. They're all run by the same manager and he noticed what kind of worker I am. He asked me if I wanted a supervisor position. He offered me a permanent full-time job."

I asked James if he liked being responsible for other employees. "I'm a good supervisor. I tell the guys, 'I'm not going to call your attention to what needs doing. Walk around and find it yourself. If you can't see what needs doing, if you need someone to find it for you, then I don't need you.'"

On a summer afternoon in 2021, James arrived early for dinner. He was with his daughter, the youngest who lived in Jamaica. He was more talkative than usual. "This is my daughter," he said, extending his arm toward her. He took his time to introduce her to each of the volunteers. "She's here for a long weekend. I'm giving her a tour of Hartford." His daughter smiled and greeted us. She took out her cell phone and showed us pictures of her children.

"My grandchildren love me," James said. "If my daughters start to pick on me, my grandchildren say to their mother, 'Leave my grandfather alone!' They defend me!"

A few weeks later, I asked James if he had heard from his daughter in North Carolina.

"Since her mother died," he said, "we talk on the phone every day. I know she's hurting, but I'm grateful it has brought us closer."

At the end of August, James arrived late one Friday afternoon. He rode his bike up the sidewalk to the door where Leah, a volunteer, and I were waiting and softly said, "My mother died two days ago." His shoulders slumped and he stared at the ground. "I knew it was coming. We talked by phone every day. I need to go to Jamaica. I need to say goodbye. I always tried to honor my mother." But James didn't make it to her funeral. There wasn't enough time to make international flight reservations while COVID-19 restrictions were still in place.

It's unusual for James to miss a Friday Gathering. He is often the last to arrive, and we don't close the doors until he comes. "If a piece of equipment is broken at the car wash, I can't ignore it like that," James said. "I don't leave work until it's repaired. Some weeks, it makes me late. But I always come, because the woman at the door says to me, 'Oh my friend, I packed a bag for you.' I don't want to disappoint her."

Leah—the woman at the door—knows James's preferences, his likes and dislikes. Before he arrives, she has already packed a bag for him. It's filled with avocados, bananas, fresh tomatoes, peppers, milk, and cheese when they're available, and an assortment of pantry supplies. Her attentiveness to detail—she remembers the diners' preferences—is how she shows them that they matter.

Before he leaves, James checks a trash barrel at the back door. The barrel collects empty bottles and cans that can be redeemed for a nickel deposit. Members of Grace and others bring them to church for diners to collect. "Lee," a member of Grace, "told me about the bin and that I could help myself. It gives me something to do when I'm not at work," James said.

***

Vicki was born in 1971 and grew up on Long Island. She's of average height and identifies as white. Her weight has fluctuated over the years between plump and slim. "I lost weight. Did you notice?" she would ask when she dropped one or two dress sizes. "I can wear these jeans now and look good," and she would swivel her hips one way, then the other, smiling and showing off her figure.

Vicki is the youngest of four siblings. She has a brother who still lives in the house she grew up in and two sisters. Her oldest sister, Judy, is about twelve years older. "Judy didn't get along with our mom. It's as if we grew up with different mothers. I was five or six when Judy left home, and she never came back."

Vicki graduated from high school, got married, and had a son named Ethan. "It wasn't a good marriage, and we got divorced," she said.

"In September 2010, I had a fight with my sister Cheryl and needed to get away. I had met a man online who lived in Hartford, and he said I could stay with him, so I came. Ethan stayed on Long Island with my brother. Ethan's all grown now. I dream we'll be reunited someday in the future.

"I came to the first Christmas Eve dinner at Grace," Vicki said. "I was still new in Hartford. I met Louisa, who helped start the Friday Gathering, and asked her if she needed volunteers. When the weekly dinners started in January, I came regularly."

"In those years," Louisa said, "Vicki was at the Gathering most Fridays. But she also stopped in frequently during the week to visit, to have a place to be, to have someone to talk to. We got to know each other quite well. I remember that she called Ethan every week. They had a regular time when she would call, and she did that for years. When her phone wasn't working, she came to Grace and borrowed the church phone or used mine. She was always trying to figure out a way to have him come live with her."

Vicki met Tyler, a Black man, and he sometimes accompanied her to the Friday Gathering. In June 2012, their daughter Kristina was born.

Vicki brought Kristina to the Friday Gathering, and we watched her grow up. We marked her developmental milestones: smiling and recognizing her name, cutting her first teeth, clapping her hands, and playing peek-a-boo. She was a quiet baby. She learned to talk, but she didn't babble. Once she started walking, she ran around the dining hall and crawled under tables out of arm's reach. She didn't shy away from the noisy, crowded room.

Vicki welcomed the aunties and uncles who vied for Kristina's attention and the break it gave her. Kristina ran around the room and diners called her name or held out their hand to beckon her over. When Kristina was about two years old, Vicki asked Bernie to take their portrait, and their picture is displayed in the dining hall. Vicki held Kristina cheek-to-cheek. Vicki was relaxed and smiling while Kristina looked wide-eyed at the camera.

"In 2013, Vicki's father was dying," Louisa said. "She offered to pay for gas if I would drive her to Long Island to see him. It meant a lot to her that her father got to see Kristina before he died. I met her son, Ethan, and her brother, and they seemed like really nice people. It could have been a much more difficult visit."

Vicki and Tyler didn't talk about it publicly at the Friday Gathering, but there were domestic troubles, and Kristina was placed in foster care. They mourned losing Kristina in their own ways. They sat apart at the Friday Gathering. Vicki sobbed through dinner. Tyler kept to himself. They were allowed supervised visits, but Kristina lived more than an hour away by car; it was nearly impossible to arrange a visit. Some weeks, Tyler showed me photos the foster mother sent him. Vicki played short videos on her phone that the foster mother sent her. Kristina started school. She had friends her age and was growing. Eventually, Vicki's and Tyler's parental rights were terminated and Kristina's foster mother adopted her.

When Vicki and I talked in January 2020, she was upbeat. "I'm writing a book for Kristina," she said. "Her adoptive mom encouraged me to write it so that Kristina will know about her birth family. I'm writing about the dreams I have for her, that I want her to grow up to be smart and strong and have a good life. I want her to know that I love her, and I want us to be a family again."

"I need family!" Vicki continued. "And I found my sister," she said emphatically. She was talking about her elder sister, Judy.

"Before my father died," she explained, "he told me to find Judy. I didn't know what that would do to my mother, so I didn't do anything. But since my mother died last year, I felt free to search. Using Facebook, I found her! She's living in Delaware. We haven't met in person yet, but we talk on the phone. When she talks about our mother, it's hard to listen to her. I'm trying to see things from her point of view."

Vicki was pleased with herself, too, because she had completed all her shifts as a bell ringer for the Salvation Army during the holidays. "We had eight-hour shifts outdoors in all kinds of weather. It's a long time to be on your feet, standing on cold cement, with no way to warm up.

"The hardest part of the job was being rejected," Vicki said. "All the people who walk past you and won't look at you, who can't even say hello. It's like you're invisible, like you're not there. Then there are the people who make excuses for not putting something in the kettle. 'I gave at the other door,' or, 'I don't have change today,' or 'I'll see you on my way back.' Being lied to—especially at Christmas—makes it worse. And the monotony. All the bodies passing one way, then passing the other way, and I can only stand in the same spot for eight hours.

"It made me think about what it's like to depend on the generosity of strangers. Not just the people who put something in the kettle. But the strangers who suddenly appeared with a cup of hot chocolate or hot coffee. Some people just said, 'Thank you.' I think they meant 'Thank you for doing this for people in need.' And it surprised me, that their little kindness to me could turn a dreary afternoon around. Such a little thing.

"I made it to every shift I was assigned. I never saw anyone I knew at the sites I worked. I'm filling out job applications now. One is to be a school bus driver. I'm motivated. I don't want to be a bell ringer again.

"I'm married now, too," Vicki said. "I'm Vicki Bonds. Changed my name." Then her voice dropped. "But he's in jail."

Months passed and we didn't see Vicki again until summertime. Her face was swollen, she had two fresh black eyes, and she was crying. One of the volunteers asked her, "Who did this to you?"

"My roommates," Vicki said. She had gotten an apartment not too far from Grace and allowed two people to stay with her. "They took my keys. They locked me out of the apartment and took my cell phone. I have nothing."

Roy, who by this time had moved away from his boarded-up family home to an apartment, was shaken at the sight of Vicki's face and invited her to stay with him for the weekend. She stayed until Roy asked her to leave. "She causes some of her own trouble," was all he said.

One afternoon, a group of diners were sitting together in the park. They were talking about how they first got to know each other at the House of Bread. "That's where I got to know Vicki," Ray said. "I used to do intake records at a shelter, and I tried to use that experience to help her. Sometimes she can be too trusting and good-natured. Then she gets mixed up with people who take advantage of her. She has a hard time being alone."

More than a year passed. Then a diner mentioned that they had seen Vicki. "She's hanging out at the gas station," they said. "She's lost weight."

***

Albert was born in 1928 and grew up in Hartford. He was a Black man, shorter than average, and a middle child among two brothers and five sisters. He passed away in December 2017, before diners' stories were recorded. The voices of his friends, neighbors, and grandson contributed to this memory of him.

Albert was more than a regular fixture at the Friday Gathering. In the early years, he made rounds during dinner, visiting every table and greeting diners. It was how he kept his finger on the pulse of the neighborhood and the city. In later years, when his health began to fail, he staked out a chair next to the table where diners picked up their name tags. If the chair was occupied when he arrived, he evicted its occupant. He held court at the Friday Gathering, and diners sought him out—to ask his advice, share a piece of gossip, or take comfort from his abiding faith in God's mercy.

Although Albert never shepherded a congregation, he was widely known as Reverend Bell. He had earned a diploma in religion and Bible studies from Ambassador College in Pasadena, California. He held a certificate in clerical training and was enrolled in the Black Ministries certification program at the Hartford Seminary.[69]

Hilda introduced Albert to the Friday Gathering in 2011. They lived in the same apartment building, and she was his home health aide. "He received a small food stamp allowance," she said, "but he didn't have a habit of going to soup kitchens. He came to the Friday Gathering because I was cooking, and of course, he liked my food. He got to know Darrell and Pastor Eva. We went together to the class she held for new members and the Wednesday Bible study she led in the community room at our apartment building."

Albert joined Grace, and every Sunday he sat up front in the third pew. He wore his best clothes: pressed trousers, a button-down shirt and tie, socks to match, loafers with tassels, and a cap or hat. "I lay them out the night before," he said. In November 2012, the congregation elected him to serve on Grace's church council. He completed his fifth year just before his death.

Albert talked about himself as both a sinner and saved by the grace of God. "I've done it all," he said.

One Friday he choked up and tears rolled down his cheeks. "My mother instilled good morals in me and I let her down." He described a childhood memory, about an opportunity he had to help an elderly man carry his packages up a steep hill. Instead, he ran away and joined his friends. "After all these years, I am still asking for forgiveness. And still learning how to receive it."

In 2014, the congregation voted to recognize Albert as an outreach minister. It was the first time Grace acknowledged such a position. On worship bulletins and monthly newsletters, his name and title were listed alongside the names of the congregation's pastor, staff, and leaders. "He wasn't perfect, nor did he argue that he was; he was a sinner and a saint as all of us may be. Albert offered himself to his family, friends, acquaintances, and strangers just as he was," Pastor Rick said.[70]

Albert carried copies of his curriculum vitae with him. He served with the US Army in the Korean War and the European theater and was honorably discharged as a private second class.[71] He was a typesetter for the Hartford Courant, responsible for the quality of the copy they produced. He was an administrative assistant for United Cerebral Palsy and an intake worker for Friends of the Street, a nonprofit that assisted people who were homeless. He served on the boards of several community organizations.

Of all his work experience, Albert was most proud of his role as a caseworker for US Senator Joseph Lieberman. He responded to constituents' problems, including questions about Social Security benefits, Medicare, and customs. Recalling Albert's time on his staff, Senator

Lieberman said:

> Al Bell served in my Senate office in the early 90s when I was first
> elected. He wasn't a typical hire—being older than my young staff
> and not having any administrative experience—but he brought a
> knowledge of and a connection to the neighborhoods I was
> committed to serving. He was a minister and brought calm to an
> office that could get frenetic. He was well liked by the staff. He
> taught them tolerance and kindness in the face of agitated
> constituents, and they attempted to teach him how to operate the
> fax machine. Neither was completely successful! I do remember
> his contribution to the annual staff picnic was a huge tub of ice
> cream, and he never showed up without a string of nephews and
> nieces and neighborhood kids tagging along. He had a joyous
> spirit, and I was privileged to know him.[72]

Albert organized a residents' association at the SANDS housing project when he lived in Hartford's North End. He urged residents to fight for responsible property managers. He refused to let drug dealers operate near his apartment. After a five-year-old child was killed by a car when she tried to cross Main Street to get to a store, Albert operated a small store out of his apartment.[73] His grandson recalled, "He sold candy, Italian ice, diapers, popcorn, and loaned people money. He wasn't a loan shark. The people loved and respected him."[74]

When Albert moved to Asylum Hill, he joined the board of the neighborhood association. Bernie, who also served on the board, said Albert "came to the monthly meetings to speak his mind. Even in doing so, he did not call a great deal of attention to himself, but rather to the cause that he was most concerned about at that moment."[75]

Albert never abandoned the struggle for justice. In the last year of his life, he was agitated about the deteriorating conditions at his apartment building, three blocks from Grace. A new group of residents left the exterior doors open, and it threatened residents' security. Albert watched drug dealers operating on the street outside his window. He and other residents battled through bed bug infestations. The rats that were gnawing through his kitchen wall were the last straw. Pastor Rick arranged a meeting at Grace with the city's mayor. Bernie recalled, "Albert did not hesitate to speak his mind clearly and forcefully."[76]

"Albert was always engaged. Worried about traffic lights and drug dealers, absentee landlords and the people living in their buildings, presidents and the woman on the street carrying a child and her groceries. Nothing passed him by, everything was in his heart and in his smile," Pastor Rick said.[77] "Albert was a fearless organizer yet was not satisfied with his ability to influence," he said to diners at the Friday Gathering.

In August, a few months before his death, Albert attended the One Thousand Ministers March for Justice in Washington, DC. The march protested continuing social and racial injustice and honored the anniversary of Dr. Martin Luther King, Jr.'s "I Have a Dream" speech. Even in DC, Albert was a force. He wore a Grace Lutheran Church t-shirt and attracted the attention of news cameras and marchers.

Albert had no biological offspring, yet he cared for three stepchildren and was a patriarch to five generations of nieces, nephews, cousins, and untold numbers of extended family.[78] He was devoted to all of them. He set aside Sunday afternoons to visit his grandson in prison. Albert worried about who would support his grandson after he was gone.

"He would visit me," his grandson wrote to me, "and tough guys would see him and be excited or even cry, saying, 'Mr. LB, you're still alive. I haven't seen you in decades.' They would tell me how he caught them stealing or misbehaving and corrected them. Universally, they all said, 'LB did not accept my bullshit.'

"He was a tough guy. Funny memory to prove my point," his grandson said. "He and I had a conversation prior to his passing about him leaving shortly. I was about to break down sobbing, and he became general-like instantly. He barked, 'Grandson! Stop that and buck up! I'm dying and I accept it, so accept it. Grandpa is still sharp in the mind, but Grandpa's body is giving out. I will be here for you until my last breath and will do all within my power for you. You have to humble yourself. You have to be smart and intelligent. You have to know when to use your smarts and when to use your intelligence. They are not one and the same.' At our last visit he was falling asleep and did not have the strength to open the door upon departing. Until he exited this realm he loved me to the highest degree."[79]

When Albert passed away, his absence was palpable at the Friday Gathering. A tribute published in the monthly *Asylum Hill News & Views* stated that Albert was the first local resident to be honored with an obituary in their paper.[80] Lamont, the church sexton, put a copy of Albert's portrait on the chair where Albert sat, next to the table where diners picked up their name tags. The portrait sat there for a month, and then the chair was moved to the stage. One of Albert's caps was placed on the chair, next to the portrait, and the memorial remained in place until the first anniversary of his passing. "He was like a father to me," Lamont said.

"I see Albert as a moral force," Pastor Rick said, "a reverend who found God in his life journey where he encountered all the elements of racism, poverty, drugs, police brutality, anger, ignorance, despair, discrimination, and being ignored and discounted. His humor, love, and strength left its mark on all who knew him, and particularly the large family who loved and admired him."[81]

***

Our culture is preoccupied with achievement and success and their hallmarks: awards, trophies, and luxuries that only lots of money can buy. From a young age, we learn that if you aren't a winner, then you're a loser. But it is in the struggle—the back-and-forth dance of failing and pursuing—where we learn and grow, and it is a process that continues all of our days. To deny the struggle or to value one struggle more than another is to reject our life and humanity. Honoring the struggle means we value the ordeals that have shaped us.

7

For the Enjoyment of Others

Happiness quite unshared can scarcely be called happiness; it has no taste.

—Charlotte Brontë, letter to W. S. Williams, March 19, 1850

Darrell said, "Hosting the Friday Gathering isn't a chore, it's fun." He left the cooking to the chefs and turned his attention to the enjoyment of the community. He did it with music. Darrell invited musicians of all abilities to perform at the Friday Gathering. One of them was Addison.

***

I met Addison in 2008 when I was searching for a church home. He was one of the people I noticed the first time I visited Grace. A tall white man, he sat near the front and used a braille book. A petite woman, also white, sat next to him and used a braille book, too. I learned later that she was his friend Janet.

Their braille books were oversized three-ring binders, about three inches thick, filled with pages of dense paper imprinted with raised dots that form the braille alphabet. When we stood during the service, Addison and Janet rested their books on the back of the pew in front of them. The books looked heavy, and their bulky size made them awkward to manage. Addison and Janet balanced the opened books with one hand while the other lightly swept across a page, sensing each line and reading the patterns of dots.

Addison was born prematurely in 1952 in Philadelphia. He was placed in an incubator with an oxygen-rich atmosphere. It was common in those years to treat preemie babies this way to increase their chances of survival. But there were side effects. In 1954, researchers established that high oxygen levels could damage the retina and cause blindness. One pediatrician estimated that from the 1940s to 1953, approximately 7,000 babies in the United States were blinded by oxygen therapy, including Addison and singer-songwriter Stevie Wonder.[82] The increase of blindness in babies was severe enough that it was called an epidemic.

Addison was the youngest of three brothers. His family loved music, and they each had their favorites that they listened to on the radio and the record player. "My parents liked big band music," Addison said. "They liked the rhythm and they danced to it. My grandparents listened to classical music and my uncle listened to jazz. My brothers played rock 'n' roll records. I liked all of it.

"We had a piano in the living room when I was growing up," Addison said. "It had belonged to my grandmother—on my father's side of the family. My mother played it, and she encouraged me to play. When I was three, I climbed up on the piano stool and started picking out tunes by ear. 'Jingle Bells' was the first song I played."

Addison began attending the Overbrook School for the Blind in Philadelphia when he was three years old. When he was seven, his family moved to Glenside, just north of Philadelphia. Addison was enrolled in Overbrook's residential program and came home on weekends.

Classes at Overbrook covered all the basic subjects—math, science, English, language arts, and social studies. The curriculum also included art, music, and gym. Addison thrived, especially in music. In third grade, he, like all the third-grade students, started learning how to read music in braille. At Overbrook, Addison took piano lessons, was the substitute organist for chapel services, and sang with the elementary school chorus and junior high choir. Overbrook is where Addison got his first taste of performing for the public. "There were annual spring and Christmas concerts," he said. "I was happy to play in groups and to play solo, and to share music with others."

When Addison was fifteen, his family moved to West Hartford, Connecticut, and he enrolled at the Oak Hill School, located in the northwest corner of Hartford, a fifteen-minute drive from home. "For the first time in years, I lived at home and commuted to school," he said. With roots extending back to the 1890s, Oak Hill, like Overbrook, served the educational needs of students who were blind. At Oak Hill, Addison continued to study music. Making music was becoming a driving force in his life, and he began to imagine himself as a professional musician. After graduating from Oak Hill, he continued to the Hartt School of Music at the University of Hartford.

At Hartt, Addison studied piano and jazz. He graduated magna cum laude in 1976 with a concentration in piano and went on to earn his artist diploma in 1978. "I've been fortunate to be able to play what I enjoy. I'm just as comfortable with pop and rock 'n' roll as I am with jazz and classical music."

Addison's career has spanned nearly fifty years. He performed throughout Connecticut, Massachusetts, and New York as a pianist with the Al Jarvis Orchestra, the Sam Pasco Orchestra, and the Jerry Carrillo

Orchestra. He was a guest DJ for jazz programs on WWUH, a radio station licensed to the University of Hartford. He accompanied ballet students at the Greater Hartford Academy of the Arts and for the Hartt School's Community Division. He gave private piano lessons, sang barbershop, and still performs solo for public and private events.

Addison has been an active member of Grace since he and his family came to Connecticut. When Darrell invited musicians to share their talents with the Friday Gathering, it was natural to include Addison. On the nights he played, his friend Janet, also a member of Grace, came, too, until she passed away in 2019.

***

Janet was born in Hartford in 1948. She and her twin sister were born almost two months premature, and like Addison, placed in incubators with oxygen-rich atmospheres. The damage to their retinas was not immediate, though. Janet had some vision that gradually faded by the time she started school.

Her sister said, "All her life, Janet remembered the color of blue and purple, she remembered the sun."

Janet's twin suffered vision loss, too, but not to the same extent. Consequently, the girls were schooled differently. At six years old, Janet began at the Oak Hill School while her sister attended public school. Janet lived at Oak Hill during the week and went home on weekends.

"It caused a separation in the family, especially between us," Janet's twin said. "My father was heartbroken. He asked the doctors if he could donate his eyes to Janet, but that wasn't possible.

"At Oak Hill, Janet learned how to be self-reliant," her sister said. "She was smart, she was fearless, and she was strong. When Janet came home on weekends, she had her own way of doing things. She was confident and knew how to take care of herself. I missed her when she was away. I didn't have the same kind of confidence, and I struggled with that difference between us. We were torn apart, and it was never the same. They should have enrolled me at Oak Hill, too, because it would have helped me learn how to be strong and independent, like Janet."

Janet was schooled in all the subjects that led to a high school diploma. She took advantage of Oak Hill's music program and learned to sing, tap dance, and play the piano. "Janet was good at harmonizing," her sister said. "On the radio, we listened to Patience and Prudence, two sisters who sang harmony together, and we wanted to be like them. Their big hit was 'Tonight You Belong to Me.' Janet sang alto and let me sing the lead. Singing brought us together."

Janet was determined to support herself. After graduating from Oak Hill in 1966, she went to New York City and trained to become a medical transcriptionist. "She lived independently in New York," her sister recalled. "She was there two years and took the bus by herself, visiting all around the city. Janet came back to Connecticut and worked at Saint Raphael's Hospital in New Haven. Then she went to Saint Francis Medical Center in Hartford and worked there for over thirty years, until she retired. She made a career of it.

"Janet loved to wear dresses," her sister remembered. "She was organized and had a system so that she could put outfits together. She knew which shoes to wear with each outfit, which blouses or scarf went well with a suit. She liked to wear jewelry, especially dangly earrings. She enjoyed knowing that she looked good. If I didn't compliment her on an outfit, she'd ask straight out: 'How do I look today?'"

When Janet retired from Saint Francis, she asked the members of Grace to start a clothing program for the neighborhood. Years later, when she was recognized as the Asylum Hill Neighborhood's Volunteer of the Month, her motivation for the clothing bank was detailed in an article for the neighborhood's newsletter: "She realized that she would no longer need the many business suits that she had acquired over the years, but rather than take them to one of the many secondhand stores that would sell them, she talked to her fellow members at Grace about starting a free clothing bank."[83]

The program was named Janet's Closet, and it opened to the public for two hours each Wednesday. More than clothing, Janet's Closet offered people another pathway to belonging. There are neighbors who collect and donate clothing and small household goods, others who sort donations and organize clothes, and still others who greet neighbors when the doors are open. It radiates a coffee klatch ambiance so that stopping in to say hello is as welcomed as browsing for clothing.

Addison and Janet met at an Oak Hill alumni event. He heard her play the piano and sing with a group of girlfriends, and their music got his attention. Addison and Janet crossed paths at other alumni programs and a friendship grew between them, shaped by their pleasure of singing and making music together. After Janet married and was later widowed, she moved closer to Hartford and joined the congregation at Grace. On Sunday mornings, she sat with Addison at worship, was a cantor for the liturgy, and sang harmony with the hymns. After she retired, she moved to the Asylum Hill neighborhood and lived nearby on Woodland Street. "She loved being within walking distance of the church," her sister remembered.[84]

When Addison played on Friday nights, Janet often came, too. She stood next to the piano and sang while Addison accompanied her. "Doo-wop and hits from the '50s, '60s, and '70s were her favorites," Addison said. "Songs like 'Teenager in Love,' 'Earth Angel,' and 'It's My Party.' We both liked 'Let Me Go to Him' by Dionne Warwick. One night we danced to 'White Christmas,' from a recording by the Drifters."

Janet liked to play the piano on Friday nights, too. When Addison took a break, it was her turn to play. "Janet loved music," her sister said.

"I knew which music she liked best," Addison said. "I miss playing for her and listening to her."

Diners at the Friday Gathering enjoyed the duo. When Janet sang, diners stopped their conversations and sang along with her. They marveled that Addison could play without seeing the keys and were even more amazed that he could play an endless stream of music from memory. "Watching him play, to see his fingers jump up and down the keyboard, it never gets old," a diner said. "I don't know how he does it."

Addison brought song lists he had printed in braille and occasionally stopped to read one before starting a new piece. Diners peeked at the text when it lay on top of the piano and were fascinated by it. When Janet wasn't singing, Addison played selections of classical and jazz music. "It seems like he can play anything," a diner said.

Addison's outlook on performing—and all the roles any of us fill—is that you should always do a good job. It doesn't matter whether you volunteered for it or whether you're paid a little or a lot. It doesn't matter what the size of the audience is.

"Martin Luther King, Jr. talked about this in a speech. Sweep streets as good as Michelangelo painted pictures," Addison said, recalling Dr. King's remark in a speech:

> If it falls your lot to be a street sweeper, sweep streets like Michelangelo painted pictures, sweep streets like Beethoven composed music, sweep streets like Leontyne Price sings before the Metropolitan Opera. Sweep streets like Shakespeare wrote poetry. Sweep streets so well that all the hosts of heaven and earth will have to pause and say: Here lived a great street sweeper who swept his job well.[85]

"This attitude applies to hospitality and to being a chef, too," Addison said. "Those who can't afford to pay deserve just as good a meal and to be welcomed just as warmly as those who pay. Some blind people expect mediocrity because they're afraid of asking for too much. They don't want to be perceived as a burden or helpless."

Addison plays for the Friday Gathering, he said, because "even people who are poor enjoy good music. Those who can't afford to pay are worthy of it just the same." Addison plays for the pleasure of his listeners regardless of their circumstances.

"What do you get out of it?" I asked him.

"When I've heard and then learned a good piece of music, it's a shame to keep it just in the practice room," Addison answered. "Good music is meant to be shared. I want the diners to have a good time, and then I have a good time, too."

***

Live music is more than entertainment at the Friday Gathering. It brings diners together. The meal is transformed and the evening becomes an event. There is a reason to linger. Conversations take a pause, the chaos subsides, and diners move in unison to the rhythm of the music. Hans Christian Andersen, a master storyteller, said, "Where words fail, music speaks."

One evening, as I was looking at the portraits in the dining hall, I was surprised to find Walter's picture there. Walter, a Black man, is the custodian in the building where I live. I hadn't noticed him at a Friday Gathering before. When I saw Walter a few days later, I said, "You came to my church for dinner and I missed you. I saw your portrait on the wall at church, and it's a great picture of you."

"I only came once," Walter said. "There were Russian ballerinas performing *The Nutcracker,* and I wanted my granddaughters to see them. I could never afford tickets to the theater. This was so much better. We were right there on the floor where they danced. When we got home, my granddaughters twirled and danced around and pretended to be ballerinas. They loved it."

All varieties of musicians made their way to the Friday Gathering: Maxine, a jazz saxophonist who had performed in New York City clubs;

Oasis, a local Christian rock band; and the KC Sisters, five sisters with perfect pitch and harmony. Darrell invited people from the neighborhood to sing while he accompanied them on guitar. A'Niya, Leah's daughter, sang when she was still in elementary school. "She's one of us," a diner said. He invited Cami, the granddaughter of a kitchen volunteer from Jamaica, and Sophie, a young Black woman who emigrated from England. The dining hall quieted to welcome their voices and erupted with applause in appreciation for their talents.

Norman, a Black man and a jazz and blues pianist, lived in the Asylum Hill neighborhood. He never had formal music education and said he couldn't read music. He played by ear and called himself a "freelance musician." Norman learned about the Friday Gathering from Chef Louis and asked if he could play on Fridays. When Louis cooked, he came out of the kitchen to sing alongside Norman.

When there was no live music, the host played recordings from CDs. Pastor Rick asked the diners for requests, and there were plenty: Ray Charles, Louis Armstrong, Aretha Franklin, Marvin Gaye, The Temptations, Dr. John, Prince, and Gladys Knight. Some nights, Sonny got up and danced along. "He's a pretty good dancer, too," Pastor Rick said.

I asked Addison, "What's the difference between live music and a recording?" and he answered immediately, "Fidelity."

"The quality of the sound is different when it comes out of a speaker, when the sound is produced by a machine. If the music is live, it comes from your body," he explained. "It's a singular moment with the musician, the room, the acoustics, and the audience."

The audience is more than spectators. They participate in the performance. There is a continuous feedback loop between the musician and the audience that weaves them together. There's a synchrony in the moment that cannot be duplicated, that makes each performance unique and intimate.

"A machine can't reproduce that," Addison said.

Magic happens when musicians click, as if they spring from the same body with lungs breathing and hearts beating in unison. It's an infectious spirit. Singers and audiences get caught up in the magic, too. There is a link between music and our brains, a connection to emotions, memory, movement, and coordination. Heads bobbing, toes tapping, shoulders rocking, fingers drumming, voices singing, all responding to the same groove.

Oliver Sacks, a neurologist and author, investigated how music influences the way we experience the world. He observed that rhythm can be contagious within a group. Writing about accompanying one of his patients to a concert as part of his research, he reflected: "I say I 'observed' all this, but I found myself unable to remain a detached observer. I realized that I, too, was moving, stamping, clapping with the music, and soon lost all my usual diffidence and inhibition and joined the crowd in communal dancing."[86] Sacks concluded that music functions in its power to "[bring] people together, producing a sense of collectivity and community."[87]

When musicians share the essence of themselves, it isn't a chore. It is fun. They bring their whole being to the moment and invite diners to be their whole selves, too. At the Friday Gathering, live music is the icing on the cake. The meal is delicious and it's plentiful. But it is music, especially live music, that expresses our collective joie de vivre. In those exhilarating moments, we belong to each other.[88]

8

Keeping the Doors Open During the Pandemic

The major problem of life is learning how to handle the costly interruptions. The door that slams shut, the plan that got sidetracked, the marriage that failed. Or that lovely poem that didn't get written because someone knocked on the door.

—Rev. Dr. Martin Luther King Jr.

In early March 2020, the Friday Gathering committee took steps to address the COVID-19 pandemic. We recognized that chefs, volunteers, and neighbors were at increased risk of illness and death due to their age, chronic health issues, poverty, race, and the neighborhood's high population density. On March 13, we suspended indoor dining and began serving the hot meal in take-out containers.

Concern for our neighbors intensified with the threats of apartment evictions, increased homelessness, and food shortages—exacerbated by closed restaurants, coffee shops, schools, soup kitchens, and food pantries. The Friday Gathering chefs were committed to ensuring that COVID-19 would not become an interruption to serving dinner. "Keeping the doors open" expressed how we adapted and maintained our connection with the neighborhood.

News spread by word of mouth that the Friday Gathering was still operating. After the second week of serving takeout, I shared these observations with the committee:

- Neighbors started gathering early, at 3 p.m.

- Neighbors expressed gratitude and relief, saying, "Thank you, thank you," and "You remembered me."

- Some made a point of telling us they were hungry. One man said he had not eaten in two days.

- Diners said several kitchens were closed and one had switched to serving sandwiches.

- People asked, "Where can I go tomorrow?"

- Several diners declined toilet paper and other supplies, saying, "I have enough. Someone else might need it more."

We made offering choice a priority. "Do you want cheese or lunch meat? A bar of Dove soap or Dial? A roll of toilet paper or paper towels? Tuna fish or spaghetti sauce? Milk or eggs? Whole wheat bread or bagels?" The ability to choose honored diners' individual preferences, shared control with them over their decision-making, and broke up the monotony. It put a little "yes" in their day. If we'd had pre-filled bags to make the distribution easier, some items might have been tossed because they were not what a diner could use. The power to exercise choice is one of our most pleasurable experiences. It validates us. Jacqueline Novogratz, who works to alleviate poverty on a global scale, drew a connection between dignity and exerting personal choice. She wrote, "The opposite of poverty is dignity. Dignity is freedom. It is choice. It is having control over decisions in our lives."[89]

Bringing diners indoors to pick up meals brought them past the dining hall where their portraits lined the walls. For the hundreds of diners we met for the first time during the twenty-nine months of serving takeout, the portraits reflected the neighborhood back to them. Welcoming diners into the church building was important. Who is allowed in conveys messages about who matters and has clout, whether those messages are intended or not. A one-way path, in one door, down a ramp, and exiting out another door brought diners past several distribution stations and the restrooms and helped us manage social distancing. At each station we greeted friends by name. "Hi, Joe. Hi, Dorothy. I'm glad to see you! How are you managing?"

Diners were welcomed in, but there were safety precautions. Some diners argued when they were asked to use hand sanitizer. "Are you calling me dirty? Is that what you think of me?"

The host at the door adapted and we learned how to set expectations while diners waited in line. We announced the menu and pantry items; shared information about free test sites, free buses, and the library; and set expectations for masks and hand sanitizer, so everyone could anticipate the process as their turn approached. Knowing what to expect eased some of their anxiety.

The serving line passed right by the washrooms, and diners didn't need to ask permission to use them. We do not know whether diners are homeless or living in shelters; our relationships aren't based on those details. We do not know how long people have been out during the day or how far they commuted to get to Grace. Public places where people used to gather were closed. We anticipated that neighbors had less access to restrooms. The Friday Gathering chefs intended for their meals to be enjoyed; giving diners privacy to care for themselves would help them relax when they ate their dinner later.

One Friday, a woman asked me, "Do you have any clothes? I only have what I'm wearing." We found two pairs of slacks and three tops in her size and invited her to use the restroom to freshen up. During the summer and fall when more people were on the move and searching for help, there were more requests for clothing. Access to the washrooms offered a safe place to change clothes for diners who carried all their belongings with them. For some, access to running water was pure pleasure. "The sound of running water and splashing it on my face rejuvenated me," a diner said.

In May—after months of isolation—some neighbors came to Grace searching for more than food. They hungered to be relevant and asked to volunteer. "I'll do anything," Elena said. I texted her a few times, but she didn't reply. We didn't see her again.

On a Friday in early June, four of us were in the kitchen, chopping vegetables, making salad, and seasoning meat for the evening meal. A woman of Asian descent appeared at the kitchen door and said, "I work in kitchen. Lee told me come today."

***

Lee, a white man, was born in Hartford in 1940. "When I was two years old, my family moved to Glastonbury [a suburb of Hartford]. I spent most of my younger years there and graduated from Glastonbury High School. I enrolled at the New Britain State Teachers College and planned to become a teacher.[90] I worked part-time for a painting contractor to help pay for tuition and discovered that I liked working with my hands. I left school with an associate degree and started my own painting business. I began learning carpentry skills and added home remodeling and repairs to my resume. I built my first house in 1963 and continued building houses until 1969, when there was a severe downturn in the residential mortgage industry. I was forced to discontinue my building business."

Lee took a hiatus from construction work, but not for long. Over the span of his career, he managed and renovated all sorts of properties that took him to Arkansas, Texas, Florida, and Rhode Island. In 1996 he moved back to Hartford. "I lived on Kenyon Street in the West End. In 2002, I took 'unofficial retirement' and moved to the Immanuel House Senior Living facility, on Woodland Street near Grace. I continued in the construction business with a longtime friend and business partner. When my friend retired in 2012, the business was disbanded."

In Hartford, Lee got involved in the West End Civic Association and served on several boards. In 2004, he was described as a neighborhood activist.[91] The *Hartford Courant* reported on his efforts to convert a corner lot into a Christmas tree nursery with its proceeds to benefit the neighborhood's Little League Program. In 2005, the West End Community Center honored him at their first Movers & Shakers Community Gala.[92] Despite the public recognition, Lee is a quiet man and shuns the spotlight.

Lee objected when I asked him how he identifies himself. "It doesn't matter what color, religion, or culture we are," he said. "We're all people. No matter who we are, we all desire the same things: comfort, a place to call home, companionship. We cry. We laugh. Color doesn't change any of that.

"The Asylum Hill neighborhood is like a mini-United Nations," Lee continued. "That's why I sit outside in front of the church. I meet all different kinds of people. I carry dog treats in my pocket and I've gotten to know all the dogs, too." He chuckled. "I like hearing about different cultures, and people from other countries share their traditions with me. I like the diversity because it's interesting and I learn something."

Lee helped bring two Alcoholics Anonymous groups to Grace, and he is their informal hospitality manager. He opens the doors for meetings, brews a pot of coffee, and serves protein bars, cookies, and fresh fruit. When people in the city ask me which church I belong to and I answer, "Grace," occasionally they say, "I know that church. I've gone to AA meetings there."

When Connecticut implemented lockdown measures in March 2020, Lee was adamant about keeping the doors open for in-person AA meetings. He said, "The isolation and loneliness can be overwhelming for people at risk of relapsing. There is no substitute for being in the presence of each other."

Lee insisted that attendees remove their face masks. He said, "I won't let masks help people cover up their deepest needs. We need to see each other's expressions." He ventilated the meeting room, limited the size of the group to ten, spaced chairs for social distancing, checked temperatures, and insisted on hand sanitizing. Not a single case of COVID-19 was reported among his groups. But when Lee and I talked, he was worried about how many with alcoholism or drug addiction might have relapsed. Although he kept the doors open, some people stopped attending meetings.

One afternoon that summer, I saw Dennis—a man I knew from the Gathering—outside city hall. He immediately asked, "How's Lee? He's my dad, you know." Then Dennis clarified that he was speaking metaphorically. He added, "I haven't talked to him in a while and I miss him. Give him my new phone number."

When Richie, another Friday Gathering diner, mentioned Lee, he started off with the same words; "He's my dad. He has a good heart. He's there for you. I can call him anytime and talk to him about anything. If he doesn't have the answer to something, he'll find it. You can trust him to keep your confidence."

Throughout the day all week long, the church doorbell rang with people asking if Lee was in. During a bitter cold spell, Jan, who was homeless again and waiting for a warming center to open, came to see him. Lee let Jan in so he could warm up. Lee found work to do—sorting clothing donations, breaking down cardboard boxes, picking up litter—and the sharing of chores chipped away at the loneliness and feeling useless. On Friday afternoons when the packaging team portioned food into take-out containers, volunteers set one aside and wrote Lee's name on it. "It's a small way to show him how much he means to me," a chef said.

Lee is a journeyman carpenter. At Grace, we could rename "Jack-of-all-trades" to "Lee-of-all-trades." He is intimately familiar with the building and has an eye for detail. He installed rollers on the kitchen prep tables, mounted new knobs on cabinet doors, opened a boarded-over fireplace, refreshed water-stained ceiling tiles, fixed the faulty hinges on a folding table, replaced broken floor tiles, and repaired toilets and leaky pipes, all while keeping the floors polished and giving the walls a fresh coat of paint.

In 2013, Louisa asked Lee if he could build benches from discarded wooden pallets. Lee said he could. Louisa wanted to install the benches in the garden and under the cherry trees so that neighbors taking shortcuts across the property would have a place to rest and visit with each other. Lee took his coffee breaks on one of the benches in front of the church. Although he called it a coffee break, he'd just shifted roles from carpenter to the Grace welcoming committee. He invited passersby to sit with him and invited them to dinner on Friday, and if they needed the restroom, a drink of water, or a bag of groceries, he saw to that, too. Although Lee didn't remember meeting the woman who appeared at the kitchen door in early June, he imagined it happened while sitting under one of the cherry trees, because this was where he often met neighbors. He told her to come on Friday morning at ten o'clock.

***

Setsuko was a small woman and soft-spoken. Her eyes peeked out above a blue disposable face mask. She wore a backpack that looked too large for her frame, and over her arm she carried a large reusable grocery bag. "Lee told me come today," she repeated. Then she pointed to the grocery bag and said, "I brought food."

The kitchen volunteers and I weren't expecting her. I found Louisa and asked if she knew what Lee had in mind. Louisa shrugged and said, "Find something for her to do."

I showed Setsuko where to stow her backpack, placed the bag of food in the refrigerator, and gave her a quick tour of the kitchen, including the sink to use for handwashing, the drawer holding the supply of disposable gloves, and where to get an apron and hair covering. Then, Setsuko and I picked up the salad materials and moved into the dining hall where we could spread out.

Before we tackled salad making, Setsuko and I walked around the hall and looked at the portraits on the walls. I pointed out a few of the pictures and told her short stories about some of the people. "He plays the piano on Friday nights; she makes name tags for people when they arrive; he always stays for the prayer circle; he's one of the chefs; that's Lamont who you met in the kitchen; he's Lamont's brother, Arnell; and this is Bernie, the man who took all these photographs."

Setsuko told me a little about herself. She was born in 1976 in southern Japan. Both of her parents and a brother were deceased. She had a sister living in Tokyo. She had been in the United States for quite a while. Her husband was Asian American, and they had been married twenty years. She didn't mention if they had children.

It was because of Setsuko that I learned about the history of the ornamental cherry trees on the front lawn of the church. "Grace has a history of connections with people from Japan," Louisa told us. "The trees have flourished in this place. Cherry trees live about forty years and ornamental cherry trees even less. These trees are almost sixty years old."

I joked with Setsuko and said, "They've been waiting for you."

Setsuko was eager to talk about her passion for dentistry. She had recently completed her studies at the University of Connecticut. After dreaming of becoming a dentist for many years, she was finally able to practice it. I asked her what she enjoyed about it. Although some people say they want to be a doctor or a nurse I never met anyone who dreamed of being a dentist. "It's such a small space, inside a mouth. You have to trust that your patients aren't going to bite you, don't you?" I half-teased her.

"People think dental work is just cosmetic," Setsuko said. "Commercials show white teeth, big smiles. It's all about being pretty. But it's more than that. Taking care of your mouth is part of healthy living. I help people be healthy." Then Setsuko asked me if I flossed every day. She wanted to know if my gums bled. She said, "Flossing helps prevent strokes and heart disease."

When COVID restrictions eased up and dental offices reopened for elective work, Setsuko was placed on a call list. She traveled to different offices to fill in when they were short-staffed. One week, she was in Manchester, another week, in New Britain. On a Thursday in July, she texted, "Today I worked at South Windsor. People are very nice so I have enjoyed." She texted a selfie of herself with a coworker, the tops of their heads tilted toward each other. They wore face shields over their face masks, and gowns to cover their street clothes. Their crinkled eyes suggested they were smiling beneath the masks.

I had never heard of dentists traveling to different offices around the state and asked Setsuko if this was routine. She texted back, "Sue! I think you're misunderstanding. I'm a dental assistant! I go everywhere in Connecticut! I'm looking for good environment and positive working people for permanent job. I graduated Tunxis Community College and did the clinical at UConn."

We laughed at my confusion. I texted back that this seemed like good experience, seeing the work styles of different dentists. But it also seemed stressful. Setsuko was always starting over, learning a new layout with new people and the social dynamics at each office. And waiting to see if people wanted her back. "It's important work. Be strong!" I texted.

Setsuko answered, "I feel like dentist. My priority is the taking care of patients," and she added a smiley face emoji.

The next morning at 6:00, Setsuko texted photos of Elizabeth Park and the flowers in bloom. "This morning I ran Elizabeth Park," she messaged. I sent her a photo of the park where I was walking. We called the parks our sanctuaries.

One week, Setsuko said she was working in a pediatric dentist's office. She said it was like babysitting, keeping the kids distracted while the dentist worked on their teeth. "However, I don't have children so I need more practice and study," she texted.

Another day she said the patient was a three-month-old baby who was born with teeth. "So tiny!" I texted back.

A few weeks later, she texted that she was working in a pediatric office again. "It is very fast paced. I can't keep up. I'm screwed. I'm little bit depressed." Each work assignment was like a performance interview.

The increased incidence of attacks on Asian Americans was reported in the media. President Trump's insistence on calling COVID-19 the China Virus wasn't just xenophobic; it fueled hostility and aggression toward people who appeared to be of Asian descent. I asked Setsuko about her safety and how she was treated on the public buses. She brushed me off and changed the subject.

Dr. Marietta Vazquez, Associate Dean for Medical Student Diversity and professor at the Yale School of Medicine in New Haven, Connecticut, called attention to the ripple effects of the president's rhetoric. She said, "Public transit riders have encountered hostile interactions and people simply walking down the street have experienced microaggressions—which I prefer to call veiled aggressions, because there is nothing 'micro' about them for the person on the receiving end. … This type of discrimination may also put their mental health at risk."[93] I wondered if any of this was impacting Setsuko's employment prospects.

Each week when Setsuko came to work in the kitchen, she brought food. "Is this food for us to give away?" I asked one week.

Setsuko nodded, "Yes."

I explained that we had to follow health guidelines and prepare the food in the church kitchen. When our work was finished for the day, I asked her to take her food home. One Friday she said, "This is for you. You take it home."

On a Thursday a few weeks later, she texted that she was bringing cooked salmon on Friday. "You can eat too. Salmon is very healthy.

Everyone deserve to eat! Little bit stink." She texted again and said she was bringing rice. "And seaweed. Make a rice ball, not too much."

The next afternoon, Setsuko showed me how to wrap the fish in nori and cover it with sticky rice. Her fingers moved quickly to form a perfectly shaped rice ball that fit in the palm of my hand. As we ate I said, "You're right. A little bit stink," and we laughed. She made a rice ball for everyone working in the kitchen, but the rice balls sat, untouched, on a plate.

On a Tuesday in July, Setsuko texted me, "I want bring something food to church. Any requests?"

I texted back, "I just want to enjoy your company."

Setsuko wrote, "I know, but when we're cooking I get really hungry. I bring something surprising."

That was it! Setsuko not only brought lunch for herself each week, she also brought enough to share. I regretted misunderstanding her thoughtfulness and tried to apologize.

In late August, there was a change in Setsuko's mood. She was sluggish and quiet. She didn't respond to text messages as quickly as before. She said she was on a new medication and it made her drowsy. Sometimes it kept her from sleeping at night, and then she was tired during the day. In the middle of cutting up vegetables, she sometimes left the kitchen, went to the dining hall, and put her head down on a table.

She missed a couple of Fridays. One week she said she had to leave early for a doctor's appointment. Then two weeks passed without any word from her. The third week, in the middle of October, I received a text message from her husband. Setsuko had hanged herself.

Of course, there was more to her story with details we will never know. Each of us replayed pieces of conversations, trying to make sense of it, and came up short. Like many families during the pandemic, we were isolated and our grief was immense. In the dining hall, Lamont set up a memorial with two stuffed teddy bears. A plaque on the front of the table read, "Our family is a circle of strength & love." I amended Pastor Rick's words from when Robert died: *We were fortunate for the time Setsuko spent among us where we could care for her.*

***

During the pandemic there were other people we met for the first time when they rang the doorbell and asked to be put to work: Rickie, Marcia, Shelly, Rita, Nicole, Tom, Raniyah, and Cecilia. Some never returned, some came only once, and a few volunteered for a month and then vanished. It was unclear how they learned about the Friday Gathering or that they could volunteer at Grace. Their disappearances were not explained either. As the calendar gave way to November, it became impractical to set up tables outdoors, tables that during the summer had been filled with books, shoes, clothing, toys, and other gently used items, anything to offer a distraction from the monotony of the lockdown. Without those extra tables and distribution points, there were fewer opportunities for volunteers to participate.

The isolation we faced the first year of the pandemic revealed how much building community is linked with putting to good use all of the offers to volunteer at the Friday Gathering. Neighbors arrived looking for places where their presence mattered, where they had purpose and a sense of belonging. Some volunteers offered to fill in where needed and others saw a need and offered to fill it.

We learned from the pandemic that besides simply staffing volunteer positions, we had to embrace the offers that are made to us. Volunteers saw needs that we had not recognized or did not know how to address. Receiving their contributions of talent and time made them part of us.

***

"I think everyone has a need to belong. It is at the very center of our nature," Darrell said. I asked how he saw that manifested at the Friday Gathering. He answered:

> Around the time we first began the Friday Gathering, the congregation had a clean-up day. Besides the traditional congregation, people attending the Friday Gathering were invited to come and help clean up around the church. Some came because they felt they were important just because they were asked to participate. Nobody paid them, nobody offered prizes that they might win by helping, nobody tried to guilt them into it, and nobody browbeat them into it. In addition to the exterior work, some noticed the kitchen floor needed attention and other interior work needed to be done. They knew they had the skills and talents to do the work and asked about doing it. All I did was get some mops, cleaners, and other equipment, and they went at it. I had to step in a little because there was some conflict and competition about who would be "the boss." Before long, it was clear that many were taking satisfaction from making "a contribution;" some people give money and others make their contribution by working. Either way, contributing is a way to experience belonging to a community or a family.
>
> Over time, some began to develop roles that involved cleaning dishes, helping the chef prepare meals, setting up tables, and making coffee. Lamont, for example, became very serious about running the kitchen and keeping it clean. He would come early and stay after the event. He came in during the week to help clean up. Some of the men formed a men's group. They had outings but also helped maintain the building. Together we painted and got grants to put in new toilets, sinks, and things of that nature. Lamont was so serious about this that I developed a job description. This helped structure, clarify, and give more

status to that role. He wasn't even being paid! It helped me realize how important a job like this is for so many people who want to have a role, a place, and a way to contribute and belong. We developed other job descriptions as well, both to clarify responsibilities and also to give structure and status to the job.

One Friday night, as I observed all the work being done—the scheduling and transportation in getting food there, the organization of the chefs, the clean-up people, the greeters and people signing people in, the servers, the musicians—I realized all this was going on each Friday night every week and every month, and nobody is being paid! They are just people who belong through what they are doing, guided by a new appreciation for the work of God's Holy Spirit. These people want to belong to something in which that spirit is present and powerfully moving.

I believe, as humans, we all have a need to belong, and we are created for community. At the same time, we live in a world where connections and relationships are fragmented and broken; a world in which people are objects to make money from or used and exploited in other ways and discarded. It's a world in which all of us, to some extent or another, are orphans with a deep need for community and belonging. We also carry with us an ancient story that The Source of all life and being that flows through this universe breaks through. The Source reverses enmity and destructiveness to bring us together as a community and to a safe place where we are valued infinitely, where our talents and utter uniqueness are free to emerge and contribute to the human adventure.[94]

9

I Can Do It Myself

Chances are, disabled or not, you don't grow all of your food. Chances are, you didn't build the car, bike, wheelchair, subway, shoes, or bus that transports you. Chances are you didn't construct your home. Chances are you didn't sew your clothing (or make the fabric and thread used to sew it). The difference between the needs that many disabled people have and the needs of people who are not labelled as disabled is that non-disabled people have had their dependencies normalized.

—A.J. Withers, *Disability Politics and Theory*

As she moves among the diners, Barb offers to clear a dirty dish or deliver an extra napkin or fork. She uses the seat and handlebars of her walker like extensions of her body, the way other volunteers use a cart to deliver desserts or a dishpan to collect dirty plates. We choose whether to "see" others—and ourselves—as whole and complete persons or as broken. Diners like Barb, Eddie, Papa Charles, Paul, and Claudia live full, meaningful lives on their own terms. To see them as less than whole is a reflection of us, not of them.

***

The bread donation arrived late one Friday during the COVID-19 pandemic. Diners were lined up, waiting to be served, but the church doors would not open until the breads and pastries were laid out. Barb and Shirley hustled to unload the cases. Barb tugged at a case to pull it closer. Shirley reached past her and said, "Let me get it."

"I can do it," Barb said in a firm voice.

"No, no. Let me," Shirley said again, more emphatically. "I'm doing it for you."

Barb matched Shirley's energy. "Really," she said, "I can do it myself."

It was no use. Shirley pushed Barb's protests aside. "It occurred to me," Barb said later, "that Shirley might want to handle the cases the same as me, because she wants to show that she can do it, too. She's considerably older than most volunteers, not that anyone would know. She really can run circles around me! Perhaps people make assumptions about her based on her age. Hmm!"

It was the kind of scene I had witnessed between Barb and other volunteers before and had participated in, too. Because Barb used a walker, it was tempting to make assumptions about what she could not do.

After dinner one week, I collected the wet towels and aprons to take home to launder.

"I'll do the laundry this week," Barb said.

"I've got it," I answered. The weight of the soaking wet towels, some the size of bath towels, flashed through my mind.

"Indeed!" Barb said. "I do laundry every week, and one more load makes no difference."

I was annoyed at myself. *Of course she can do the laundry. I know better than this,* I thought. From then on, Barb and I took turns. She did the laundry one week, and the next week was my turn.

Barb and her husband, Rich, have lived in the neighborhood since 1996. When they retired about twenty years later, they still had an appetite for volunteer work, which had been a part of their lives during their careers. Retirement afforded them the time to develop new connections in the neighborhood.

Barb began volunteering at the Friday Gathering in 2017. "The first time I came, one of the kitchen volunteers looked at my walker and me and told me to have a seat and enjoy myself and that I was welcome to stay for dinner. Months later, after we got to know each other, I talked to him about it, and we both had a good laugh. I had just finished taking a tray full of dirty cups, plates, and utensils to the kitchen when our eyes met. I teasingly said to him, 'And to think that when we first met, you looked at me as if to say, *What am I going to do with you?*' I wagged my finger at him and said, 'See?'"

Like many diners, Barb was not assigned a role when she started volunteering. She was encouraged to spend time chatting with neighbors and get to know them. The volunteers began to know her too and invited her to join the serving line. "I loved this because I could see everybody who was present. There was time to say hello and have a brief chat." When the meal was finished, she helped clear the dishes, grabbed a bucket of soapy water, and washed the tables.

After dinner, volunteers filled empty cartons with leftover breads and desserts. Sometimes, Barb joined them, using the seat of her walker to hold a box while she filled it up. "Occasionally a volunteer tries to step in and take over for me. I try to use a little humor and tell them that I know: In the time it takes me to fill one box, they will have finished with the rest of it. It's a matter of pride and stubbornness. I want to show that I'm able.

"However," Barb continued, "sometimes the energy is not there to do it. When that happens, I leave it to the others. I don't want to get in the way of what needs to be done. I want to do everything, but I need to be realistic about it."

I asked Barb about how she identifies herself. She said, "I don't want to be labeled white, and I work very hard to not use 'Black' or 'white' as a description, but clearly, I do. It really pains me to do that, and it pains me even more when I hear a person referred to as a 'big Black guy' or a 'Black lady' when skin color has nothing to do with it.

"I recently taught a literacy class on vocabulary to use to appropriately describe people. I showed the students a book with pictures that teaches children about why people have different skin tones. I held a white piece of paper next to my arm and asked, 'Am I white?' I held up a black piece of paper, and no one in the class was really black. Everybody got it that 'white' and 'Black' are meaningless descriptions. This is why I don't want to be labeled as white.

"I take some pleasure in speaking of a person to someone who is dying to know the race, yet I won't use the word. I had forgotten how much I dislike the white and Black thing in this country!"

Barb's parents were immigrants. As children, they came to Canada with their families; her dad from Scotland and her mom from Northern Ireland. Barb was born in 1950—their only child—just as her father finished graduate school in Massachusetts. Her mother was a registered nurse. When Barb was three years old, her father took a job with Alcoa and moved the family to Belleville, Illinois, a predominantly white community eight miles from downtown St. Louis. Barb's parents didn't expect to remain in the United States, but that idea eventually faded. First her mother became a US citizen, and later her father did, too.

"Growing up," Barb said, "I had a neighborhood reputation as a tomboy. I could ride a bike, climb trees, and run like the boys, and was proud of it. It was so different from the excruciatingly shy girl I was in school, who never made a peep in class. Later, when I worked in Brooklyn, New York, I took pride in my Double Dutch jump-roping skills when I played with sixth-grade girls during recess. They were pretty impressed!"

Barb's mother had a temper. "She usually didn't hesitate to use it toward family and others in public. My mother had fears that prevented her from offering help to strangers."

Her mother worked every other Saturday, so Barb and her father had the day to themselves. "We almost always had grilled cheese sandwiches and Campbell's soup for lunch. I felt closer to my dad.

"I knew he would rarely stand up to my mother. In later years, he said he had learned early on that his life was hell when he did."

As a young adult, Barb noticed her mother consuming more alcohol. "As time went on, her emotional state became more depressive and demanding. She was less involved in life around her. Once I started college, I did not live near my parents, so it was Dad who dealt with it firsthand." Barb was forty-two when her mother died and fifty-three when her father passed. "I don't like to admit it, but it was like having a cloud lifted when Mom died. And it was the saddest day of my life when my dad died."

Barb met Rich at Western Illinois University, and they married while they were still students. After graduation, they worked in the Chicago area and later earned master of social work degrees at the University of Illinois. Barb pursued a career as a clinical social worker in a medical center but later switched to education.

"I worked one year in the Cicero [Illinois] school system, in a town with a long history of overt racism and organized crime. Some of the students and families celebrated Hitler's birthday, some students attended a Nazi youth camp, and some boys were given guns on their birthdays. It was difficult to be exposed to this ideology from kids. The administration wouldn't allow me to make home visits alone. The rise of white supremacy in recent years fills me with such revulsion and sorrow. It goes back so far in the history of this country and the world!"

In the 1980s, Rich and Barb worked in New York City, then relocated near New Haven, Connecticut, where Barb worked in an upper-middle-income school system. "It was an eye-opener," she said. "I quickly realized that the priorities of some of the families differed from my previous experiences. They were more interested in ensuring that their children had the latest computers, attended certain summer camps, and were accepted at choice colleges. There was a child dressed in a sweatshirt that said on the front, 'Harvard Class of —' with the year that the child would presumably graduate.

"Once I arrived at a student's home for an appointment and found the mother breaking up chairs and burning them in the fireplace to heat the house. She was divorced and didn't want people to know how destitute she and her four children were, so she agreed to meet me at her home instead of coming into the school. Maybe it was that she could avoid the chance of running into parents and school staff who might have asked questions about how she was doing or she was afraid of being put on the spot or breaking down in front of people who did not know her circumstances. By this time, I think she must have felt that I could be trusted.

"On another occasion, I visited the home of a student who received speech and language services. The only furniture on the main floor of the house was a card table and chairs. This was the sacrifice the family willingly made to afford to live in that community. At the time, I didn't get it and was really puzzled. I came to the conclusion that everything is relative. Most of us want happiness and success, but what that looks like and how we set priorities to achieve it is different for each of us."

Barb and Rich took a year off to travel and returned to New York in 1987, "loving the city," Barb said.

"The next two and a half years were the most draining of my career and the most beloved." She worked with children and their families who were homeless and temporarily housed in a converted hotel; the children attended the nearby school. "The day often started at 7 a.m. and finished twelve hours later. The school's hours were long to accommodate the needs of the students, such as meals, homework time, and some recreation.

"Many of the adults were employed. But it was often the case—and still is—that there was a serious shortage of affordable housing. Families depended on the city's housing authority for help. It often meant they were moved from one place to another multiple times. Oh, did that disrupt a family! There was no feeling of belonging at home or in school.

"One day when I arrived home, Rich asked me how the day was, and I burst into tears. A boy—he was new at school and at the hotel—told me that his family had lived in their own apartment. They had just moved the day before because a rat came through the plumbing when they flushed the toilet. That incident put me over the edge. Those tears were the culmination of stories of children and their families living with such dreadful circumstances."

During this time in the city, Barb was diagnosed with multiple sclerosis. "When I was diagnosed at age thirty-nine, my biggest fears were losing my independence and being worried about what people would think of me, especially if they had not known me before. I was still accustomed to running, jumping, and flying up and down stairs. I always thought that maybe I could do that again if a cure was found, but now my age would prevent me from doing those things anyway. I'm not sure exactly when that realization hit me. Independence? I've still got it, but over time, I learned that it's not all tied to physical skills.

"It's been more than thirty years," Barb said. "It's always impaired my walking in a slow progressive manner. I don't let it stop me from doing most things I want to do. But it entails doing many tasks in different ways than a completely able-bodied person. I still miss long walks and hiking. That's when I remind myself of the many things I can do! Yes, my *cap*abilities and not my *dis*abilities."

In 1989, Rich accepted an offer that brought them back to Connecticut. Barb took a position in a public school near Hartford. It gave her the flexibility and opportunity to initiate new projects.

"I wanted to start a disability awareness program. The Americans with Disabilities Act [ADA] had just gone into effect, and the school system was making physical changes to its facilities, such as ramping and accessible parking. I had lots of support, and I loved the feedback from students, the staff, and parents.

"Several years later, when I was conducting an after-school group for kids who had siblings with disabilities, I brought up the fact that there was a person in the room with us who had a disability. None of the kids could figure out who it was. I told them, 'It's me.'

"One boy asked, 'You do?'

"I could have kissed him!" Barb said. "This was a measure of success! Next to me were my walker and cane. Also in the room was an electric scooter that I used to move quickly in the long hallways. The kids saw me every day with these devices. But it was me, not my disability, that they saw!

"There was no doubt that we'd live in Hartford," Barb said. "We're city people. Traffic doesn't bother me. I like hearing the sounds of people. The constant movement. The energy. I love the hum of the city and feeling the pulse of activity. I might be the only person you meet who tells you the sound of traffic and noise doesn't bother them." Barb pointed out that their condo faces busy Woodland Street—half a block from Grace—which is a main artery for emergency vehicles traveling to the Saint Francis Medical Center.

It's unusual for Barb to miss a Friday Gathering. I asked her, "What keeps you coming back?"

"I feel a real dedication, a commitment to the diners I've gotten to know. If I don't see someone, I wonder if they're okay. I always tell them, 'I'm so glad to see you.' Seeing them is how I know they're okay.

"There's one older man, Isaac. He's a curmudgeon, and I've been determined to find something that may produce a smile from him. I discovered that he likes rye bread. On Friday nights, I look for a loaf of it and set it aside for him. Such a little thing.

"One winter evening during the pandemic, as I was leaving the church, the headlights of my car picked Isaac out, sitting on a bench, eating his dinner alone in the cold, dark night. My first thought was that I wanted to take him home with me, but I knew that I couldn't because of health issues and the pandemic.

"It's been a few months since I last saw him, and it has me so worried. When I drive around Hartford, I watch for him. Actually, I keep an eye open for any diners I might see. I know it makes me feel good to be greeted by people, especially someone I don't see often, and I assume that applies to them also.

"Friday evenings are a tiny piece of the week that has to be good for them," Barb added. "It's not just the food, which obviously is important, but also being in a familiar place that holds positive memories for them; feeling welcomed by familiar faces who provide unconditional care and interest in how their week has been. We have the ability to take the edge off their day. That's what brings me back on Fridays."

***

Eddie is one of the diners Barb looks forward to seeing. He's been coming to the Gathering for years. At six feet three inches tall, he towers over most of us. Accentuating his height is his long, blond hair that looks like it's just been blow-dried.

Eddie is a white man born in 1960 in West Hartford. He carries a backpack slung over his left shoulder, on the side where his arm was amputated just above the elbow. "I had cancer when I was twenty-two," he explained.

"I'm a man, not a white man," Eddie said. "I can't stand that, describing people as Black or white. It stirs up trouble. There will always be prejudice. I know I've got some of it in me. Everybody does. We should push tolerance. There will always be people you don't like, and you've got to learn how to get along."

All the volunteers know Eddie. He entertains them each week with a fresh set of jokes.

"As a boy, I loved building sandcastles with my grandfather," Eddie said without a trace of humor.

"Until my mother took the urn away," came the punchline.

When I texted Eddie, I began with, "This is Sue from Grace."

Eddie turned it into a nickname. On Fridays, he greeted me, "Hi, Sue-from-Grace."

One week he texted, "Hello Sue from Grease." Eddie has a knack for twisting words around and making something funny out of them.

One Friday during the pandemic, Eddie arrived at the station where Barb was serving. He rested his backpack on the table to open it and filled it with a boxed dinner and a loaf of bread.

Craig, a volunteer who was directing diners to the exit, shouted, "Get that backpack off the table!

"I was worried about the virus," Craig explained later, "and keeping the table germ-free. People shouldn't be touching the table!"

Craig and Eddie shouted back and forth until Eddie left, leaving everything behind except his backpack. Barb held up the boxed dinner for Eddie to take. Instead, he ran up the stairs and shouted over his shoulder, "I don't need your dinner, and I won't be back."

I hurried after Eddie and apologized for the incident. Eddie said he didn't need the dinner. "I come for the company," he said.

"I tried to volunteer," Eddie continued. "People think I can't do anything. No one will give me a chance."

Two weeks later, Eddie was back, but his humor was gone. He picked up his meal and left without speaking.

I walked with him again. He talked about the stove in his apartment that didn't work and how the landlord didn't respond until he threatened to complain at city hall. He said the man living above him was loud and kept him up all night. And he was going through a series of tests at the hospital. Doctors wanted to biopsy a spot on his lung.

A few weeks later, as Eddie opened his backpack, Barb asked, "Can I help you with that?"

"No," Eddie answered. "You wouldn't let me help you when you had packages."

Then they looked at each other and burst out laughing. "Of course," Barb chuckled. "We're both capable. We understand each other," and they laughed again.

When Eddie had the tumor—and part of his lung—removed, Louisa, Leah, and other volunteers checked on him. The tumor was benign, but it was a painful operation. The hospital stay and his recovery were longer than he expected. He accepted rides to doctor appointments and to go grocery shopping and the food that Leah left at his door. Slowly he recuperated. When Eddie felt better, he began looking for a new apartment.

Months later, Eddie was at Grace when Louisa and Leah arrived with a van full of food. Leah retrieved a utility cart from the church, and the three of them loaded it with cartons. Eddie handled the heavy objects with ease. The next week, Eddie was waiting when Louisa and Leah arrived with another load of food. When the Friday Gathering committee met a few weeks later, Louisa reported that Eddie was volunteering and helping with food deliveries.

***

A few diners use electric wheelchairs. One of them is Papa Charles, who stayed one wintery night in January 2020, just before the pandemic, to talk about his life. He was born in 1952 and identifies as African American. He is quick to smile and say hello. I was curious about who called him Papa and what it was like to get around Hartford in a wheelchair.

"I was born in Hartford, although my mother lived in Yonkers, New York. When the time was near for me to be born, my mother came to Hartford to be with her mother. After I was born, the two of us went back to Yonkers. A few years later, when I was still a toddler, we moved here permanently.

"I was very close to my grandmother, and we had a special relationship. She was my protector. She was strict and made sure no one, not even my mother or my uncles, put a finger on me. In later years she was senile, but she broke out in a big smile when she saw me. We lived in Bellevue Square in the North End.[95] I went to Job Corps instead of high school."

Job Corps is a residential career training program that operates in all fifty states, Puerto Rico, and the District of Columbia. Young people ages sixteen through twenty-four can earn their high school diploma or equivalency and college credits. They receive technical skills training in careers focused on construction, culinary arts, hospitality, and automotive repair, among others. For up to three years, Job Corps offers students tuition-free housing, basic health care, and transitional support.[96]

"They flew me out there on a plane—it was my first plane ride—to Colorado," Papa Charles said. "I only stayed six months; I didn't like Colorado. You had to shake your sheets out at night to be sure there were no critters hiding there. I transferred to a Job Corps site in Corpus Christi, Texas. I learned all the trades for construction and operated heavy equipment like giant bulldozers. We lived in a dorm and built a house from the ground up. That's how you learn all the trades, building a house from scratch. I finished Job Corps in two years and came back to Hartford because this is where my family is.

"I got work doing carpentry," Papa Charles continued. "One day, I was working on a second-story porch when it collapsed. The wood was rotten underneath, but I didn't know it, and the porch gave way. I landed on concrete. The injury caused a neuropathy that runs from my neck to my toes. For a while I could walk on my own, but then I needed a walker. It just got progressively worse. After about twelve years, I was in a wheelchair all the time.

"In 2016, there was a fire in my apartment building on Laurel Street [in the Asylum Hill neighborhood]. I couldn't use the elevator because of the fire, and I couldn't use the stairs on my own. The halls were filled with smoke, and it was terrifying. Finally, a neighbor helped me down the stairs. After the fire, the building was condemned, and I couldn't move back. Three months later, my blood pressure was high, and I started having heart attacks." Papa Charles explained that he couldn't get permanent housing because his health situation was unstable. Between hospital stays, he lived at one of Hartford's shelters for homeless men. He was living in one when he started coming to the Friday Gathering.

"Every morning, I ride this wheelchair up Main Street to Bellevue Square," he said. "I have a friend there with three kids. I call them my grandchildren. They're five, ten, and fifteen years old. I wait with them for the school bus. They're good kids. They need someone they can talk to. Even more, they need someone who will listen to them. Kids should never be hit. If you develop trust and respect, then they will have a place to turn for help. I want all three of them to grow up and have a good life. Kids having kids before they're grown, I want more than that for them."

Our conversation turned back to Papa Charles's wheelchair. It's more than two miles from the shelter to Bellevue Square. I asked him how he navigated the sidewalks and thought about the cracks and seams that rise and fall like frost heaves.

"Winter is only half of it," he said. "It isn't just the snow and ice. It's the garbage that people throw on the ground. The furniture and junk that's abandoned at the curb. A trash can left in the middle of the sidewalk that I can't scoot around. And dog crap. It gets up inside my wheels, and then I bring it indoors. I don't want to run over it the same as people don't want to step in it. People should be responsible for picking up after themselves."

Papa Charles set off early in the morning when the shelter ejected its boarders. He used the road instead of the sidewalk. "I get a kick out of seeing how fast this thing can go. When it's fully charged, it's pretty fast."

A few weeks after our conversation, sit-down dining was suspended due to the pandemic. Papa Charles came a few times for a take-out dinner, but our visits were brief. By the end of summer, he stopped coming.

Late in the second spring of the pandemic, Papa Charles was back. He was upbeat and friendly. The quick smile was there. "I got my own apartment now," he said.

Papa Charles explained that he had been in and out of the hospital. "The shelter was contaminated with black mold. The mold triggered asthma attacks, and that aggravated the heart. The doctor at the emergency room noticed that I kept returning and got involved. He contacted the shelter. Told them that they needed to provide permanent housing for me and get me out of there. He wouldn't discharge me if I was only going back to the black mold. He kept calling the shelter until they moved me to one of the hotels they converted for homeless people. A few months later, I got my own apartment.

"It's made all the difference," Papa Charles said. "For four years, my blood pressure was 200 to 220. Now, it's 117, and I feel good."

Papa Charles said the neuropathy in his legs had worsened. Some days his feet hurt, and some days he couldn't feel them at all. He could manage his daily needs, except the laundry. "I'm particular about my laundry. I need to use fabric softener. When you sit all day, you need to make sure you're clean and that the fabric next to your skin is soft. But I need a nurse's help to stand up now. It's getting the laundry done that I'm struggling with the most.

"I have a friend, and I babysit her two-year-old son. We met when she was homeless and I was still in the shelter. Her son was two months old then. She was so frazzled that I told her to let the baby's father take him for a day and I paid for her to have a hotel room. She could sleep, take a long bath, watch TV. Just pamper herself for a day.

"One day, that little boy called me Grandpa Charles. It was the first time I heard him talk. He has a lot of energy and he gets frustrated easily. He pouts, and I tell him, 'Come over here.' He crawls up on me, and I just hold him. I'm teaching him to use words to say how he's feeling. I can just look at that child, and he knows to calm himself down.

"I still see those grandchildren in Bellevue Square as often as I can. The boy got in trouble at school, and his grandmother told me about it. I told him to knock it off. 'Don't waste this chance you have.' Even though I'm in a wheelchair, my word carries weight, and he settled down. Those kids mean the world to me."

In the spring of 2022, Papa Charles met me in the park and introduced me to his friend Coco. She was a cook at the Chrysalis Center, where he went for breakfast and lunch; they had been friends for years. Coco told me how much she appreciated Papa Charles's kindness and gentleness. When she cooked on the weekends, she often brought him a plate. While we were talking, a few of Papa Charles's friends joined us. And then a young woman appeared, carrying a sleeping child about four years old. It was the boy who first called him Grandpa Charles. His mother slipped him into Papa Charles's arms and joined our conversation.

***

Lily is a middle-aged white woman, and she is profoundly deaf. When Bernie took her portrait, she smiled at the camera and made the sign for love with her right hand.

Lily is fluent in American Sign Language. There was a volunteer who could converse with her, but that volunteer came to the Friday Gathering sporadically. When I signed hello to Lily, she got excited and forgot that I did not know ASL. She made signs and murmurs that I didn't understand, which frustrated both of us. We tried to communicate in writing, but our conversations were brief. I learned that Lily had a grown son and she was looking for paid work. "Give me a chance!" she wrote.

Sitting with Lily in the dining hall made me aware of how isolated she was at the Gathering. Looking around the room, I saw that most diners had someone to talk to except Lily. I sat with her when the host made announcements and transcribed on paper what was said. The back-and-forth exchange between announcements and diners' remarks moved rapidly, and I couldn't capture all of it on paper. I was more than Lily's translator. I was her editor, and she was limited by my choices—what to record, what to ignore—made on her behalf.

It's been years since Lily came to dinner. Occasionally I see her walking downtown but we haven't connected; we weren't close enough to make eye contact.

***

Paul, a white man, was born in 1943 in Bristol, Connecticut. He moved to Hartford in his thirties, and in 2014 to the apartment building where Hilda, Albert, and other diners lived. He attended Grace's Christmas Eve dinner in 2010.

"I don't remember how I learned about it. I might have seen a flyer or heard about it at an AA meeting," he said. He got to know Pastor Eva. "She made an impression on me. I started coming regularly for dinner. I made some friends, men who like to read as much as me. We sit together on Friday nights, and as you know, our discussions can get pretty lively. I joined Grace and came for services on Sunday for a while.

"I'm compulsive about books," Paul said, "and how they can make people feel more human, more connected. When you read something good, you don't feel all alone. A good book takes you somewhere else. It's an escape, and you imagine you can be anything. Not all books do that. In third grade, we read a poem by Emily Dickinson that had a lasting effect on me," and he recited the opening lines:

There is no Frigate like a Book
To take us Lands away[97]

"At that moment, I knew literature and history would always fascinate me. They became a way that I could distinguish myself." Later, a love for Beethoven and classical music and art and art galleries opened up new worlds where Paul was comfortable being himself.

By the time Paul was four years old, he was painfully aware that he was different. His right hand was deformed. "Doctors were always looking at it. Everyone noticed it. Strangers stopped to ask about it. I was someplace with my father when a man asked him, 'What happened to his hand?' My father was annoyed and said it was none of the man's business. My hand caused too much attention, and it made me feel inferior."

Doctors call the condition amniotic band syndrome. It occurs when a fibrous band from the amniotic sac of a developing fetus gets tangled up, usually around a hand or foot, and constricts the growth of the limb.[98] In Paul's case, it prevented his thumb and fingers from developing.

"My parents took me to Newington Children's Hospital to see what could be done to give me more use of the hand. At the time, most of the children there were being treated for polio. It was terrifying to see its effects. There were children in wheelchairs and others who walked with braces. I knew a girl who had polio and used braces. At that age, I couldn't distinguish between their conditions and mine. Until the vaccine became available, we lived in fear of polio. We were hypochondriacs and worried about every ailment.[99]

"When I was seven, my parents and I were sent to a hospital in Newark, New Jersey. With a skin graft from my leg, they separated a small section of skin where the thumb should be. It gave me some flexibility with those joints, and I learned how to use what I had. When I was older, I mowed the lawn, raked leaves, climbed a ladder, and cleaned the gutters. But I still felt inferior. I decided I would make up for the hand in other ways.

"When I was ten, I started a neighborhood newspaper. I knocked on neighbors' doors and asked them if they had any news to share. I wrote the newspaper out longhand. My dad bought me a mimeograph machine so that I could print copies. Then he got me a typewriter. I don't remember now if I charged anything for the paper.

"I wrote an article about a boy who lived in our neighborhood. Today, we would say the boy had an intellectual disability. He climbed a telephone pole that held high-tension wires. The pole had climbing steps, and he kept climbing higher and higher. A crowd gathered to watch. People shouted, 'Don't touch the wires! Don't touch the wires!' But a person like that, it's a miracle he didn't touch them anyway. He eventually climbed down but not right away. It's still frightening to think about what could have happened to him.

"When I was eleven, my parents took me to President Franklin Roosevelt's home in Hyde Park, New York. It was known by then that polio had paralyzed his legs. When we made the trip, the polio vaccine was still not available. I remember seeing FDR's car and how it was modified with hand controls so that he could drive it. We saw the wheelchair that he used. After that visit, I fell into a depression. It's something I've had to deal with my whole life.

"At school, I felt like an idiot in gym class," Paul said. "We played baseball, and I could catch a ball okay. But I had to throw it with my left hand, and I'm not left-handed. People think you adapt, but some things just are the way they are. I'm right-handed in my brain. When I threw the ball to first base, it would go wide, and the first baseman couldn't catch it. It was humiliating.

"I walked around with my hand in my pocket to keep it hidden. I wondered, *Why am I different? It's not fair.* It didn't help to hear that there were people with worse troubles than mine. People didn't know how to react when they saw my hand. When you're young, you don't have enough experience to put things in perspective. Now, I realize adolescence is tough anyway."

Paul graduated from high school and completed thirty credits at Central Connecticut State University. Then he dropped out. "I had no idea where my life was going. No idea about what I could do, what jobs were available for someone like me. I couldn't imagine that any woman would want to be with me. It was traumatic. I turned to alcohol to make things better."

Paul worked as a proofreader for Eastern Typesetting, the Hartford Courant, and New England Typographic. "One time, I failed to notice a misspelled word in an ad. The company told me it was an $8,000 mistake, and they let me go."

Paul totaled his car in a snowstorm while commuting to work, so he moved to Hartford to make commuting easier. He taught himself to read Spanish and volunteered with the Hartford nonprofit group Revitalization Corps. He traveled to Mexico and Colombia. "I fell in love with Mexico City and wanted to stay. I foolishly called the Courant and resigned. Two weeks later, I ran out of money. My parents paid to get me home. I tried to get my job back at the Courant, but they said, 'No.'"

Paul got a job driving for the Yellow Cab company. "They told me I'd have trouble lifting people's luggage in and out of the trunk, but it wasn't a problem," he said. Paul met Janet—the Grace member who inspired Janet's Closet—and started chauffeuring her when she worked night shifts at Saint Francis. "People said Janet was good with the buses, and she probably took them when she worked the day shift. But at night the buses stopped running. If I was on duty and Janet called for a taxi, they gave the route to me. She was a real nice person, easy to talk to. When we arrived at the medical center, I escorted her to the door."

Paul went back to school. In 1983, he graduated from Charter Oak State College with a bachelor of arts in literature. In 1987, he got a job driving for Connecticut National Bank. "It was a great job. I made deliveries to branches all across the state," Paul said. Then the 1990 recession hit. "To save money, the bank outsourced some jobs. My department was eliminated. About fifty drivers were let go. You think you're going to be there for the rest of your life, and then poof, it's all gone."

Paul went back to driving a taxi. "In thirty years of driving, I was only robbed two or three times. Never with a gun. I just gave them the money. I knew a couple of guys who were killed on the job."

To supplement his income, Paul tried substitute teaching for Hartford Public Schools. "I substituted at half of the schools in Hartford. I never taught the students anything. There was a fifth-grade class, and the kids were smooching in the cloakroom. Another time, a female student wore a low-cut shirt, and I could see her cleavage. She tried to flirt with me, and it scared me. I could see jail time right in front of me. I couldn't look at her. One day the students were so out of control and riotous that I screamed at them. The assistant principal heard it down the hall. He came to the room and told me I could go home. After two and a half years of substitute teaching, I didn't go back.

"I could see that the students had a lot of things going against them. Broken homes. Street crime. Poverty. But I couldn't keep discipline in the classroom. They knew that and took advantage of it.

"I've always wanted to improve my mind," Paul said, describing the authors and books that capture his imagination. "Harriet Beecher Stowe's sister, Catharine, published *A Treatise on Domestic Economy for the Use of Young Ladies,* a book with standards about how to run a household. Think about what a different time that was," he said.

"Charles Dudley Warner was a friend of Mark Twain's and an editor of the *Hartford Courant.* He coauthored *The Gilded Age* with Twain. He wrote *My Winter on the Nile,* and I found a second edition copy of it, published in 1881.

"Before Louisa May Alcott wrote *Little Women,* she went to Washington, DC, to nurse wounded Union soldiers. She kept a journal that was published called *Hospital Sketches.* She wrote so graphically about the filthy conditions and the pain the soldiers were in—there was no anesthesia—it almost made me feel like crying. You get a sense of the scale of the war.

"On Main Street in the North End of Hartford, across from the Old North Cemetery, is the 1865 Widows' Homes, built for the widows and children of Civil War soldiers.[100] No one notices things like this today. Driving a taxi, I got to know Hartford up close.

"George Brinley was a wealthy man who lived in Hartford in the mid-1800s," Paul continued. "Brinley collected all things Americana, especially books. The book he coveted most was *Bay Psalm*. It was published in Cambridge, Massachusetts, in 1640—the first book printed in North America. Brinley eventually found a widow who owned a copy of it. He purchased the book from her on a promise to supply her with coal for the winter. He also had a copy of the first translation of the Bible into Native American languages. Learning about these people and their lives is fascinating to me," Paul said.

"I've been sober thirty-five years. I still go to AA meetings. I'd be a basket case if I didn't. I made some good friends there. It's easy to forget the bad stuff. In the beginning, I thought drinking made me feel better. Then I realized it didn't. At AA, you hear people's stories; you remember your own, that you've been there. AA is wonderful for that. People don't tell everything. They don't want to look like fools. You go to AA because you want to know that things can be better. It's easy to get isolated, to spend too much time alone. I know that's not good for me. We're social creatures. AA gives me a place to be with people I 'get' and who 'get' me. I've met teachers, people with PhD's, an architect, and lawyers. When I had a car, I used to drive people to meetings. It made me feel good to help them. People want to be useful.

"A man in our building died two weeks ago," Paul said. I knew him, too. He and his friend Iris, who also lives in the building, came early on Fridays for the prayer circle.

"He had two dogs," Paul continued. "When he died, the dogs started barking and wouldn't stop. When neighbors complained, management checked his apartment and found him dead. He was in his early fifties. It was probably drugs. His friends were people who are addicted. I'm grateful for my friends at AA."

***

Two diners are published authors, and another is a published illustrator. They all live in the neighborhood. Claudia is one of them. With her permission, the following dialogue is a composite of our conversations and correspondence and her blog postings.

One Friday early in the pandemic, when conversations about wearing face masks were contentious, I saw Claudia walking toward the church wearing a plastic Halloween mask. She marched up to me and said, "Will this do? I'm wearing a mask."

Before I could answer, she pushed the Halloween mask up, waved a cloth mask in front of me, and started laughing. It was easy to laugh with her. Over the next month, Claudia wore a different face covering each week. First, it was swimmer's goggles and the next week, chemical safety glasses with side shields. She topped them off with colorful hats, scarves, and mouth coverings. Her favorite—and Louisa's and mine, too—was the pink cowgirl hat with feathers and rhinestones. Claudia added a welcomed light-heartedness to our day.

Claudia was born in 1966, in La Banda, Santiago del Estero, Argentina. Her parents were of Italian descent, and she identifies as Argentinian of Italian descent. "Identifying myself as 'white' is not something I would do," Claudia said.

Claudia lives "with the effects of autism," she wrote. She rejects being called autistic because the label is subjective. "As far back as I can remember, there has never been a place to which I belonged. When I say 'place,' I mean less a geographical location and more a group of people with whom I am connected and to whom I belong.

"Living with the effects of autism is like being the 'Caged Bird' in Maya Angelou's poem," she said.[101] She quoted an interpretation by Amber

O'Neal Johnston, an author whose work focuses on appreciating our differences. "Maya Angelou wrote that a bird confined to a limiting cage struggles to see beyond the rage induced by its confinement. He's bound and stripped of his ability to spread his wings and fly, 'so he opens his throat to sing' of freedom.[102]

"I relate some of autism's confinement to that idea because being autistic is like living in a cage, so I opened my eyes to read books," Claudia said.

"Understanding our relationship to autism is as urgent today as it has ever been," she explained. The clinical definition relies on imprecise behavioral assessments and making judgments about how a person handles social situations. Claudia challenges the idea that sociability can be measured and that it is deemed disordered at some arbitrary point. These artificial measurements produce a system of categorizing and labeling that inevitably leads to stereotyping and stigmatization. "Central to my philosophy is the assumption that neurodiversity is a natural condition," Claudia said.[103] By measuring sociability, we come to value some degrees of it more than others.

Claudia wrote about how she experiences the world. Face-to-face interactions can be too intense. "I have such a kind of autism that if I am confused by contradictory ideas and pushed too far, I lock up like a shopping cart's wheels."[104] She prefers to communicate through writing. "Please text, don't call," she told me. "Sometimes I feel myself getting into situations where I can't think. I've always found my brain to be dissipated in a thousand little pieces. I am constantly bombarded by sensory information that I do not coordinate very effectively.[105]

"From my earliest memory, I've been in a separate universe," Claudia said. "I couldn't tolerate noise, especially the laughing and screaming of other children. When I couldn't isolate myself, I covered my ears with my hands. At age twelve, I was still largely uncommunicative. People feared I wouldn't be able to find my way in the world."[106]

At age seventeen, Claudia moved to Buenos Aires; two years later, she enrolled at the Institute Grafotectico to study journalism. "The city was just too overwhelming for me," she said. "I spent most of the time riding the bus because it was quiet."[107] She also took walks in a park with a golf course and learned about the game. She wrote a paper about the history of golf for one of her classes.

Claudia's photographic memory and fascination with players' performance statistics led to a career as a golf historian, researcher, and journalist. She wanted to be independent, to prove that she could look after herself. "Only then, finally, did I feel the umbilical cord had been truly cut," she said.

She wrote for Argentine newspapers and golfing magazines and helped organize the Library of the Argentina Golf Association. She taught herself English by reading *Golf Digest;* applied for and received Italian citizenship; traveled to London, Scotland, and Madrid; and visited the United States for the Grand Slam championships and the Ryder Cup.

Claudia's social circle was exclusive to golf. "The world outside—beyond golf—was out of sight, and therefore out of mind," she said. "Ignoring the outside world was relatively easy because listening requires active engagement, and I was not looking for relationships and understanding. We choose who we hear from, and we can't just move through life expecting a diversity of messages to automatically penetrate. I needed to train my brain to think differently.

"I dreamed of discovering the hidden element that transforms talented pro golfers into great champions and wanted to write a book about their gifts. My dream was not that far-fetched, but I struggled without having the right connections."

Claudia eventually found a literary agent in New York City but couldn't afford to live there. Instead, she came to Hartford in December 2005 and rented a room near the Hartford Seminary. At the school's library, she listened to the stories of others. She spent so much time at the library that students thought she was a member of the staff.

"Although I had never been a 'people person' in Argentina, when I moved to the United States I went out of my way to be sociable. I joined Saint Patrick Saint Anthony, a Roman Catholic Church in downtown Hartford, and frequently volunteered with them. It was essential to mix with all types of people if I was going to learn social skills. I undertook this journey not only as a voyage of self-discovery but also to learn about other people's lives, to gain experience, and improve my understanding of the world. Then, hopefully, I would be able to get all the thoughts that were whirling around in my head down on paper and turn them into a book."

She went through a rough time when she ran out of money. She took odd jobs—one was as a dishwasher at a store in West Hartford—to support herself. "I was there two years and four months but it was not going to work out for me. I had other goals in life." In February 2010, she was unemployed and could not afford rent; she stayed "here and there" for the next two years. Her pastor, Father Thomas, became aware of her housing situation and talked to the Sisters of Mercy about it.[108] The Sisters offered her an apartment in the Parkville neighborhood. It was October 2012.

While at the Hartford Seminary, Claudia met Pastor Martin, a Lutheran from Germany who was spending his three-month sabbatical at Grace. He invited her to the Friday Gathering.

Before the pandemic, when diners sat down together to eat, Claudia would arrive late. "I realized that when you have a developmental disability, you tend to be uncomfortable in social situations. You don't know what to say, you don't know where to look, you don't know how to treat other people, and you don't know whether they feel pity for you when pity is the last thing you want," she said.[109] By arriving late, she avoided the most crowded and noisy time of the evening.

As Claudia became more comfortable at Grace, she began volunteering with Janet's Closet. "She has a real drive to help people," Louisa said. The atmosphere was easygoing and quiet. There was space to spread out.

Claudia and Lee got to know each other. Lee welcomed neighbors to Janet's Closet while Claudia sorted the clothing. She noticed which garments were soiled and took them home to launder. People gave Claudia clothing donations, which she brought to Grace. She refilled the coat racks in the hallway with men's and women's clothing. If there was an overabundance of some items, she took them to another clothing bank. She kept the space organized and tidy.

In March 2020, when COVID-19 restrictions were implemented, Janet's Closet was put on hold. This presented Claudia with a paradox: "As a person with autism, I endured all my life the ultimate in social distancing. When social distancing became the law, I was altogether enamored of this part of the crisis. Society was not fashionable any more. Autism had been given the thing it always wanted: the chance to reject community. I adjusted nicely."[110]

However, Claudia struggled when she discovered that the places where she felt accepted and comfortable were shuttered and closed indefinitely. "At last, there was no way to avoid losing all my social skills," she wrote.[111]

Claudia asked Louisa for a volunteer job. The Friday Gathering was too chaotic and not a good fit. Meanwhile, new bags of donated clothing had piled up. Claudia and Lee lobbied to reopen Janet's Closet. They would take all the necessary precautions to keep themselves and others safe. In August 2020, when Janet's Closet reopened, Claudia was there to keep it organized while Lee checked temperatures and welcomed neighbors back.

Claudia's book, *Legendary Lessons: More Than One Hundred Golf Teachings from Walter Hagan, Bobby Jones, Grantland Rice, Harry Vardon, and More* was published in 2016 by Skyhorse Publishing. Her success was reported in the *Hartford Courant,* but it didn't make her a celebrity in Hartford, at the Friday Gathering, or among golfers.[112] "I've been through frustration and rejection," Claudia wrote to me. "It is certainly true to say that I still have to 'make it' in the golf industry."[113]

In 2021, Brad Klein, a journalist for *The Golfer's Journal*, wrote:

> [Claudia is] one of the most brilliant and confounding golf historians and aspiring journalists I've ever met. … While she is yet to be publicly rewarded in terms of permanent employment, recognition, financial success and the accumulation of material goods that are traditionally associated with 'making it,' I have come to believe that says more about our difficulty as a society in respecting difference than it says anything about her.[114]

Presently, Claudia is a "profesora" of the History of Golf, online at the PGA of Argentina. Since August 2020, she has worked in bindery for a nearby printing company. "I appreciate the independence it gives me while I research and plan my next book," she said.

"I believe that God made us to be different," Claudia said. "As I see it, this follows logically: if a person is chronically 'ordinary,' there is something wrong. Something is missing."[115]

***

The norms of a community define what it values. The desire to see the humanity in each other—and the resolve to value the contributions of each other—inspires the Friday Gathering. This is different from making accommodations, which tend to leave barriers in place, are reactive instead of universal, and isolate or marginalize individuals. Seeing the dignity in each other compels us to save a loaf of rye bread for a lonely man, tell jokes and laugh together, nurture a neighbor's child, talk about books with a table of diners, serve at Janet's Closet, and appreciate the merit of these contributions. They aren't trivial. They express what it means to belong: we do not try to be the same as everybody else or settle for just fitting in.

10

Belonging to Each Other

Let the globe, if nothing else, say this is true:

That even as we grieved, we grew,

That even as we hurt, we hoped,

That even as we tired, we tried.

That we'll forever be tied together.

—Amanda Gorman, *The Hill We Climb: An Inaugural Poem for the Country*

Periodically I ask diners, "What is it about the Friday Gathering that brings you back?" Their responses keep me grounded in their perspectives and realities.

There are people who come because they are hungry. Others need to stretch their cash resources, and a free dinner puts a little elasticity in their budget. There are diners with disabilities—physical, intellectual, or psychological. Many neighbors do not have access to an automobile. Planning, shopping, transporting groceries, and preparing a meal is arduous for some of them. Some live in unfurnished apartments and lack plates, utensils, or a pot for cooking. Some diners are homeless, and some live in shelters. They all need to eat.

Dig deeper, and other motivations emerge. Dennis, a white man in his fifties, struggled with severe depression. During some episodes, he said, "Coming to the Friday Gathering is the only time I leave my apartment." Others reply that this is where they meet their friends. Occasionally, a diner said, "On Friday nights, my friends go to the bars. Coming here is a better option for me. I don't have to choose between that and being alone." Philip, a white man in his sixties, said, "It's embarrassing. I can afford to feed myself. But I'm so lonely, being here makes me feel better."

Occasionally, when I ask, "What brings you back?" a diner raises their arm in a giant sweep of the room and says, "The photos. The people. I fit in here." Lamont was one of the first diners who sat for a portrait and agreed to display it on the wall. Lamont doesn't just belong; he offers belonging to the neighborhood.

***

In 2011, Lamont's friend Woody saw a flyer about a free supper at Grace and suggested they check it out. Lamont and Woody came for dinner, and then Lamont told his childhood friends Richie and his brother Jesus, and they came to dinner. Lamont invited more friends, and they came, too. By word of mouth, invitations to the Friday Gathering rippled through the neighborhood. In an interview for the *Asylum Hill News & Views,* Lamont recalled that they liked the food and the people seemed nice enough, so they kept returning until it became routine.

Even now, after all these years, Lamont still tells newcomers, "The food isn't bad." Then he laughs because it's an understatement. He is proud of the food that's served and that he helped prepare it. For Lamont, Grace is home, and he is cooking for family.

Lamont was born in Hartford in 1967. He's a Black man of average height, lean, with a slender, compact build. His brother Arnell, one year older, is built the same way. There is a strong resemblance between them. Lamont has a restless spirit. He is nearly always on the go, dashing here or there, talking to himself, counting off all the things he needs to remember.

Arnell's manner is just the opposite. His sense of purpose is measured, restrained, and quiet. He watches out for Lamont. When Lamont gets stressed, Arnell soothes him. Arnell stands nearby, where his brother can see him. They don't need to speak to communicate. Arnell doesn't tell Lamont what to do. The closeness is reassurance enough. I have observed this exchange a few times and witnessed the calming effect that Arnell has on Lamont. I am drawn to the bond between these brothers because it's been tested.

"Arnell taught me how to be the brother I am. How to be strong," Lamont said. "I can be pretty demanding."

"You're spoiled," Arnell countered in a soft voice, and the brothers laughed.

Lamont is the youngest of four children. He and Arnell have an older brother, and the eldest of the siblings was a sister. She worked as an underwriter for the Travelers Insurance company. She died in 2010 when she was forty-seven. "I was shocked when they told me," Lamont said. "I couldn't believe it; she had an aneurysm."

The memory of his sister shook Lamont up. His voice trembled, his hands fluttered, and his words were fragments of unfinished sentences. I asked him if he had been able to see his sister before she died.

"Oh yes," he said. "She lived a few more years." Even though the aneurysm and his sister's death were several years apart, his memories of the two events were linked and inseparable. The memory of her passing was as fresh as if it had just happened.

I asked Lamont and Arnell if they had been close to their sister.

"She was like a mother to us," Lamont said. "She could be bossy, telling us what to do and what not to do. She had a temper like our mother. But Arnell could break her spell. He knew how to make her smile. My sister couldn't stay angry at him."

"She took us places," Arnell continued. "One time, she took us to the mall in West Hartford. We stayed all day, and it was amazing. We ate breakfast, lunch, and dinner there and stayed until it closed. We didn't just window shop. We each saw things we liked. We were curious about who liked what. It was fun to take our time planning our purchases and, at the end of the day, buying something for each other."

"She took us to New Haven, flea markets, places like that," Lamont added.

"She had 'the look,' you know," Lamont said, and the brothers laughed again. "She wouldn't take 'no' for an answer. She took me to Red Lobster once, and I didn't have money to pay for my dinner. I didn't know what to order because I couldn't pay. She gave me 'the look' and told me to order what I pleased. We always knew we were family. That's what mattered."

One afternoon during the pandemic, Lamont and I sat side by side distributing dinners. After a while, the stream of diners slowed until there was a lull. We were alone and it was quiet. We weren't talking about anything in particular when Lamont blurted out, "My mother was shot and killed when I was growing up."

The loss of his birth mother was the missing link in a story that had not made sense to me. Over the decade I had known Lamont, he often mentioned his mother. One time he referred to her as his foster mother. Another time he said he was adopted. Sometimes he said his mother was dead, and other times he said he was going to Waterbury to visit her. One day, he said it was the anniversary of his mother's death. I couldn't make sense of the bits and pieces he shared. But it wasn't important to our friendship, and I didn't press him.

Sometimes when Lamont talked about his mother, he meant Dolores, his mother's friend. Dolores was born in Cuba, grew up in Jamaica, and attended private schools. She immigrated to the United States in 1946 and became a citizen. She and her husband settled in Hartford and raised nine children. She was a nurse and worked at the Hebrew Home & Hospital until she retired. And she looked after Lamont and his siblings in the years leading up to their mother's death. "God bless her," Lamont said. "She did it because she knew my mother."

Lamont was eleven years old when his mother, Rosetta, was murdered in a "domestic dispute," as reported in the *Hartford Courant*. Around 11 p.m., she was shot in the chest and died a few hours later at the hospital. Lamont wasn't home when it happened. He was staying with Dolores. Arnell and their older brother were with their father in Waterbury. Their sister wasn't home, either. She was at a friend's house.

Lamont and Arnell became quiet, retreating into memories of Rosetta. "She loved how Dorothy Moore sang 'Misty Blue,'" Arnell said. "Every morning, she listened to that record. We woke up to it playing over and over. She liked to party." The brothers hummed a few bars from the song. "I listen to it when I'm thinking of her," Lamont said.

> Oh, it's been such a long, long time
> Look like I'd get you off of my mind
> But I can't
> Just the thought of you (just the thought of you)
> Turns my whole world misty blue (misty blue)[116]

After Rosetta's death, the children were split up. Lamont's two brothers moved to Waterbury and grew up with their father and his wife—their stepmother, Irma—and their children. Arnell graduated from high school there. Their sister lived with her father and his family in East Hartford. Lamont's father had disappeared long before, so Dolores and her husband, Guy, became his foster parents. When the foster care system tried to move Lamont to another home, Dolores and Guy adopted him. Dolores told

Lamont, "We're going to do this right."

These women—Rosetta, Dolores, and Irma—are mothers to Lamont. "I would do anything for them," he said. He especially revered his memories of Dolores and Guy. "I loved them both very, very much. They were good people."

Lamont and his adoptive parents lived in Hartford's Frog Hollow neighborhood, which was becoming known for its Puerto Rican community. Lamont lived close enough to walk to the elementary school and made friends with Richie and his younger brother, Jesus. From elementary school through high school, the boys were in and out of each other's houses and ate at each other's dinner tables. Dolores was strict and kept Lamont close to home, especially during high school. "She made it impossible for me to get into trouble," Lamont said.

Dolores and Guy not only cared for Lamont but also nurtured the bonds between the siblings. "Guy drove me to East Hartford, so I could visit my sister," Lamont remembered. "Arnell came from Waterbury to visit me, and I went to Waterbury to see my brothers." In Waterbury, Lamont became another son to Irma, and he called her Mom.

"One weekend, there was a family gathering in Waterbury," Lamont said. "There were people there who didn't know me. Arnell and I overheard a woman ask Mom, 'How's he your son?'

"Mom told her, 'That's my child. None o' your business how he's my child,'" Lamont mimicked Irma's voice, and the brothers burst into laughter.

I asked Arnell to describe Irma, and he answered without hesitating. "She's a churchgoing lady who will beat you with the Bible! When something is important to her, that's what she says. 'I'll beat you with the Bible.'"

"Irma told me," Lamont added, "Don't you call me Irma, call me Mom, or I'll beat you with the Bible," and the brothers laughed again.

"She'll throw the holy water on you in a minute," Arnell laughed.

"She's a good lady," he added soberly.

Lamont graduated from Hartford High School and went to work in the fast-food industry, first for Wendy's, then for McDonald's. Along the way, he met Woody.

Woody, a Black man, was born in 1955 in Richland, Georgia, a rural town near the border with Alabama. He and his twin brother were the second and third oldest of eleven children. His father was a farmer, and he grew collards, peppers, corn, and squash. In eleventh grade, Woody left school to help out at home. He did the dishes, swept the floor, and cared for the younger children.

"We lived next to a cemetery," Woody said, "and I knew there were ghosts in there. When I was fourteen years old, I saw ghosts running into a headstone." Woody usually joked around and laughed about everything. But as he talked about the cemetery and the ghosts, he was solemn and quiet. Then he explained, "I was born with the veil.[117] I can see spirits.

"It was scary living by the cemetery. There was no running water in our house. Every night, my brothers and me walked half a mile to the spring and filled up buckets with water. 'Get home before the ghosts get ya.' That's what we said."

In 1975, when Woody was twenty, his father was killed in a car accident. The next year, his mother died from cirrhosis of the liver. Woody headed north. His aunt—his mother's sister—lived in Hartford. She took Woody in, but their arrangement did not work out.

Woody was living on the streets when he met Lamont. "He was not in good shape," Lamont said. "I felt God calling me to take him in, the way Dolores and Guy had done it for me, to show him the way and how to get back on his feet." Dolores and Guy treated Woody like a son and made him family. In time, Lamont helped Woody apply for disability benefits and Section 8 housing.

When Lamont's parents became ill, he quit work to care for them. In

2004, Guy died of a heart attack. In 2007, Dolores died of complications from diabetes. The next years were an unsettled time for Lamont. The recession hit. His sister died. He found part-time work. Lamont moved in with Woody. "I made him my family and gave him a home, just like he did for me," Woody said.

When Woody saw the flyer for the Friday Gathering, he told Lamont, and they came for dinner. They heard Darrell's message, "We're building community here. This is the place where you want to belong."

"I fell in love with this church," Lamont said, "and I decided to make Grace my home. I love cooking, being loved by all the people here, becoming the kitchen supervisor. I would still love it if I couldn't be the kitchen supervisor. Nothing lasts forever. The people I love would still be here. When I invite people to Grace, I tell them, 'I'm going to bring you home,' and I mean bring them to Grace. Grace is the place to be."

"It's my home, too," Woody chimed in. "I can always come here. When I die, I want to come home to be buried here."

Lamont and Woody came to church on Sundays and in a short while became members. Lamont took on acolyte duties. At Grace's annual meeting in 2013, they volunteered to serve on the church council and were elected to it. When the sexton retired, Lamont was hired. Lamont tells his neighbors, "That's my church. It's my home. All of us made it our place to be."

On Friday mornings, Lamont is in the kitchen working alongside the chefs. "I'm at home in the kitchen," he said. The banter between the chefs and Lamont moves back and forth between chitchatting and affectionate scolding. The chefs ask him to lift the heavy pots and pans, retrieve an item from the pantry or freezer, and chop vegetables, and gently chide him if he wasn't at church early enough to unlock the door for them in the morning. The talk is seasoned with laughter and teasing. The chefs share their wisdom with Lamont about how to deal with life's struggles. They encourage him to take better care of his health. Get more rest. Slow down. Fussing at Lamont is how they show they care about him.

"They treat me like family," Lamont said. "We might fight. We might argue. But being a family means we can do this! At the end of the day, we're still family."

***

Richie claims Lamont as family, too. "He's my brother," Richie said.

The two men have been in each other's lives since their boyhoods. They grew up in the same neighborhood, went to school together, took turns buying ice cream sandwiches for each other at lunch, and were in and out of each other's childhood homes. They know each other's secrets. "My mother loved Lamont," Richie said. "She always told him, 'You're the son I never had.'"

Richie shrugged at the memory. "It hurt a little," he said, still uncertain about what she meant. "My mother loved all of us," he concluded.

Richie was born in 1966 in Puerto Rico. His mother was Puerto Rican, and his father was Black. They met when his mother was in Miami. When his mother moved back to Puerto Rico, his father followed, and they were married there. "My mother taught him how to speak Spanish," Richie said. "If he didn't learn it, then she could talk about him, and he would have to sit there and agree with her. He wouldn't know what she was saying."

Richie identifies as "other," not Latino or Hispanic, Black, or white, and claims his Puerto Rican and Black heritages. "I got the best of both," he said.

Richie is the middle child, with an older brother and sister, a younger sister, and a younger brother named Jesus. When Richie was six months old, his family came to Hartford and settled in the Frog Hollow neighborhood. Richie and Jesus grew up speaking Spanish at home and English at school. They joined a wave of migration that dramatically transformed the ethnic makeup of the city.[118]

In the 1950s, Connecticut's tobacco farmers recruited Puerto Ricans to work their fields. In the 1960s, Puerto Ricans turned to unskilled blue-collar jobs at industrial sites like Pratt & Whitney, an aircraft engine manufacturer.[119] Along Park Street in Hartford, in the Frog Hollow neighborhood where Richie and Lamont grew up, the business district was increasingly Spanish-speaking. As Susan Campbell, journalist and author, points out, "By 1970 Frog Hollow was overwhelmingly—70 percent—Hispanic, 18 percent African American, and about 7 percent Caucasian."[120] Richie's father had a friend in Hartford who worked in construction, and that connection drew them north.

Richie remembered meeting Lamont at the market on Park Street, two blocks from their homes. "In those days, you could get a Tootsie Roll for a penny. If you had a nickel, you could buy five and have enough for yourself and some to share. Jesus and I were probably buying candy at the store the day I met Lamont," Richie said.

It was Jesus who recognized Lamont and pointed him out to Richie. Their mother knew Lamont's mother, Dolores, and Jesus had seen Lamont in the market with her. Richie and Lamont were a year apart but in the same grade at school. The boys became friends. Richie walked to Lamont's house in the morning on school days. If Richie was late, Lamont walked to his house. Then they set out for school.

"Lamont was a scrawny kid and picked on at school," Richie said. He couldn't put up with two or three bullies ganging up on one kid, so he became Lamont's "big brother" and took on the bullies. Sometimes he could handle it without a fight. "Why you bothering my brother?" Richie asked them, and ended it with, "Don't let it happen again."

Richie's father demanded respect. "My parents taught me to be respectful no matter what. Respect means everything. With respect comes responsibility. Being worthy of respect means that others can count on you."

When Richie was in ninth grade, he had a disagreement with a teacher. The teacher said he talked back and called his parents to come in for a conference. His father took time off from work to go; his mother stayed home. Richie and his dad met with the teacher. "My dad was calm and polite. He didn't argue. He listened, and then it was over. We got in the car and went home. I thought the worst of it was past and went to my room. I took a shower. When I came out, dripping wet, my father belted me.

"It was the only time he hit me," Richie said. "My father didn't believe in hitting. He was the type to sit down and talk it out. He believed in punishment, though. We couldn't watch TV or play the radio. We weren't allowed to go out until punishment was ended."

Richie dreamed of being an airplane pilot, like the ones he saw in the old army movies he watched with his dad and uncle. "It's amazing how they can stay up in the air and they can carry jeeps and trucks," he said. He also was afraid of flying. "What if the plane runs out of fuel? What if the pilot wakes up on the wrong side of the bed? What if we get lost in the Bermuda Triangle?" Richie asked. "Do you believe the Bermuda Triangle is for real?"

When he was growing up, Richie's mother and siblings returned to Puerto Rico to visit family. "I never went with them, because I was afraid of flying." A flood of memories came rushing back. He had celebrated his fourteenth birthday there. He remembered driving to the airport and that they flew on Eastern Air Lines. Richie named the foods that were prepared for his birthday dinner. "They made empanadillas with different fillings and stuffed Rellenos. They had a pig roast. Of course, there was cake and ice cream, and soda. It lasted all day. It was my two cousins' birthdays, too. We celebrated together." Richie shook his head. "I just don't remember being on a plane."

A few weeks later, Richie said, "I asked my older sister if she knew how they got me on the plane. She said they crushed up a sleeping pill and mixed it with soda. Since it was my birthday, they told me I could have all the soda I wanted. It was just like Mr. T on [the television series] the A-Team. His character was afraid of flying, and his friends had to invent ways to get him on an airplane."

Richie was expelled from high school before he could graduate. The assistant principal found him and a group of teens fighting in the restroom at school. Richie wouldn't tell what they were fighting about. He was suspended, and then the suspension became permanent.

Hartford was "the best," Richie said, remembering his childhood. "There was crime but not like today. The gangs were different then. They looked out for you. If you graduated from high school, they threw a neighborhood party for you. They celebrated what was good. The cops were good, too. If you were in the park after dark, they brought you home." After the cops brought Richie home for the eighth time, his father told him to stop bothering them and let them do their job. "'They're not there just for you,' my dad said. 'They're there for everybody.'

"Today, times have changed. At every level of society, people are out for themselves. Everybody has a grudge, and they just want to get even."

Richie never joined a gang. "I didn't think it was worth it. Your family is your gang," he said.

"In high school, the first time a girl said she loved me, it scared me. I thought 'I love you' was just for family, for your father, your mother, and your relatives. I didn't know what love meant if it wasn't about family."

After high school, Richie worked in shipping and receiving. He tried living in New York City, but he wasn't comfortable there. "You could get lost in the subways," he said. He went to Louisville, Kentucky, and worked in the kitchen at a Waffle House. When his father had a heart attack, Richie came back to Hartford. "It took two days by bus because I wouldn't fly." His father lived a short time until he slipped into a coma and passed away.

Richie went back to Louisville and got his old job back. When his sister called to say his mother wasn't well, he came home again. "She died in her sleep with her dog, Pebbles, a chihuahua, in her arms. I didn't know she was gone until she didn't answer me. I called 911 and they came. She was already cold." I asked Richie how he dealt with losing his parents. "My mother told us, 'You're not promised tomorrow.'"

Initially, Richie expected to return to Louisville, but it didn't work out. He and Jesus experienced stretches of homelessness. They sometimes found refuge at the ImmaCare Shelter, housed in the former Immaculate Conception Roman Catholic Church in their childhood neighborhood. They slept in the park. Friends like Lamont and Woody took them in. The Salvation Army gave them shelter, too. A few times they sneaked into Grace for the night. When they were caught, it compromised the congregation's trust in them. "We didn't have any other way to cope," Richie said.

Richie and Jesus came to Grace for more than dinner in the early years of the Friday Gathering. Lamont organized a men's group, and they met at Grace on Saturday mornings. They cooked breakfast and ate together, did projects around the church, and organized fun activities. They went hiking, toured the Nautilus Museum, had a cookout, and tried fishing and sailing. They experienced what it meant to be responsible to one another when one man was late and it held the whole group up, or when the person in charge of the cookout forgot to bring a spatula to flip the burgers. There was the time a water valve wasn't properly shut off and the floor in the men's room flooded. Richie and Jesus worshipped with the congregation on Sundays. When Louisa and Lee started making benches out of pallets, they learned about furniture making and working with wood.

Richie started coming to Grace for Alcoholics Anonymous meetings and worked with Lee to make benches. When orders for benches increased, the operation outgrew the workspace at Grace. It moved to the other end of Niles Street, into the basement of Trinity Episcopal Church. When winter came, Richie worried about Lee walking the extra distance at night to get home. He knew Lee had cataracts, and it was more difficult to see after sunset. "Like clockwork," Lee said, "Richie waited every day for me, and then he walked me home."

On Saturdays, Richie meets Lee at the church. He tackles the chores that Lee assigns him, and then they do Lee's weekly shopping. "I make sure I'm there, so I can carry his packages," Richie said.

In 2019, Jesus's alcohol addiction worsened, pushing his diabetes out of control. Richie turned to Lee and Pastor Rick for help, and they used their connections to get Jesus into the Salvation Army's rehabilitation program. "Richie and Jesus had become like sons to me," Lee said, "and it hurt to see the toll it was taking on Jesus."

"At first, no one told me where Jesus was," Richie said. "He's my brother! I look after him. We hadn't been separated since I came back from Louisville. He wasn't allowed visitors for three months. We were only allowed to talk once a week on the phone."

"The separation was hard on Richie," Lee said. "I understood. I missed Jesus, too. Richie was lost without his brother. Depressed. He had been sober for about four years, and I worried he would relapse.

"People work at their own pace through the program," Lee continued. "A lot of times, folks only last a month or two before they drop out."

"After seven months, Jesus graduated," Richie said. "I went to his graduation, and Lorraine—our friend—came, too." Jesus moved to an assisted care facility near Grace. Richie and Jesus have seen each other almost daily since then, except during the pandemic when the facility closed to all visitors.

Richie didn't go to church when he was growing up and said he didn't have strong ideas about the existence of God. In February 2014, he decided to be baptized at Grace. He still isn't sure he believes in God. "Everyone is out for themselves, the pastors, too," he said. "They don't live in the neighborhood. What does that tell you?

"How can God allow so much suffering?" Richie continued.

"How can God allow women and children to be abused? The elderly who are alone and abandoned? The police start off good, and then the system abuses them, and they abuse the people they were sworn to protect. How does God allow a three-year-old and a fifteen-year-old in the North End to be shot and killed?"

Richie turned to talking about his own children, and his agitation melted away. He smiled to himself and held his arms as if he were cuddling one of them. "Being a dad is the best feeling in the world," he began. "They told me I wouldn't be able to have children. I was hit in the groin with a baseball.

"I met Diana when she was pregnant with Joshua. He's in high school now and has a part-time job. Diana was new to Hartford then; she moved here from Florida. It made me proud when Joshua called me Dad." Then came Tommy, Manny, and Athena.

"I was in the delivery room when Athena was born. I had to get scrubbed and gowned before they let me go in, and then I thought I'd be sick. Seeing a child born. Knowing it's mine and that I helped make that little baby. Even now, it brings tears to my eyes." In the dining hall at Grace, Richie pointed out where all the portraits of him and the kids were hung. "There's me and Tommy, and me and Athena. There's Tommy and Manny together. There are two portraits of Manny by himself and one of Tommy by himself."

"Tommy calls me Grandpa," Lee added. "I'm teaching him how to paint and how to use power tools. He's growing up."

"Diana and I are friends," Richie said. "I know she wants more out of the relationship, but we're good at coparenting. Things are good the way they are. Why mess it up?

"When I get to the house, if the kids call me Richie, I know everything is okay. If they call me Daddy, then I know they're in trouble with their mother. They want me to talk her out of their punishment. I talk to them. I hear their side of what happened. I don't believe in hitting. I tell them to do what their mother tells them. Then, in private, I tell Diana that she can't turn everything into a battle. If there's too much arguing, I walk away.

"I'm the one who goes to the parent-teacher conferences at school," Richie continued. "The teachers say the kids are smart. They follow directions and do their work. They don't cause trouble. It makes me proud of them. Except when the teacher says they didn't turn in their homework."

Richie pulled a bronze token out of his pocket and handed it to me. "I've been sober six years," he said. The token was marked "VI" in roman numerals on one side and with the Serenity Prayer on the other. "Six years clean," Richie repeated.

"It means a lot to me that Lee knows he can count on me. I can kid around with him. I can make a joke about buying a six-pack, and he gets it. If I'm really, *really* tempted, I think, 'What would Lee say?'

"'The choice is yours.' That's what he says," Richie finished.

I asked Lee to explain, and he nodded in agreement. "What I mean is, you know the difference between right and wrong. Take responsibility for your choices."

"He's my dad. I can count on him, and he can count on me," Richie said.

***

Lorraine is part of Richie's family, too. "She's my sister," Richie declared one afternoon. "She's my bestie."

"We have that 'eye' thing, you know? We don't need words. We just look at each other and know what the other one is thinking. She just knows," Richie said.

Lorraine nodded in agreement. "I don't have to explain myself to Richie," she said. "We understand each other."

Lorraine was born in 1958. "I hate being labeled as colored," she said. "People of color. I hate that term, too. White is a color. There are lots of different whites, but they don't make a deal out of that. I don't want to be called Black either. I'm not black. My color is bronze. I have freckles. You should see my kids. One is darker than me. Is he black? No, he's not. Everybody looks at you and wants to put a label on you. Black people do that to one another, too."

Lorraine and I got to know each other a decade ago when we volunteered to clean up Niles Street, the side street where the church and the neighborhood elementary school are located. We spent a couple of hours going up one side of the street and down the other, picking up trash. We bonded over our shared identities as mothers. I often participated in clean-up projects and knew how difficult it is to enlist volunteers to pick up other people's garbage; I was grateful for Lorraine's generosity. It was easy to enjoy her company. She was thoughtful and strong and cared about things that mattered to me.

Lorraine is the second oldest of six children. Her parents migrated north from Selma, Alabama, seeking better opportunities for themselves and their children. "My mother said I wouldn't have survived if I was born down there. She said my mouth was too sassy," Lorraine recalled. She doesn't know why her parents chose Connecticut or Hartford. They didn't have family here. "Everybody else went west. After my older brother was born, my parents said they wouldn't have any more kids down there. So, they came north. I was born in Hartford.

"My father dropped out of school in the sixth grade, but he could read and write. My mother finished school. She was no fool. She rode motorcycles. When she was twenty-one years old, she gave her life to God and said it changed her. She became a pillar in the church and in the community. Everybody knew her. They had a lot of respect for her.

"My mother and father loved each other. Mom always said, 'Go check on your dad. Take him something to eat.' She never talked bad about him. When he was drinking, she said, 'Leave him alone. God'll fix him.' She meant that God would either take him out or heal him. It wasn't up to us."

Lorraine's father worked for Waybest Chicken, a poultry distributor. "He was a truck driver and made deliveries for them. He delivered furniture, too. He was a hard worker. He loved playing the bass guitar. He would set up and play in the living room. Sometimes my brother played guitar with him. My dad was a good guy." Then Lorraine's voice quieted. "He was abusive and alcoholic, too. He didn't get along with his family in Alabama and was already drinking when they moved to Hartford.

"I loved my dad," Lorraine said. "He had a lot of demons in him, a lot of sadness. Sometimes my mom said, 'Go find your father and bring him home.'"

Lorraine's mother cleaned houses and was a short-order cook for the posh G. Fox department store downtown. "She was up at 4 a.m. to catch the bus to get to G. Fox to open up the kitchen. I worried about her in the winter. She had to walk down a steep hill to get to the employee entrance on Market Street. I was afraid she'd slip and fall on the ice.

"Mother brought the leftovers home for us. Or, if she was working overtime, she'd send for one of us to come down and pick up the food. Dad would be out somewhere."

The family lived in the North End of Hartford. Their first home was in Stowe Village, Hartford's second-largest housing project with six hundred units. It was brand new in 1952 and plagued with scandal from the start. The units were built on swampland and incurred cost overruns to stabilize the foundations. In January 1953, the chairman of the Housing Authority described the facilities as "grossly inadequate."[121]

"By the age of three, my mother was preparing me to be the mother to my siblings," Lorraine said. "I was a parent before I was a child. By the time I was five, I was grocery shopping. My mother worked all the time to make ends meet. When I was older, it fell to me to get the younger kids off to school. I never did the childhood things that my siblings got to do—go to the beach, the amusement parks, the prom, school trips. My sister got her driver's license. The next week was my turn. My mother told me to cancel the appointment. She couldn't afford it. I took the brunt of things and made it easier for the others.

"My older brother—he was two years older than me—stuttered and was teased about it. My mother said, 'Leave that boy alone.' We were close. He was everything a big brother is supposed to be. He tried to be the man of the house. Tried to protect us. He stole pompoms for me to wear in my hair so I could have the latest things that my friends at school had."

When Lorraine was nine years old, her mother left her father and moved with the children to California. "She was tired and wanted to get away from the abuse," Lorraine said. They went by bus. Lorraine's uncle—her mother's brother—had married Lorraine's father's baby sister, and they lived near Los Angeles. Lorraine's mother settled with her children in Riverside, a working-class community east of LA.

"There were fruit trees in front of our house and a dairy farm across the street. We could buy an ice cream cone for three cents," Lorraine remembered. "There was a white boy named Sammy in my class who liked me. I liked him, too. No one paid attention to the color of our skin."

They stayed for three years in California. "My mother was always out, always working, trying to hold things together," Lorraine said.

This was 1967-1970, when protests and calls for reform consumed Hartford and the nation. Residents in the North End of Hartford marched to demonstrate against housing conditions and the shooting of a Black youth by a police officer.[122] Gunfire, arson, and other violence impacted daily life. When Lorraine's father purchased a home on Cleveland Avenue—a tree-lined street of single-family homes with driveways and private off-street parking—still in the North End but out of the projects, Lorraine's mother moved back to Hartford. Her mother lived in the house until she passed away in 2006.

"'We got a house now,' my father said. We had our own front yard and a backyard. No one could tell us we can't play, sit, stand, or walk on the grass. At Stowe Village, they had all those rules."

In 1976, Lorraine graduated from Hartford Public High School. "I wanted to be a nun and go to the Oral Roberts University. I thought about joining the army. I did everything but get sworn in. I wanted to go to Outward Bound, but I had to stay home and be the parent. I had dreams of going to college. I wanted to be a physical therapist."

Lorraine's first son was born the September after her high school graduation. The baby was due in December, but he came early. Not until December did he gain enough weight for Lorraine to bring him home.

Although the protests in Hartford had subsided by this time, poverty prevailed. The US Department of Housing and Urban Development undertook a program to improve the quality of life of public housing residents. A survey that assessed the level of unemployment in the North End of Hartford concluded that in 1979—only a few years after Lorraine had graduated—unemployment was 44 percent, compared to 4 percent in the surrounding towns. In addition, the report stated that "Fifty percent of those who had completed federal job-training programs were unable to find work, and 57 percent of the 17–20-year-old age group in the North End was unemployed."[123]

"My brother was two years ahead of me," Lorraine said. "Imagine what it was like for him.

"When times were bad—and some days were terrible—we looked out for each other. We went to church every day. I grew up in the church. Church was everything. We prayed together. We had to do the best we could with what we had."

Lorraine said that in her early twenties, "I was having a hard time. My mother told me to go to Alabama for the weekend. She thought the change would do me good. I ended up staying longer. I wanted a new start. I was tired of the abuse. I wanted out of the projects.

"Everything was cool for a while." But eventually Lorraine decided her mother was right. "I couldn't survive down there." Lorraine returned to Hartford. A second son was born, and a decade later, a daughter. She waitressed and worked as a teacher's aide for the Community Renewal Team. Lorraine married, then came to terms with her husband's depression, alcoholism, and abuse. They separated, and he later died.

When Lorraine was twenty-five, her older brother collapsed at a friend's home. He had sickle cell disease, and doctors said it triggered a heart attack. "My oldest brother died in the arms of my youngest brother," Lorraine said. "It was devastating. Three years later, my father died. They said it was cirrhosis of the liver. But I know he died of a broken heart. He didn't get over losing his firstborn. Dad was only forty-nine years old.

"When I was in my thirties, my mother apologized to me," Lorraine said. "She wasn't well. We talked every day and were becoming friends. In those days, everyone called each other Auntie 'this' or Auntie 'that.' There was Auntie Gloria, Auntie Lottie, and Auntie Celeste. But I was just Auntie. No one called me Auntie Lorraine. One day I pointed this out to my mother, and she finally understood how much I had sacrificed. She said, 'I'm sorry, Lorraine, for all the things I put you through, that you had to stand in my place. I'm sorry for depriving you of your childhood.'

"I don't know who I am," Lorraine said. "I had dreams. Things I wanted to do. Everybody wanted a piece of me."

One sister went to Cheyney University in Pennsylvania and made a career working in information technology. Her younger brother retired after a thirty-year career in human resources with the State of Connecticut. "He loved to travel the world," Lorraine remembered. "He would say, 'I sat and ate with the best.'" Another sister retired from the army and went back to college. She completed two bachelor's degrees. One sister lives with a disability. "I'm the matriarch of the family now," Lorraine said, "and it doesn't bring me any peace."

One afternoon, Richie and Lorraine got acquainted when he noticed her walking her dogs. "Romeo, come on, Romeo," she called to one of the chihuahuas. Richie started mimicking her. "Romeo, oh Romeo," Richie echoed, and his nickname for Lorraine stuck.

When Louisa visited the Loaves & Fishes soup kitchen and invited neighbors to dinner at Grace, Lorraine was there. Richie learned about the Friday dinner from Lamont. When Lorraine and Richie came to dinner at Grace, they were neighbor greeting neighbor, and it felt like home.

Lorraine joined the congregation and became a member of Grace. "One day, Evelyn asked if I'd like to help." Evelyn is one of the chefs and a member of the congregation. "Church is everything to me, and I said 'yes.' Why did she invite *me?* Evelyn has always been good to me," Lorraine said. Evelyn showed her how to set up the altar for Sunday services, where the linens are stored, how to arrange the communion trays and fill the baptismal font with water, and the extra touches needed for special occasions.

When Janet's Closet opened in 2013, Lorraine and Leah ran it together. They coordinated with other volunteers. Leah made lunch for them each week. The team of women was comparable to the men's group that Lamont had organized.

Lorraine invited Richie to help her prepare the altar until one day, a member of the congregation questioned what they were doing. "It was insulting," Lorraine said. "Trust is a two-way street, and to have my integrity questioned changed my relationship with them. I didn't feel comfortable there anymore."

In recent years, Lorraine has dealt with housing and health problems. In 2018, the local housing authority—the agency providing rental assistance to low-income families—forced her to move. Lorraine had lived in the Asylum Hill neighborhood in the same two-bedroom apartment for twenty-three years. She raised her children there. When the landlord's property maintenance was called to the attention of the housing authority, the landlord made the repairs. No other tenants receiving rental assistance were forced to move, but the housing authority ruled that Lorraine needed to downsize to a one-bedroom apartment.

Louisa accompanied Lorraine to meetings with the housing authority, hoping she could help navigate the system. "It was awful to go through this with her," Louisa said. "Lorraine had such a pretty apartment. She had sunny windows filled with plants. In the end, she lost her apartment, and I couldn't help her."

"They took my home," Lorraine said. She was under a time limit to find a new apartment or lose her housing certificate. She moved to the South End of Hartford, out of the neighborhood where some of her neighbors had become like family. "I'm back to existing day to day. It doesn't feel like home. There's a rodent infestation. The mice have ruined my clothes, and the city inspector told me to take the landlord to small claims court. When you walk around the apartment, you need to make noise so that the mice scurry and you don't step on one."

Lorraine began experiencing blackouts. Doctors said her brain activity showed she had been having seizures for some time. They prescribed medications and gave her a medical alert necklace to wear.

Lorraine fingered the necklace around her neck. "It made me cry to have to wear this thing," she said. "It's heavy. If I'm passed out, how am I supposed to use it? I try to think of it as costume jewelry, and it's not so bad."

Lorraine is nervous that she'll have an episode while riding the city bus. She prefers to sit in the front, in the seat reserved for people with disabilities. "One time, a bus driver yelled at me to move to another seat. He yelled that the seat was reserved for people with disabilities. I told him, 'I'm disabled,' but it didn't matter. Didn't Rosa Parks win this battle? Why can't I sit in the front of the bus?"

One of Lorraine's legs went numb, and she had surgery on her back to repair a disc. She can't always afford the medications the doctors prescribe. When her leg is acting up, she has trouble using the stairs to get on and off the bus. "I don't look disabled, so people assume I'm not. It's made me aware of how much people judge each other based on appearances."

To ease Lorraine's anxiety about going out, Richie accompanies her. He goes with her to medical appointments. He carries her packages when she has things to pick up. He makes sure she can get on and off the bus. He calls her in the morning and asks if she took her pills. He knows her kids and grandchildren. When Richie needs a place to stay or someone to talk to, he can turn to Lorraine. "She would bend over backward to help you," Richie said.

I asked Lorraine what a good day looks like for her. "A good day is when my house is clean," she said. "I want peace and quiet. No cars blasting their music or fireworks shooting off. I enjoy doing jigsaw puzzles, taking care of my plants and the dogs. And family. It's all about staying connected with family."

***

In 2013, The Hartford insurance company—an Asylum Hill neighbor—engaged the Harwood Institute to conduct a study of the neighborhood. They surveyed people who lived and worked in Asylum Hill, asking them what would strengthen the neighborhood. Three themes emerged. One concerned crime and another focused on building trust between different sectors in the neighborhood. The third finding—which underpinned the full report—was that people wanted "places in the neighborhood where they can meet and get to know each other."[124]

> Residents said repeatedly that they want to be able to go outside their homes and have safe, welcoming places where they can meet, socialize and work with their neighbors. ... Having the ability to gather with others is critical to building a neighborhood where people can support one another. Time and again in these conversations, residents expressed their desire for "more

togetherness," the ability to "rely on our neighbors," and a place "where we all look out for each other."[125]

It's one thing to walk down the street and recognize a neighbor and another to "know" them. The Friday Gathering offers a space where neighbors can be themselves and where old and new friendships can flourish. Diners join together in conversation, enjoying music, pitching in, adding their portrait to the wall, singing happy birthday, taking a meal to a shut-in, and simply showing up. This was how we learned to belong to each other.

***

One afternoon when Lamont and I were looking at portraits in the dining hall, he pointed to one of them and said, "They call me grandson." It was a picture of Ethel and her mother, Maude. Lamont met them at the Friday Gathering. During the pandemic, he ran over to their apartment on Fridays and dropped off two boxed dinners. When Maude died in the second spring of the pandemic—she was ninety-four years old—Lamont and I took a bouquet of flowers to Ethel. When Lamont rang the buzzer to her apartment, I overheard him say, "Grandson is here." Without another word, Ethel buzzed us in.

11

Home Is Where One Starts From

To be at home is to be known. It is to be loved for who you are. It is to share a
sense of common ground, common interests, pursuits, and values with others
who truly care about you. In community after community, I met lonely people
who felt homeless even though they had a roof over their heads.

—Vivek H. Murthy, M.D., *Together: The Healing Power of Human Connection in a
Sometimes Lonely World*

"Where is home?" I asked.

Todd laughed and said, "That's a good one! There's no one place that's
home. It's that spot where you feel content, safe, and loved. It's something
deep inside of you that, if you're lucky, stays with you."

Our childhood circumstances shape our idea of what "home"
represents. Home is where we first formed emotional attachments. It is
where we learned to talk and took our first steps. It is where we began to
make sense of the world, our place in it, and how to take care of ourselves.

Our concept of home shapes our present and the homes we create in adulthood.

***

"I first noticed Louisa when I saw her working in the garden at Grace," Todd said. "I used to cut through the parking lot on my way to the Loaves & Fishes soup kitchen. I heard she wasn't American and wondered where she was from. She was friendly and easy to talk to, so I made a point of looking for her when I was in the area. I have great respect for her, for the work she does to help others. The wholesomeness of her heart drew me to her and to the Friday Gathering."

Louisa invited Todd to join her and Lee and others from the neighborhood in building benches from discarded wooden pallets. "He's a natural," Lee said. "Todd's got a feel for working with his hands and a sense for how a piece of wood will respond to his touch. I could tell within a few minutes the first time we worked together. It's a knack that some people have, an aptitude that can't be taught."

Todd, who identifies as Black, was born in Hartford in 1955. He's about six feet tall and muscular. "My mother told me I had perfect eyebrows," he said, laughing. Todd's mother lived in a second-floor apartment in the North End of Hartford; he was her only child.

"I was a lively kid, always on the go. My mother kept to herself, but I was curious and independent. Even before I started school, I was running around on my own. I was too young to be left unsupervised, so my godmother, who lived downstairs, raised me. I called her Ma.

"Ma was born in Americus, Georgia. She had a biological son named Frank. He was already grown and married when I was born. Ma was a foster mother to wards of the state and raised seventeen children, including me. She loved kids and wanted us to have a good life. She made sure we ate well. Everybody looked up to her and came to her for counseling. Even when she was getting on in years, people came to talk with her.

"My godmother owned the three-family house we lived in. She was a resourceful, business-minded woman. She was a landlord and owned other properties, too—another house in Hartford and a house in Marlborough that she rented to a physician.

"It made all the difference, growing up in a house that my godmother owned. It was a family house. After I was grown, I moved back and lived with my mother for a while. When she died of cancer, I was in a house surrounded by family. I didn't have a landlord telling me I had to leave.

"In 1963, when the turbulence started in Hartford, Ma moved me—and the other kids she was looking after—to a house she owned in Ellington to get away from it. The Ellington house had sixteen rooms. There were apple and pear trees, a blackberry patch, two old shacks, and room for a baseball diamond. A Jewish man lived on the adjacent property. He was our family physician and a friend to us. Ma said, 'Blacks and Jews know each other's struggles. We have to stick together.'"

Ellington is about seventeen miles northeast of Hartford, a small, predominantly white, rural town. "There was only one other Black family in the area where we lived, and they had wards, too. We felt like we were the lesser because we were the minority. The others had power because they were the majority; but we had street smarts. We had to make adjustments to keep things cool. My brothers and sisters and me—the ones Ma took in—we didn't lose our roots. We spent our summers back in Hartford.

"I had white friends at school and we got along okay. We hung out together. My best friend at school was white. Some nights I stayed at his house and some nights he came to my house and stayed over.

"I can see the good and I can see the bad, in white people and in my own people. People are people. This comes from my belief in God. People have problems with people, but God loves all of us.

"In Ellington, I had a paper route and delivered newspapers. When I was around thirteen, I won a contest with the Hartford Courant for adding the most new customers to a route. Four or five other kids won, too. The prize was an airplane ride from Bradley International to JFK in New York.

"It was an old plane. It had regular seats, like a bus. The engines were noisy and the ride was bumpy. It was scary. I had more fun on the ground, riding around JFK and getting a tour of the airport. The return flight was just as bad. I haven't flown since and I won't. I refuse to get on an airplane.

"When I was in fifth or sixth grade, I started playing the trumpet and taking private lessons with Max Kabrick. I wanted to play the way Herb Alpert did in 'A Taste of Honey.' When I heard Miles Davis, Louis Armstrong, and Quincy Jones, I knew I got the right instrument. I could play jazz.

"In junior high, Max asked me to play Echo Taps with him at funerals. He played at the graveside while I stood behind a tree and played the echo. Max was a Shriner and he asked me and other students to play with them in the Manchester parade. My first paid job was playing a duet piece for the Vernon Methodist Church. They paid me $35.

"Uncle Frank—that's what I called Ma's son—was a musician. He played keyboards and bass. There were pictures of him playing in Vegas hanging on the wall in Ma's dining room.

"Uncle Frank gave me a Gibson Hollow Body electric bass guitar, and I taught myself to play it. The guitar looked like B.B. King's, except it was a bass. I put together a small neighborhood band when we were in junior high. The school held a talent show and our band played Grand Funk Railroad's 'Closer to Home' and Creedence Clearwater's 'Down on the Corner.'

"In high school, I had teachers who wanted to push me academically; they wanted me to go to college. The band teacher said I had talent. I played in the high school marching band and first chair with the school's concert band. Music was the center of my world, and that's the direction I wanted to go in. It was more important to me than going to college. Music was how I expressed myself. It was how I gave of myself.

"In high school, I started a rock-jazz band called Too Much Too Soon. We had horns and could play like Blood Sweat & Tears, Chicago, and Earth, Wind & Fire.

"In 1974, Tower of Power performed at the Palace Theater in Waterbury. Our band manager—the father of two of the musicians in the band—was a professional musician and played the circuit. He invited Tower of Power to his house in Ellington. It was a social visit, a break from touring and the hotel life. We got to hang out with them, play basketball, and eat soul food. They did a little workshop with our horn and rhythm section, showed us how to stay tight. On the car ride back to Waterbury, I sat next to Lenny Williams. When Gladys Knight and the Pips came on the radio, he sang along to her hit, 'Midnight Train to Georgia.' Lenny Williams sang with an anointed voice.

"I was always on the go," Todd said. "In my high school yearbook, they wrote, 'A comer and a goer in a six-man band' underneath my picture." It was a reference to the lyrics in The Association's 1968 recording, "Six Man Band."

While he was in high school, weeks before he turned sixteen, Todd's son, Michael, was born. "I met Pamela in high school," he said, adding that she was his girlfriend. "We had been in the same kindergarten class on Vine Street in Hartford. She remembered me and still had the class photograph of us to prove it. Her family moved to Ellington before I did. They lived in a different area of town, and we didn't meet again until high school.

"When Pamela discovered she was pregnant, we didn't tell our families. When she started to show, she wore baggy clothes. Pamela went into labor at home on a Saturday morning. She started screaming, and that's how her mother found out she was pregnant. They called an ambulance for her. I didn't find out that Michael was born until the next day when her brother showed up at the house to tell me.

"Michael was born premature," Todd said. "They kept him at the hospital in an incubator until he was strong enough to come home. Pamela's family didn't want to raise him, so he grew up in my godmother's home. My sisters were like mothers to him.

"While we were still in high school, Pam's parents came around, and gradually, she started picking Michael up and taking him home for the weekend. We both finished high school and graduated with our class.

"Pamela went to Briarwood College, and I had my music and my band," Todd said. "I had a new girlfriend, Debbie. She was jealous of the amount of time I put into the band. She wanted all of me to herself, and I wanted desperately to be loved. To keep Debbie, I quit the band. I went from a player of music to a lover of music to a superfan of music and bands. I stayed on top of the new music that was being produced. It didn't work out with Debbie, though. After we broke up, I went into a depression.

"Uncle Frank pushed me to get out of the house," Todd said. "He took me to a few of his gigs. He told me that even though I'd broken up with a girl, life goes on. 'You still gotta live a life worth living,' he said.

"Pamela and I gradually made amends and started to date again. When she was pregnant the second time, we were older, and I wanted to make us a family. I wanted to do the right thing, so we got married. Michael stayed with my godmother; it was the home he knew. Pamela and I were married about four years, but we weren't suited for each other. I wasn't home enough. I was partying, hanging out with the guys, and drinking. Pamela left and took my second son, Wayne, with her. We made another go at it. I said I was going to try to make it work this time, but I was still running the streets. After all these years, Wayne has nothing to do with me. It hurts."

Todd worked a variety of jobs. "I had to make a living. I had to eat, and there are a lot of starving musicians out there." He was a host and a bouncer at disco lounges when music and dance clubs dominated Hartford's culture in the 1970s and '80s. Gradually, making music was less at the center of his life.

He operated the historic carousel in Bushnell Park. Later he lived at Open Hearth—a nonprofit that assists men experiencing homelessness—and processed intake records. "I was literate, and I could talk to people, so they paid me to be a clerk.

"No matter what else was going on, I visited Michael. I listened to him. We've always kept our connection." Their relationship contrasts with what he experienced growing up.

"When I was in my late twenties, Ma called me up one day. She said Frank was in the hospital. He'd had a heart attack and wasn't going to make it. She told me I had to go visit him. I got dressed up, wore a shirt and tie, and went. Ma didn't tell my foster brothers and sisters that they had to visit; she only told me. She didn't explain why, but I knew. Frank was probably my father, even though no one ever said so. Ma said she was my godmother, but she was probably my grandmother. To this day, I don't know if Frank was my father. My mother had already passed when Frank died.

"At the hospital, Frank called me 'nephew' and wouldn't acknowledge our relationship. It cut deep. After he died, I separated myself from Ma and the rest of her family. I didn't hear that she had died. When I sobered up and went looking for them, everyone was gone. The house in Ellington, too.

"When I started coming to the Friday Gathering, I was working at a laundromat in the Frog Hollow neighborhood. Before that, I had worked for a landscaping company and got laid off when the weather turned cold. Without income, I was homeless. I started doing deliveries with a man named Roger, and he let me sleep overnight in his delivery truck. The truck gave me shelter and guaranteed I'd be on the job in the morning.

"Roger owned a laundromat and the thrift store next to it. He needed someone he could trust to watch the businesses while he was out doing deliveries. I watched the laundromat and the store, and he let me sleep in the basement at the laundromat. Roger and I became good friends, and I had that job ten years.

"I knew people on the street, and on Friday afternoons, the word was, 'I'm on my way to Grace.' Grace was the place to go, and I went, too. In the beginning, I came for the food. I knew a few people, but I came for the home cooking and a hot meal.

"I've been clean and sober seven years. I'm a changed man. I didn't get serious about life until I stopped drinking and doing drugs. Lee convinced me to seek help and go to AA meetings. He encouraged me to use the meetings to better my life. It wasn't just about getting clean but about learning how to let go of emotions. I would like to do the same thing for several friends, but they aren't open to it. I was searching for something better, and they aren't searching for that yet.

"I was on the city bus one day and noticed a man reading. He saw me looking at his book and told me it was the Bible. 'You should read this,' the man said. He was prophetic. I study the Bible every day now. I've come to know God through his word. My relationship with God is so much more intimate now.

"I went through a terrible depression. For months, I couldn't make myself get off the couch. I thought I was going to die. It was New Year's Eve, and I was at the apartment I shared with Louisa, lying on the couch, covered in blankets. Louisa said that Lynn, a neighbor in the building, was coming over. I was not in the mood for anyone's company.

"Then, in came Lynn. A white-haired white lady in a wheelchair. She had multiple sclerosis, and she was so happy and upbeat and charming. She brought sparkling apple cider and gluten-free brownies, and Louisa made food, too. Lynn brought Mardi Gras necklaces for us to wear. I looked at her in her wheelchair. I saw how happy she was, and decided it was time to get on with my life. She helped me recover from that depression.

"Reverend Bell helped me, too. When I couldn't leave the apartment, he came to me. He sat with me and talked with me. He helped me move away from the isolation that was overwhelming me. Even with being sober, there are difficult times. I'm spontaneous. I just get up and do things. If I get irritated, annoyed, or stressed, I go off by myself until I can work it through.

"Being a dad to my son means everything to me. It keeps me on the straight and narrow because I have to be there for him. Michael gets his disability social security check, but we all need something more than that. We have to be anchored to something; otherwise, we'll sink and drown. We need to be attached to each other. It makes us stronger when we don't go it alone. I'm in a position now where I can reach back, and Michael can latch on to me. There are times when I want to be flamboyant. But I stay focused on God. God is my anchor."

Todd and I talked the week of his sixty-sixth birthday. A close friend had died of cancer a few weeks earlier. He counted off the names of other friends he had lost. "I went up to Capen Street last week, to the house where I lived with my mother. The house is being renovated. They didn't tear it down like so many others, like the house in Ellington. The Capen Street house is not gone. Even though the inside of the house won't look like it did when we lived there, I get a sense of peace visiting the place where my mother lived. Every so often, I go up there and sit and look at the house."

***

Alfred began coming to the Friday Gathering in the summer of 2019. When the discussion group, E-Talks, was launched the following January, he attended every week until the pandemic lockdown.

"Alfred is my real name," he said. "I don't need an alias for my story because no one knows that my real name is Alfred."

The name doesn't appear on any legal documents. Alfred's birth certificate was altered, and a judge ordered it sealed. He can't access any record with his birth name on it, and no one calls him Alfred.

Born in 1967, Alfred is lively and engaging. He identifies as white and is five feet seven inches tall. He wears his hair long, down past his shoulders.

It's brown and turning gray, and it blends in with his long beard.

Alfred clicked through the details of his early childhood matter-of-factly. He was from Robbinsdale, a small town near Minneapolis, Minnesota. He was the second-born child and had a sister who was five years older. He also had two younger brothers and twin sisters.

"My older sister was named Kimberly," Alfred said. "Or, Rosa. They changed her name, too, and I don't remember which was her real name. My brothers were Sam and Joey."

When Alfred was five years old, two soldiers came to the house and said his father was dead. "He died in Vietnam. I don't have any memories of him," Alfred said.

His mother was from the Chicago area, so she took the children and moved to be near her family. "My grandmother—my mother's mother—lived with us when we moved back," he said.

"I'm Apache, Irish, and German. The Apache comes from my grandmother. You could see the Indian in her face, but you can't see it in me. My grandmother had lived on a reservation in Arizona. I don't know how she ended up in Illinois.

"When I was seven," Alfred said, "two cops came to the house. They told Rosa that my mother had crashed the car. She and at least one of the twins, maybe both of them, died. They took Rosa, my brothers, and me into custody and put us in foster care. I never saw my grandmother again. I have no idea what became of her. I don't have any photographs of me or my family. The time I spent with them was not nearly enough.

"From 1974 to 1981," Alfred said, "I had twenty-three sets of foster parents.

"After the first foster family, none of us ever lived together again. I spent one weekend with Rosa and one weekend with Joey. They were moving us to different foster homes. One of us moved in on a Friday and the other moved out the next Monday."

Alfred's tone shifted when he started describing his adventures in foster care. He laughed at the pranks he pulled.

"I lived with a family on a farm in McHenry, Illinois. They had one biological son named Jack. We were the same age and couldn't stand each other. He was bigger than me, but that didn't make any difference. I beat him up. I had a belly full of mean. At school, I'd find the biggest bullies and beat them up. I wasn't afraid of getting whipped by them or getting kicked out of school.

"Kevin was my best friend. We hit it off right away. One day we skipped school and climbed up a grain silo and found a diamond-shaped piece of concrete there, a few feet tall. We got the idea to chisel it out. It took a few attempts until we finally pried it loose. Why no one saw what we were doing or tried to stop us, I don't know. Only one of us could carry the thing down, and that was me. It must have weighed twenty-five or fifty pounds. Kevin took the diamond home and I went back to the farm. I never asked him—or I don't remember—what he did with it.

"After six months of me, Jack's family said, 'That's it,' and called it quits. I was sent to a foster home in Alaska by way of Los Angeles. The home in Alaska wasn't ready yet, so I stayed with a family in LA. The same thing happened when I came back. I spent nine months in Alaska and came back to Illinois with a layover in LA. I stayed with the same family. Both times, we went to see the rock band Journey before they made it big. That made an impression on me."

Alfred spent time in foster homes in Colorado and Nevada. "Someone wrote in my record, 'Does not play well with others,'" he said. "And because of that, others didn't play well with me, either.

"Somewhere else they wrote, 'Does not do well with discipline.'"

Alfred returned to the Chicago area, to the Camelot Care Center, a

184

ranch group home for children, and stayed two and a half years. About fifty children, a mix of boys and girls, lived there. Alfred grinned mischievously and talked about how he beat the system.

"Every month, I got a check." He didn't know if it was a survivor benefit from his father's military service or his deceased mother. "They said it was for foster child upkeep. The money wasn't spent; it was deposited in an account for me.

"The account grew to $4,000. It was my money, and I wanted to buy a horse so I wouldn't have to share with anybody. I bought Twiggy, a retired racehorse. I owned a horse when I was ten years old! Do you know anyone who's done that?" he asked, laughing.

"I got in big trouble with that horse, for riding it to school. I used the bite strap to tie it to a bike rack, like in the old Western movies. That confused a few kids who rode bikes to school. I felt sorry for the school janitors. They had to clean up the horse's dump. The horse was there for six hours, and you can imagine the size of the pile.

"Boy, was that principal mad! The idea that I could piss off someone that high up in the chain made it worth it!

"After that, I'm sure they made a new rule: No bringing horses to school. Before me, they didn't need a rule like that! I can think of things to do that no one has written a rule for yet." Alfred laughed again.

Turning somber, he said, "The Camelot Care Center is my favorite place.

"Do you know the movie *The Green Mile?* There's a moment in the film when one of the men facing death row asks Tom Hanks, who plays a prison guard, 'Do you think after you die it's possible to go back to the time that was happiest for you and live there forever?'"[126]

The scene comes just before the man is executed, and Tom Hank's character says yes, he thinks it's possible.

Alfred continued, "The guard and the inmate talk about how that must be what it's like to go to heaven, to go back to your happiest place. It was a kind thing the guard did for the man, giving him hope. I don't know that I believe there are guards who would do that. Owning Twiggy was the happiest time in my life. That's the time I'd go back to."

Alfred resumed talking about his foster homes. "Although I changed locations, Kevin and I stayed friends. We talked on the phone. Sometimes I'd change homes and we didn't talk for a while. But then we'd find each other again. I was at the Camelot Care Center when they told me, 'We found you a foster family.'

"'But,' they said, 'they're moving to Rhode Island.'

"It was Kevin's family. His stepfather had a new job in Providence. Over Christmas vacation I flew out so we could have a trial period. We drove to Virginia to visit Kevin's mother's family for the holidays. Kevin's grandmother lived in the Shenandoah Valley, and on Christmas morning, I stepped out the back door and saw the Blue Ridge Mountains. Her property ended where the national park started. I don't know if it was legit that they took me out of state on that trial visit, but I'll never forget how the mountains looked on Christmas Day.

"After about two weeks, I flew back to Illinois. There were papers and other stuff that had to be arranged for me to move. And I had a horse to sell! I got to Rhode Island in April. My brother Joey arrived at Camelot on a Friday and I moved to Rhode Island the next Monday.

"Kevin and I didn't stay friends. We were going in different directions. When I was fourteen, I took the social security money I was entitled to and ran away. It was the day after Ronald Reagan's inauguration: January 21, 1981. My stay with Kevin's family was the longest time I spent with a family in the foster care system.

"In Springfield, Massachusetts, I found a hotel that would give me a room. You can imagine how seedy it was if they let a fourteen-year-old book a room. I stayed about three months, until my money ran out. Then I checked myself in with an adoption agency. On October 4, 1981, I was adopted." Alfred's first name was changed to David, and he took the adoptive family's surname.

"We lived in a small town, midway between Springfield and Worcester. I went to a vocational school for three years and made honor roll. There were twelve different kinds of shop classes. Students had to rotate through all of them. My favorite ones were culinary arts, electronics, and drafting. I liked electronics because it was the only shop that wasn't held on campus. You had to take a bus off campus, and I liked getting out to see the world.

"In my freshman year, I was in thirteen fights. Six of them were knife fights. Of course, there was a rule at school: no knives allowed.

"After the first fight, I was checked every day to see if I had a knife on me. I volunteered for the checks and asked the teachers to search me as soon as I got to school. I never carried a knife, but I was good at self-defense. I knew how to disarm the other guy. When I got the knife away from them, I held the blade in the palm of my hand and offered the handle to the teacher. That was my way of showing I wasn't a threat. I was only a threat to the guy who was a threat to me, until he was disarmed. I didn't carry a grudge about it. If someone wants to start a fight, though, I'm not going to run away from it. I still have a belly full of mean, but I know how to control it now.

"At school, I liked culinary best, but they didn't want me to take the culinary classes because of all the French chef knives in the kitchen.

"When I was seventeen, my sister Rosa contacted me. She was old enough to access the court records about our family. She traced me to the adoption agency in Springfield, and they connected Rosa and me. She discovered that I'd been spelling our surname wrong, using a *k* when it was supposed to be a c. The teachers would take points off my grades if I didn't spell it the way they told me to. I don't know which way is correct, just that the court's records and all my other records don't match.

"Rosa was living in Aurora, Illinois, with her husband. She had two kids, and they were in foster care. They monitor kids like us who've been in the foster care system and keep tabs on us. They look for repeat patterns. They don't want foster kids having kids.

"Rosa said she had pancreatic cancer, and that the doctors had given her three months to live."

Alfred quit school and went to Aurora. "Since the age of fourteen, I worked and saved my money. Thanks to Summer Youth Employment programs, I had experience working in restaurants, like C.J.'s and Friendly's. I was a service room attendant, which is basically a dishwasher. I paid for my own airline ticket and flew to Chicago. My adoptive parents drove me to Bradley International Airport in Hartford.

"Rosa's husband picked me up in Chicago. I lived with them and got a job working in a restaurant. Rosa ended up living nine months.

"I'm glad I went," Alfred said. "It was a turbulent time. We had both changed over the course of growing up. But we were family. It was the last time I saw any family."

After Rosa passed away, Alfred wanted to return to Massachusetts, but he didn't go straight back. He volunteered for the army and went to Fort Benning in Georgia. "I almost made it through basic training," he said. "The last week of training, they x-rayed my spine and decided I had severe scoliosis. They gave me an honorable discharge."

After the army, Alfred went back to Massachusetts and worked for Dunkin' Donuts. "Our store did the baking for four other stores. I worked twelve-hour shifts and walked six miles to and from work. I was a baker's assistant and a finisher. After the donuts were baked, I added the icing and decoration."

Alfred stayed about seven years at Dunkin' Donuts, then set off again. He went to New Mexico and later followed a girlfriend back to New Haven,

Connecticut. They began an on-and-off twenty-year relationship. He took the high school equivalency exam. "I didn't study for it, just took the test and passed."

He worked for the Public Works Department and picked up trash. "Legally, I never drove. Illegally, I drove every day. The trucks had two steering wheels, and I got to operate the truck from the passenger side. We never went speeding down the street. But I was using that steering wheel just the same. There weren't so many rules in those days. Technically, I was the helper, not the driver. I didn't need a driver's license to be a helper."

Alfred shared an apartment with his girlfriend. When they weren't getting along, he moved out.

"I found a Sea Ray® luxury cruiser with a twenty-six-foot Cuddy Cabin in dry dock, behind a factory in New Haven, and moved in. I got a jump box—you can get them at Walmart—and recharged the battery at the library. The jump box was powerful enough to run the microwave, a fan in the summertime, the stove, and the refrigerator. As long as you keep the refrigerator door closed, you can keep food cold for a day. I lived on the Sea Ray® for four years."

Alfred pulled out his laptop and turned it on. His desktop image was a photo of the cruiser propped up on jacks. It was sleek and long. With all of the hull exposed above ground, it was an impressive vessel. Alfred pointed out blotches on his desktop image and said, "Someone spray-painted profanity on the hull, and I blotted those parts out.

"To get to the factory yard, I crossed a bridge from Grand Avenue, climbed a fence, and took two steps in the direction of downtown. As soon as I jumped off the fence into the lot, no one could see me. The factory was abandoned and no one went down there. I lived alone. A few times, I invited three or four friends who were homeless to spend the night, until they got something better.

"When they brought in an excavator to tear down the building, they demolished the Sea Ray® with it. The excavator had a giant claw, and it ripped right through the building and the boat."

Alfred made his way to Hartford. "At the South Park Inn shelter, they helped me get assistance. I was diagnosed with several disabilities, including Asperger's and seizures. They helped me get disability checks."

In 2019, Alfred picked up a copy of the Charter Oak Cultural Center's *Beat of the Street* newspaper and its listing of soup kitchens. He saw an entry for the Friday Gathering and came.

"I was staying at the McKinney Shelter when the pandemic forced the shelters to close. We were moved to a Best Western hotel that was converted into temporary housing. They thought they could slow or prevent the spread of COVID-19 if they separated us. I had my own room, but I had to share it with a roommate.

"There were rules, and the staff got a lot of pleasure out of enforcing them," Alfred said. "Unless you had a job, you had to be in by 7 p.m. Unless you had a job, you weren't allowed out before 7 a.m. You couldn't leave the grounds without permission, couldn't go to McDonald's or get a coffee. You had to stay in your room. The staff had their favorites and they adjusted the rules for them. It didn't include me.

"There was one staff person who always caused me trouble. She started arguments, and I tried to get her fired. My stay at the Best Western came to an end when one of the residents put their hands on me and I slammed him against a wall. He hit his head and it knocked him out. Even though he started it, I was blamed, and I moved out."

That summer, Alfred came often to the Friday Gathering. He told us he had a hideout and was living outdoors. "The fewer people around, the fewer to flip off," he said. "I can be in a room of thirty people and tune twenty-eight of them out, like they don't exist. There's always someone who can get under my skin. It's better if I keep to myself." When the weather turned cold, he stopped coming to Grace on Fridays.

In March, I ran into Alfred at the library. He came for an hour each day, he said, to get out of the weather, watch videos, and keep up with the news. Alfred and I left the library and went to a deli for lunch. As we were talking, he asked, "Are you up for a hike? Do you want to see where I live?"

We took off and made our way down side streets toward the Connecticut River. Along a trail that paralleled the highway, behind some bushes, there was a small opening. We ducked under the highway and disappeared from view. We scooted along the dirt and gravel slope to where the hillside fell away and we could stand upright again.

A little farther on, we reached a spot where a few tents were set up. "I call this the hideout," Alfred said, and he explained that six people lived here. He pointed to a blue tent and said, "That's the one Louisa gave me."

It was just past noon, and no one was around. Alfred gave me a tour, rattling off the names of his neighbors, and showed me the odds and ends they had collected. He explained that here, no one bothered them and they were protected from the rain and wind. It was deafening, though, the sound of trucks and cars speeding by above us and the thud of vehicles hitting the struts of the overpass.

"I'd rather be on a twenty-six-by-ten-foot houseboat than under a bridge," he said.

I didn't see Alfred again until the end of the summer. He said he left the hideout soon after our visit. He was living downtown in a hotel that the city had acquired. He had a small two-room apartment with a kitchenette and a TV in each room. This time, he didn't have to share it with a roommate. His disabilities qualified him for a rent subsidy, and social security covered the rest. He liked his landlord and got along with him. Alfred said he mostly stayed in and watched TV. He only left to pick up meals at the different soup kitchens, and the distance to Grace was more than he could handle.

Alfred often brought up that he was frustrated because he couldn't access the account where his social security checks were deposited. "I'm going to be rich," he said when we first met in 2019, "with all those checks piling up." He lost his ID number, and when he went to the social security office, they promised to help him, but he still couldn't access his money. He went back and forth between making light of how much money he'd eventually get his hands on and his helplessness from being at the mercy of the Social Security Administration. During the first year of COVID-19, their offices were closed to the public and there was no one he could sit down with to sort it out.

"Even now," Alfred said, in December 2021, "you have to get an appointment with the SSA. When it's time for your appointment, they send the guard down to unlock the door and let you in. Do you know what it's like, to try to get an appointment with them? Everything is done on smartphones, and if you don't have an ID number and password, you're at a dead end."

The apartment didn't feel like home to Alfred. His relationship with the landlord could sour. The social security payments might get lost. Troublesome neighbors could move in.

"What does home mean to you?" I asked him.

"Home," Alfred said, "is someplace private, where I can let my guard down and relax, because when I'm with other people, I have to watch out. It's a twenty-six-by-ten-foot Cuddy Cabin on a boat, preferably on the Connecticut River, that I can run off a jump box. I'm keeping my eyes open for one."

***

Kenny was born in 1959 in Minnesota. At six feet two inches, he's a tall, slender man. "Some people call me Slim. I've never been able to put on weight," he said. His hair is wavy and dark brown, pulled together in a ponytail at the base of his neck. Only his beard has a hint of gray.

Kenny's mother belonged to the Chippewa tribe. His father was part

Chippewa and part African American. Kenny identifies as Native American, although he did not experience that culture growing up.

"Years after I came to Connecticut, I visited the Mashantucket Pequot Reservation. It wasn't too far from where I lived in New London. A group of men I hung out with named me One Feather," Kenny said, and he pointed to the single feather that hung from his backpack.

"My mother was an alcoholic. I never knew her. She gave me up when I was born. People told me later that it was probably good that she did. When I was older and got a copy of my original birth record, I found out that she had died of alcohol poisoning.

"The first home I remember was with Mrs. Bartlett. She and her husband lived in Lincoln, Nebraska. They took in children and cared for them until they were placed with adoptive families. I had a brother, Ronnie, who was two or three years older than me. He lived at the Bartletts', too. Mrs. Bartlett told us that we had more brothers and sisters. I later met my brother Larry, but I never met the others. Mrs. Bartlett told me that someday when I was grown, I needed to pass it on and care for abandoned children myself.

"Mrs. Bartlett was the best cook. She once cooked for the Harlem Globetrotters. She cooked for the University of Nebraska football team. On Sundays, everyone came to their house to eat. Even the pastor. Sundays were fun because of all the people who came to dinner.

"When I was three or four, the Martins adopted Ronnie and me, and we moved to Omaha, Nebraska. We were their only children. The Martins were an African American couple from Georgia. Mr. Martin worked with cattle and was away a lot of the time. After he took a job in Denver, he was away for even longer stretches. Mrs. Martin didn't like that, and she took it out on Ronnie.

"Mrs. Martin beat Ronnie regularly. She poured her hostility out on him, but she didn't touch me. Ronnie ran away from the Martins, and the police brought him back. Finally he ran away for good. I heard that he made it all the way to Mrs. Bartlett's. The day I realized that Ronnie wasn't coming back was one of the saddest days of my life. Mrs. Martin turned her attention on me.

"I ran away, too, and learned to get by on my own. My best friend was a mean junkyard dog. He was a German Shepherd, and boy, did he smell. I fed him; stole food so that I could feed him. Canned Vienna sausages were his favorite. I fed him before I fed myself, and sometimes there was nothing left for me. The police would come looking for me at the junkyard, but they wouldn't go near that dog. I hid in the junkyard and slept there at night. That dog was my buddy.

"I went to the police for help a few times. I knew that Mrs. Martin beating me was wrong, but the police didn't listen to me. They put me in a patrol car and took me back. It was terrifying and I didn't want to go. When they brought me home, I went in the front door, out the back door, and headed to the junkyard.

"I went to a juvenile detention center and asked them for help. A couple of times they let me sleep overnight, then sent me home the next day. They told me that I couldn't get a bed there. Sometimes I lay down on the sidewalk and slept there or went to the junkyard. No one listened to me.

"One night, the people at the detention center told me to take a shower and clean up. That's when they saw the scars on my back, from the whuppings." Mrs. Martin used a switch, a strap, or a piece of conveyor belt; Kenny supposed that she must have gotten it from Mr. Martin. "They sent me back to Mrs. Martin and told her that if she ever beat me again, they'd charge her. I still kept running away, and the beatings didn't stop."

As Kenny talked, tears rolled down his cheeks. He looked at the table, then looked at me and said, "No one ever listened to me. Why?

"One day, just as Mrs. Martin slammed the heel of her shoe into the palm of my hand, a social worker came to the door and witnessed it. The social worker took me with her that day, and I went back to live with the Bartletts. I was seven or eight years old. It's Mrs. Bartlett I think of when I think of having a mother.

"Mr. Bartlett liked to fish, and sometimes I went with him. One time, I felt a tug on the fishing pole and started yelling, 'I got one! I got one!' That fish started pulling me down the riverbank. Mr. Bartlett yelled, 'Hold on to that pole,' until he could get to me. When we finally brought the fish in, it was *this big.*" Kenny stretched out his hands two feet or more to show me and laughed at the memory. "I got one! I got one! That's what I remember!

"Around the time I was twelve, I went to Boys Town. Have you heard of it?" Kenny asked. "Did you see the movie with Spencer Tracy and Mickey Rooney? We lived in dormitories; it's different now. Boys Town is where I learned to cook."

The 1938 film titled *Boys Town* is based on the real-life Boys Town orphanage located near Omaha, Nebraska. While the main plot of the film is fictional, it portrays the outlook of its founder, Father Flanagan, a Roman Catholic priest. He was a social reformer who believed that all children, regardless of race or social standing, should be valued and deserve the opportunity to succeed.[127] Tracy won the Academy Award for Best Actor for his performance as Father Flanagan.

"Boys Town was a ranch, a big property, and we worked it," Kenny said. "They must have had thirty or forty horses. One day, a group of us decided to take the horses out for a ride. I had my own horse, named Shadow Gray. On this day, I took a small palomino instead. We went at a slow pace and were out about a mile when my horse started acting crazy, going in circles, and took off racing toward home. I kept pulling on the reins to get him to stop, but nothing worked. A man rode up beside me and said, 'Jump over here!' He wanted me to jump to his horse. No way was I doing that! He yelled at me to pull on the reins but I was already doing that. When we got to the barn, the horse just stopped and stood still. Suddenly everything was quiet. I remember the silence. We just stood there, the horse and me.

"Another day, I was walking behind a horse when one of the ranchers told me to never walk behind a horse. Right at that moment, the horse kicked me. I lay in horse shit for half an hour before I could move. I couldn't walk for at least a week, and I smelled like horse shit for a week, too.

"There was always somebody looking for a fight at Boys Town, and it didn't matter who started it. By the time I was seventeen, they told me to leave, and they arranged for me to go to Job Corps in Utah. I went and completed their culinary program.

"In Utah, I met a girl from Connecticut. In 1982, when she moved back home, I followed her. I settled in the New London area, and we stayed friends.

"I've had a few long-term relationships," Kenny said. "I had a daughter with my first wife and another with my second wife. I fulfilled my promise to Mrs. Bartlett. Over the years, I looked after six kids who didn't have a father figure in their life. I explained to my wife what I was doing and why, that I was going to do it one way or the other. I think of those kids the same as my daughters. It means a lot to me to do what Mrs. Bartlett told me, to pass it on. I wouldn't change a thing.

"When my daughters were growing up, our house was known as the Kool-Aid house. We had that sugary red drink mix that kids like. We were the house where all the kids on the block wanted to hang out. We called them the Sugar Hill gang. We had a VCR room, and all the kids came to watch movies: *The Wizard of Oz, Star Wars,* movies like that. Parents would show up at our door and ask, 'Do you have our kids?'

"I was a welder at Electric Boat. I ended up losing that job because the school where the kids went called me to come in when there were problems. I took too much time off, and Electric Boat let me go. I worked as a yard jockey for Allied Van Lines. One day, the boss asked me if I'd take the cab and get gas. I said, 'Yes!' I started driving long haul, Connecticut to California and back. I wasn't home much, and that took a toll on us.

"I promised myself that I wouldn't leave my kids like my parents left me," Kenny said. "My kids would always know who I was. They would know they had a father. Even when I was driving long haul, the kids knew when I'd be home.

"My first daughter is named Kamena, and my second daughter is named Amorica; everyone calls her Rica. It's a combination of words that means deeply loved. I knew I wasn't going to be able to give my kids riches, so I gave them names no one else has.

"Rica's mother says she's just like me. When she was a teenager, she took a baseball bat and broke all the windows in the house. It cost a lot of money to replace them. I didn't get mad about it. Rica tried to explain what was going on in her mind, and I always listened. I tried to be that kind of parent, understanding how hard it is to grow up.

"I used to be so concerned about what they were going to turn out to be. I didn't really have a dad, so I tried to be like the dads on TV, like *Leave It to Beaver,* Ben Cartwright on *Bonanza,* Bill Cosby when he was a family man. I wanted to be a good father. I worked every day. The kids weren't raggedy or shabby.

"I've lived that Huckleberry Finn life. I've been a nomad—a hobo, you know—traveling from one place to another, with no destination in mind, content with what comes along.

"I'm not mad at the world. Just because you were dealt a hard blow, don't hold onto it. It'll just hold you back. You waste your time being mad when you could be making other choices. What good does it do you to be mad? Just be happy for what you got. I don't think I turned out so bad.

"Home, to me, is the memories, like Christmas at the Bartletts' and making Christmas for my kids; staying up late, putting their toys together, a few pieces you can't figure out where they go, but making it work anyway. I never whupped my kids. I have no regrets."

***

Like Todd, Alfred, and Kenny, Nicky grew up without his father. Nicky was born in Newark, New Jersey, in 1958. "I have a sister who was born in 1952 and another sister born in 1954. I'm the baby in the family. Nicky was my nickname when I was a kid.

"The last time I saw my father was 1965. I was seven years old, and he tried to get me to go live with him. I didn't see him again until his funeral. I learned that he had remarried and had a whole other family. It was 1988."

"My mother was half Shoshone, which came from her mother, and half Korean, which came from her father. My father was part Shoshone and part Dutch," Nicky said. "I identify as Indigenous.

"I don't call myself Indian because that's the name Christopher Columbus used. Columbus thought he had discovered a shortcut to India and called us Indians. The name was a mistake because he didn't know where he was. When people talk about Indians, they have to explain which continent they're talking about. We inherited this problem from Columbus.

"I don't call myself Native American either because the name America came from Amerigo Vespucci, an Italian like Columbus. The title 'America' erases the names of sovereign nations that existed here before the Europeans arrived.

"It's different in Jamaica," Nicky said. "The Native people, the Arawaks, lived there when Columbus arrived. They called their island Xaymaca. The Spanish killed the Native people, but the Arawak name survived.

"I call myself Indigenous. It means 'original people.'

"I don't call people white, either. I say 'people of European descent.' Whites come from different tribes, like the Irish, the French, the English, and the Dutch. There's no single tribe that is white.

"My mother was short, and her eyes were almond-shaped. People asked if she was Japanese and called her a demon because of the shape of her eyes. She was born in 1919 in Wyoming. She had a black belt in taekwondo and competed in wrestling matches. She was known as the Ferocious Tiger. I didn't know this about her until I was grown. My sister showed me pictures of our mother from the 1940s, when she was in her twenties. The opportunity to perform in wrestling brought her East.

"From my earliest memory, my mother always wore Native clothes. She had deerskin skirts and vests and wore them with ribbon shirts. She wore a silk band around her head and lots of turquoise jewelry. Some of it was passed down through her family. She sewed some of her clothes and bought some from reservations in the Midwest. My mother would dance and put on shows for us."

Before Nicky turned a year old, his mother moved to a reservation in Wyoming and took Nicky and his sisters with her. "I don't remember living on the reservation. I was too young. Around the time I was three or four, we moved back to New Jersey. My mother came back because there were no jobs on the reservation.

"We lived in East Orange, which is right next door to Newark. Our neighborhood was mostly African American. When I went to school, my mother always had me wear something Native. When I was seven, she put a bolo tie around my neck. As soon as I got around the corner from home, I took it off. I was a kid and wanted to do kid things.

"My mother called me Running Bear because I was always climbing, moving, and pulling things down. She was from the Bear Clan, and she must have imagined that I was, too. When I was eight, she took me to a naming ceremony. It was held on native land in Scotch Plains, New Jersey.

"There might have been a hundred people there. The holy man looked deep inside me to see what qualities I had. It was his job to choose an animal name that reflected my gifts and would give me protection. The holy man said I had sharp eyesight and an unusual ability to see in the dark. He named me Red Hawk.

"The hawk is a sacred bird, like the eagle. Indigenous people believe that the Creator sent the hawk and the eagle to watch over the earth. Because they fly so high, they can see things from a broad perspective and use their powerful vision to focus on what matters.

"My mother was proud of her heritage, and she taught me to be proud of it. In fourth grade, the teacher gave us a test about the history of Columbus Day. There was a question, 'Who discovered America?' and I wrote 'Me.' The teacher gave me an F. I stood up for what I believed, even though it didn't change my grade. Around that time—I was about eleven—I started wearing Native clothes.

"The 1960s were a rough time. In Newark there were riots. Soldiers were in the streets. There were curfews, and we had to stay in the house. Martin Luther King, Jr., was assassinated. While they protested the way African Americans were treated, they called my mother a savage. When you're afraid of something, you give it power. This was when I started to learn about the relationship between fear and power.

"There was an Italian family in our neighborhood, and they didn't want to share the local park with us. They called the cops, and the cops said, 'It's a public park.' I learned to stand up for my rights. I had a friend at school whose mother was white, and her father was Black. She was harassed because her mother wasn't Black. That's when I really began to get into my Native culture. It gave me strength.

"In the early '70s, we moved to New York City. We lived in Brooklyn, and then we moved to Queens. I graduated from Bayside High School. My sisters are still there. My mother died in 2013 at the age of ninety-four. Her grave is on Long Island, under a tree and next to a private airport that only the celebrities use.

"In 1976, I won the lightweight division karate championship at Madison Square Garden. I was eighteen years old. I liked competing, the crowd cheering, and winning. I taught karate for a few years. Ray—who comes to the Friday Gathering—saw my picture on the cover of a magazine online. I didn't even know it existed. I was shocked when he showed it to me.

"I couldn't get a job in New York. The discrimination was too great. I applied for a job at La Guardia Airport, to clean planes, to do anything. When I went to the interview, the man said, 'Look at the way you dress.' Immigrants and illegals get more help than me," Nicky said.

"The only job I could get was working security on the third shift. I did it for about fifteen years, five of them at the World Trade Center. I still kept my hair long and wore face paint. Another security guard was from India, and he wore a turban. They had to overlook our dress because it was a cultural thing.

"After the World Trade Center fell, I was harassed on the subway for wearing a t-shirt with an image of the American flag upside down. It's not a sign of disrespect. It's an SOS, a call for help. A soldier who was there and saw it gave me a thumbs up.

"I got a job with the Mashantucket Pequot at the Foxwoods casino in Connecticut. I traveled back and forth on the bus that brought in customers, and the bus company gave me a discount because I was an employee. It was a long commute, so in 2006, I came to Connecticut. Donna, who I had known since we were teenagers, came with me. We were married in 2010.

"I met Donna in 1976," Nicky said. "She's been a mother to my two sons. The oldest is thirty-two and lives in a group home for special needs adults in Massachusetts. He's autistic and has a mind like an eight-year-old. They cut his hair and won't let him grow it out.

"My other son graduated from Weaver High School in Hartford. He works at a restaurant in West Hartford. He hasn't cut his hair. He wears it pulled back in a bun, and sometimes he wears face paint. People ask him, 'Are you for real?' Donna and I have a good relationship with him. He comes to us when he needs to talk.

"I have a daughter, but she doesn't know me. After she was born, her mother moved to a reservation in Wisconsin, and she grew up without me.

"Donna is part Cherokee and Blackfoot. She's also part Scotch, French, and Irish. Her family fought on both sides of the Civil War. Donna doesn't always dress in Native clothes. When she does, people call her Pocahontas. When we're out together, some people tap their open palm over their mouth and mimic making a war cry. Karate taught me how to be self-disciplined and not get tangled up in these slurs. It's harder for Donna."

Nicky paints his face and carries a walking stick that displays the symbols that are meaningful to him. When I ask people, "Have you seen Nicky?" some reply, "You mean the Indian?"

"I wear my hair in braids," Nicky said, "because Native people do not cut their hair. Many cultures respect hair as a symbol of strength and virility. If you shave a male lion and cut off his mane, you break his spirit. Many Indigenous people don't cut their hair so that their spirit stays resilient. Sometimes people cut their hair up to their shoulders, when there is a death in the family, as a sign of respect."

A beaded headband circles Nicky's forehead, with the image of an eagle in the center. Pointing to it, he said, "All animals are sacred to Indigenous peoples. The headband is a reminder to always treat animals with respect because God made them first."

Slashes of paint cut across Nicky's cheeks. "I put white paint on my cheek to symbolize purity. It represents the condition of the earth at the time of creation, before it was contaminated. The red paint represents spilled blood. It's the blood of Indigenous people who died to defend their homeland and their families."

Sometimes there is a third streak of paint, colored blue. "People see the red, white, and blue and think it represents the American flag, but it doesn't. Blue represents the sky, and the earth underneath the sky we think of as pregnant with new life."

Nicky always carries a walking stick made from a single piece of wood over four feet long. The top of the stick is a carving of a man wearing a headdress of feathers painted in different colors. He explained, "Each feather represented people killed in battle. Native peoples wore their rank on their heads. This stick was carved by an Apache."

Nicky painted his stick and covered it with symbols. "There are turtles, which represent good luck, eagles for protection, the sky filled with trees, and lots of different kinds of birds. There is a red cardinal. Cardinals are providers; they collect things."

He pointed to a section and said, "These markings represent smoke. When Indigenous people pray, they use smoke to call the spirits and create a blessing. The Catholics have a ritual like this, too. They burn incense. Indigenous people burn sage to make the smoke, which becomes a prayer for peace. We pray in four directions, so there can be peace in all lands."

Traditionally, a walking stick conferred status on the person carrying it. "I'm not a holy man or a chief," Nicky said. "I just try to be spiritual. I ask God to bless others."

Nicky returned to the memory of his fourth-grade teacher and the test question about who discovered America. "Holidays are difficult for Native people who honor their ancestors," he said. "At Thanksgiving, magazines are full of pictures of Europeans bringing food to the Indians. But it was the other way around. Native peoples shared what they had and taught Europeans how to farm. Some people think that the turkey is a symbol of Native people, and images of carving the turkey are symbolic of destroying the Indian nations.

"Independence Day—July 4th—is another one," Nicky said. "How can Indigenous people celebrate that? One nation under God? One nation after the others were decimated.

"I believe in spirit," Nicky said. "The body is a vessel that holds the spirit. The spirit is what connects us to all of creation. You have to be careful. Some spirits are evil.

"A few weeks ago, I saw a homeless woman near the entrance to the supermarket. Someone had bought her a sandwich, but she said it was too dry to eat. She wanted to get a packet of mayonnaise, but the security guard wouldn't let her come in. She had the receipt for the sandwich in her hand. I offered to get the mayonnaise for her, and the guard put his hand on my shopping cart to block me from entering. I waved a $10 bill to show him I had money, but he said I wasn't allowed in the store. Pointing to the woman, he said, 'We don't want her kind hanging around here. Your talking to her just encourages her.'

"She's a human being," Nicky said. "I complained to the store manager, and he told me that I have to take my complaint to the head of the security company. I'm not going to give up on this. What he did isn't right.

"I see things other people can't see. I can feel the presence of ancestors. I wear my grandmother's turquoise ring to remind me that I am descended from noble people. It doesn't matter where you live, you carry those ancestors with you. Home is a spirit you carry in your heart."

***

For some people, the idea of home stirs up sentimental images of warm, cozy places where we are loved and protected. But home is also where we first experience pain and loss, because all families have their flaws and limitations. Home is where we learn to cope with life's imperfections, both in ourselves and in others. When we find the place where we feel like we belong, where we can be our whole selves without having to cover up our shortcomings, we realize, "This is home." It may be a physical location or an emotional attachment. Home is where we are at peace and take shelter from life's storms.

12

Changing What We Cannot Accept

I have learned now that while those who speak about one's miseries usually hurt, those who keep silence hurt more.

—C. S. Lewis, *Collected Letters of C. S. Lewis*

Some diners come to the Friday Gathering because this is where they choose to "give back." Giving back expresses their desire for a more kind and just society. They are mindful of the advantages that have favored them while also aware that others suffer from a lack of those privileges. The stories of chefs Gladys and Louis and sisters Sharon and Cheryl begin with how they came to learn about the Friday Gathering, the networks of relationships, and the invitation to stand with our community. Beneath their stories of giving back are stories of protest against the inequitable systems that shackle all of us.

***

"I learned about the Friday Gathering from Pastor Darrell," chef Gladys said, "at a women's conference at Gloria Dei Lutheran Church. I organized a group from my congregation, and we went together. Pastor Darrell was a guest speaker, and he talked to us about serving in the inner city."

Darrell said the invitation to speak came about because of his connection with Tracy, a member at Gloria Dei. The conference was held in May 2013.

"Tracy knew about Grace's Friday Gathering because she helped me get grants for it," Darrell said. "She introduced us to Thrivent Action Teams, which helps us cover the costs of supplies that aren't donated. She helped make it possible for the volunteers to attend a free weekend retreat at Camp Calumet as a way to say thank you to them and for us to purchase the audiovisual system that's used in the dining hall. Tracy wanted the women's group to know about our program, so she invited me to speak at their conference."

Only a month earlier, Darrell's wife, Nancy, led a seminar about the correlation between climate change, poverty, and justice. Gladys and others from Christ the King Lutheran Church were there.

"Gladys and her friends were impressed that one of our Lutheran congregations was so outspoken on environmental issues and provided a symposium of that caliber," Darrell said. "Gladys said she put the two events together—the environmental justice program and the Friday Gathering—and decided to come investigate. I remember when she did. She came with a delegation from her congregation to experience what was going on at Grace."

"I was hooked right away the first time I came," Gladys said. "You meet all these people and they tell you their stories. If it weren't for the Friday Gathering, I never would have come in contact with them. We have a good time getting to know each other. They want to have real conversations, and I can ask them questions. This is a big deal: they want to talk to me. They remember my name, they remember that my husband isn't well, and they want to know how I'm doing as much as I want to know how they're doing. We're a community."

Gladys—an American of African descent—was born in 1943 in McComb, Mississippi. She grew up with a younger brother and a house full of grandmothers, aunts, uncles, cousins, and cherished guests, including Medgar Evers and Bob Moses.

Medgar Evers and Robert Parris Moses were prominent civil rights activists in Mississippi. Evers was a veteran of World War II and the Battle of Normandy. Later, in Mississippi, he led efforts to desegregate public schools and investigate the murder of Emmett Till. He was the first National Association for the Advancement of Colored People field officer in Mississippi.[128] Bob Moses was a principal organizer of the 1964 Mississippi Freedom Summer Project and a leader in the Student Nonviolent Coordinating Committee. Both men led Black voter registration drives. Evers was assassinated in 1963 at the age of thirty-seven. Moses lived to eighty-six. He earned a PhD from Harvard, received a MacArthur Fellowship, and went on to develop the Algebra Project, a math literacy program.[129]

"Medgar Evers came often to our house," Gladys said, "and Bob Moses lived with us when he was in Mississippi. He would drive seventy miles to Jackson for a meeting and then drive back so that he could stay with my parents.

"My parents were always helping someone. It wasn't just at church. They served the community, reaching out to people and sharing. I desired to continue to do the work that my parents did. This is how I've tried to live my life.

Gladys grew up immersed in the civil rights movement and the struggle for social justice. Her father, C.C. Bryant, Sr., led by example.[130]

Curtis Conway Bryant, Sr., filled many roles. He was a deacon at the Society Hill Missionary Baptist Church in McComb. He was a crane operator for the Illinois Central Railroad and president of the local railroad union. He was president of the Mississippi Pike County Branch of the NAACP from 1954 to 1988 and vice president of its Mississippi State Conference. He organized voter education and registration programs for African Americans. In 1968, he was the principle litigant in a lawsuit with the Illinois Central Railroad. He sued for discrimination and segregation practices and won in federal court; the ruling set a precedent for violations of Title VII of the Civil Rights Act of 1964.[131]

"From a very young age, even before I started school, I went to meetings with my father. Everywhere my daddy went, I went, too. When I was six or seven months old, he started taking me to his Sunday school classes; he was the teacher. He packed a diaper and a bottle for me, and off we went.

"Regardless of how inconvenient it was, I accompanied Dad. There were always people who wanted to talk with him after a meeting, so I had to wait until he was finished. There was usually a bench where I could sit. I played games and every now and then, fell asleep. I got to know everybody. They teased me and called me Granny. Was I a daddy's girl? Yes, I was!" Gladys laughed.

"On longer trips, we stayed at people's homes. There were no hotels or very few who served African Americans. I was intent on going with my dad, no matter what. Every year we attended the statewide NAACP meeting in Jackson, and every year we stayed with the Wells family; they were leaders in the Jackson branch of the NAACP. All the leaders became friends of mine. I met Thurgood Marshall several times. I shared a bedroom with Ruby Hurley. She was a hero to me," Gladys said.

Thurgood Marshall was the first African American Supreme Court Justice and served from 1967 to 1991. In 1954, he successfully argued Brown v. Board of Education, in which the court ruled that racial segregation in public schools was unconstitutional.[132] Ruby Hurley was a civil rights activist. She worked for the NAACP and is credited with greatly expanding the organization's membership. She served as director of the Southeast Regional branch.[133]

"I grew up with a lot of family around me. On my mother's side, there were my grandmother and great-grandmother. My maternal great-grandmother lived to be eighty-six. She died tragically in a car accident when a neighbor hit the car she was riding in.

"My great-grandmother, Emily Jefferson, on my dad's side, was born into slavery in 1850. Her daughter, Anna—my father's mother—was born in 1893. They were progressive people and valued education. To them, literacy and freedom went hand in hand. All of my great-grandmother Emily's children got a high school education. My grandmother Anna had planned to continue her education at the Tuskegee Institute. When her mother died, those plans were abandoned. Anna passed on her reverence for education to all of her children, including my father."

Gladys's father was educated at a Rosenwald school. Julius Rosenwald, a German Jewish immigrant who made his fortune as the CEO and a part owner of Sears, Roebuck and Company, collaborated with Booker T. Washington, an educator and founder of the Tuskegee Institute, to build schoolhouses in rural Southern states. Rosenwald established a fund that, between 1917 and 1932, provided the seed money, in partnership with local communities, to build more than five thousand schools for African American children across the South.[134]

Jim Crow laws and the legalization of racial segregation prevented many Black children from receiving an education. Literacy tests and poll taxes prevented Black people from voting. The Rosenwald schools addressed that inequality. By 1928, Rosenwald schools served a third of rural Black schoolchildren across the South and raised a new generation of leaders. In addition to Gladys's father, Medgar Evers, Maya Angelou, and Congressman John Lewis were Rosenwald alumni.

Rosenwald schools were abandoned after the US Supreme Court ruled that segregation in education was unconstitutional. Since 2002, the National Trust for Historic Preservation has provided grants and assistance to save the remaining structures and raise awareness of their role in education and the communities they served.[135]

Although Gladys did not have the opportunity to attend a Rosenwald school, she began her formal education when she was four. "I told my mother that I was ready for school and insisted that she let me go. Everything they were teaching the kids at school, I already knew how to do. I could read and write, and I wanted to learn cursive. I convinced my mother that I was capable. I persisted, and she really didn't have a choice.

"Mom would cut out words and numbers that were printed in the newspaper. She selected large-size text from advertisements that were easy to read. I learned to recognize the words. Then I arranged them to make sentences, and that's how I learned to read. Later on, my dad bought me a typewriter. By the age of ten, I was typing affidavits and participating in the civil rights movement.

"Education was very important to my family. My mother was president of the McComb PTA [Parent Teacher Association] and later president at the state level. She traveled to Jackson to attend conferences. She was well-connected in her own right."

There was a PTA for white schools and a PTA for Black schools. "The PTA wanted the town to build a new school for Black children. Our school was in an old wooden, two-story structure. It had an outhouse instead of indoor toilets. The old heating unit was situated in an underground tunnel. I attended that school through the third grade. The PTA said, 'We don't need to fix this school. We need a new one.' The local churches hosted the different grades until the new school was built. My mother led that effort. It took several years.

"I was always listening to the adults talk," Gladys said. "My father had a barbershop next door to our house. He ran it on weekends when he wasn't working at the railroad. Even after he was done for the day and the shop was closed, people stopped in to visit. I was there, too, drawn to their stories.

"The barbershop was located in a two-room building. My dad tore down the wall between the rooms and built a library with bookcases on one side. He collected all kinds of books, and people came to the barbershop to borrow them. Men who worked on the railroad collected newspapers from across the country and brought them to the barbershop to share. My dad subscribed to newspapers, too, especially the ones written by African Americans. People visited his barbershop to read, to discuss problems, and to socialize. This was how we knew what was going on in the world and with each other."

Gladys recalled a series of incidents demonstrating her father's inner moral compass and the legacy she is determined to pass on. In his private life, C.C. Bryant, Sr., was as committed to the pursuit of justice as in his public life. "He never shunned it," Gladys said, "as a man, as a teacher, as a leader.

"When I was about nine years old, a man was hiding in the bushes next to our house. It set the dogs to barking. My father went out and chased the man away. He was a white policeman, probably part of the KKK [Ku Klux Klan], and spying on us. I never saw my father afraid of anyone.

"Behind our house there was a big field with a path running through it," Gladys continued. "The path was well-worn because so many people walked it. One night when I was about ten, a man's screaming on that path woke me up. Some men were beating him because he was homosexual. Daddy got the lights on and went out. He told the men to stop. He said, 'I don't want to ever hear you attacking him again. I'll have you arrested.' To my dad, that man was a human being. It didn't make any difference that he was homosexual.

"Another time, Daddy got out of a prayer meeting and saw the police beating a Black man. A crowd of men were watching. Daddy said to the police, 'No, you won't. Don't you hit him again.' And they stopped beating the man. Daddy wasn't afraid to stand up for what's right.

"People really trusted Dad," Gladys said. "He was a giving man. People came to him for help. On the job, white men sought him out for advice. People felt that he would give them the right information.

"My mother was a staunch supporter of my dad. People called her Shotgun Annie. She sat on the porch with a shotgun across her lap so that Dad could get a good night's rest. She was the perfect housekeeper, too, and perfectly dressed. Nothing was ever out of place. Interior decorators could have learned something from my mother."

Gladys first got acquainted with Hartford when her uncle—her father's younger brother—settled in the city, following his service in the military. Then her aunt moved north and joined him. As a teenager, Gladys accompanied her grandmother, Anna, on train trips to visit them. In 1961 Gladys moved north, too. "There was nothing to do in Mississippi after high school, so I came to Hartford. We lived on Addison Street.

"It was a pretty, tree-lined street and an integrated neighborhood when I arrived," Gladys said. It was located in the north of the city near the Windsor town line. The wooded Keney Park was around the corner. The Oak Hill School for the Blind and the University of Hartford were a short distance to the west. It was on Addison Street where Gladys met her future husband, Billie.

"Billie's brother was friends with the people who lived above us. The young men sat on the porch and talked, and that's how Billie and I got acquainted." In 1964 when Billie got his draft notice, they married.

Across Mississippi that year, voter registration efforts intensified. The 1964 Freedom Summer project engaged Northern white student volunteers to come to Mississippi to work for civil rights. Violent resistance to their efforts and intimidation tactics increased. Civil rights workers were beaten and murdered. Poll taxes, literacy tests, and false arrests subverted voter registration efforts. Cross burnings and firebombs were frequent enough in

McComb that the city was called the bombing capital of the world.[136]

In January 1964, a cross was burned on C.C. Bryant's front lawn. In April, a firebomb landed in his barbershop. The building—unoccupied at the time—sustained interior damage. No one was held accountable.[137]

"In June, I was still in Connecticut when they bombed my parents' house," Gladys said. "My mom called before I could hear about it on the news. She told me to not be upset, to sit down and listen. Mom had a controlled voice, especially in times of danger. As a child, I was exposed to things like this. We never talked about it, but each time Daddy went out, we knew he might not come home."

The bomb exploded on the lawn, and no one was injured. In July, shots were fired at the house from a passing car. Again, no one was injured. Again, no one was held responsible.[138]

"Soon after we were married, Billie went overseas," Gladys said. "He was assigned to NATO in Europe. I had a baby on the way, so I went home to Mississippi until his service was finished. I worked with my father and registered people to vote.

"My father never wavered in his commitment. He believed in justice, in righteousness, in treating your fellow man the way you want to be treated: with respect. People of all races would come to this man—my dad—and ask him for guidance. He told them the truth. He never misspoke. At his funeral in 2007, an older white man who had worked with him at the railroad told me how everyone looked up to him. My dad believed that it was possible for whites and Blacks to live together peaceably."

When Billie completed his military service, he returned to Hartford, and Gladys came north with their daughter, Judith. They had a second child, Billie Jr. Gladys's husband, Bill Sr., worked for Pratt & Whitney, the aircraft engine manufacturer, and then became a Hartford firefighter. Gladys and her family moved to Windsor and bought a home four miles north of Addison Street in Hartford. They were the only Black family in their neighborhood at the time.

On Sundays, they came back to Hartford for church services. Gladys wanted her children to have the same Sunday school experience she'd had growing up. One Sunday, Gladys had car trouble and could not get to church. Literally in her backyard was Christ the King Lutheran Church, so Gladys took the children there instead. They became members and were among the first Black families to join the congregation.

Gladys and her husband agreed that she would stay home and raise the kids. "Raised the neighborhood, too," Gladys said, laughing. "Parents knew there would always be someone home at our house. Their kids were welcomed here. One time, a child was sick at school and sent home. He stayed with us because both of his parents needed to work.

"All the kids in the neighborhood ended up at our house. One spring, we put in a swimming pool and then removed it at the end of summer. We realized it was too risky when we went away for the day and found the pool full of kids when we got home. Even though we had a fence around the pool, the kids went in anyway."

When Billie Jr. was five years old, Gladys went back to work. First she was a scheduler for what was then the University of Connecticut Burgdorf Health Center, located in the North End of Hartford. Later she managed a group home for women with disabilities. Then she spent twenty years as a manager for a home healthcare organization. "To my dad, all life was precious. He said, 'You need to respect life.' I have tried to continue in his path in all the directions my life has led me," Gladys said.

By 2015, Gladys wanted to be a chef for the Friday Gathering. She needed to complete a food handling certification course. The program was offered at the House of Bread soup kitchen. "Hilda attended the program with me," Gladys said. "I met Roy at the House of Bread and some days gave him a ride home after lunch. We sat and talked in the car in front of his house and got to know each other. At that time, he was still living in his childhood home. The water and electricity had been shut off.

"When Roy started coming to the Friday Gathering, I gave him rides home at night. He always brought that big suitcase with him, and getting it in and out of the trunk wasn't easy. He made a habit of calling me early, before sunrise, every morning and reading a chapter from the Book of Proverbs. He was an intelligent man, and I enjoyed his company. He was always a gentleman."

I asked Gladys, "How do you handle fear? How do you make sense of the world today, of Black Lives Matter and the murder of George Floyd?"

"I don't have any fear," Gladys said. "I never saw my father afraid. I never saw my mother afraid. You have to stand up for what you believe in. You can't be a coward because something is difficult. When I was growing up, our parents did everything they could to shield us from racism. The community was pulled in tight around us.

"I'm more fearful now," Gladys continued, "of the things I can't control, like my husband's health and well-being. In 2006 he had a stroke. In 2019, he needed to move to an assisted living facility. In 2020, he had COVID-19. Being dependent on Medicaid and Medicare is a big challenge. I'm afraid that as I get older, I might not have the same courage to adapt.

"Nothing stays the same. Because of that, we are forced to change. People come along, like Martin Luther King, Jr., and leave us a blueprint for how to move forward. George Floyd exposed the racial ugliness that still exists. We are recording a racial history that cannot be denied. In some ways, society is getting better. But the moral decay in the world is sad.

"There are obstacles that come into your life, and you persevere. You trust in God. I believe in hope. I'm a hopeful person. My grandson Julian—Judith's son—he's my hope, too. Even with all this new technology, young people are learning how to use it in new ways. They're creating new careers for themselves. Young people, for the most part, want peace. They're our hope for the future."

***

Like Gladys, Louis learned about the Friday Gathering because his church, First Calvary Baptist Church, had a relationship with Grace. First Calvary worshiped at Grace on Sundays following Grace's services. Afterward, they served a hot meal and invited the neighborhood to join them. First Pastor Eva, then Pastor Rick got to know Louis and his wife, Carmen, through his cooking. "Pastor Rick made a habit, before heading home on Sundays, of stopping in the kitchen and taste testing," Louis said. "About four years ago, when he asked if I would be interested in cooking for the Friday Gathering, I said 'Yes.'"

"Yes," Pastor Rick agreed. "I was involved in drafting Louis as a chef. In fact, I bugged him about it until he said yes. At least, that's my recollection. I love his cooking, and I enjoy his company. On Fridays, when he's the chef, he always brings a sample up to my office before dinner is served so that I can have a taste and know what is on the menu. It's very special, and I love it."

Louis was born in 1954 in Kentucky, in the southeastern corner of the state near the border with Tennessee. On his mother's side, he is descended from the Cherokee and the Dutch. On his father's side, he's a mix of Blackfoot and African American. He never knew his birth father; the man never claimed him.

Louis's mother married a coal miner from Bluefield, West Virginia, and his half sister, two years younger, followed. Louis's stepfather was the only father he ever knew, and Louis called him Dad.

When Louis was about seven years old, the family moved to Hartford. The owner of the mine where his father worked lived in Connecticut, and Louis supposed that his father linked his future with the owner's and came north. "Dad was a ladies' man," Louis said, "and the owner of the mine was a woman. He followed her north. For my mother, coming north meant she could get away from her family. They made things difficult for her after I was born. I never felt like I was welcomed by that side of the family."

Like Gladys, Louis arrived in Hartford in the early 1960s. A series of public projects were well under way, and they would transform the city. The elevated Interstate 91 was completed as a north–south corridor along the city's eastern edge, parallel to the Connecticut River. Interstate 84, an east–west route, was built and bisected Hartford, dividing it economically and ethnically. Neighborhoods were demolished to make room for highway entrance and exit ramps, and government-subsidized housing projects were constructed. Andrew Walsh, associate director of the Greenberg Center at Trinity College in Hartford and a historian, observed: "The North End became a public housing corridor with a concentration of very low-income residents, increasingly cut off from access to jobs or local retail."[139] This is where Louis and other diners—including Albert, Lorraine, Papa Charles, Carmelita, and Edith—grew up.

"We lived on Avon Street," Louis said, about two miles south of the tree-lined neighborhood of single-family homes where Gladys's family lived. "But it doesn't exist anymore; you won't find it on a map. The city took it to build the SAND housing project, and we moved a few blocks away. I grew up in the Bellevue Square housing project."[140]

In elementary and middle school, Louis had a hard time fitting in. "I was chased a lot by the other kids," he said. Then he laughed. "I was probably the instigator as much as they were." Compared to some classmates, he was light-skinned, and his friends were light-skinned, too. "In middle school one day, a few kids started talking in Spanish to me. They found out I wasn't Spanish when I couldn't answer them. Because of my skin color, they thought I was Hispanic. People, Black people, too, look at skin color and make assumptions about where you fit in. To some people in my family, because of my mother's Dutch ancestry, I'm the white boy.

"I don't like to say I'm Black. I'm African American or Black American. I can't ever be just American. If I say I'm African American, then I lose the

Native American part of me. If I say I'm Native American, then I lose the Dutch and African American part of me. When I was young, it hurt. It hurt for a long time. I didn't know where I belonged. Putting labels on people messes everything up."

In the 1960s, Hartford's prosperity was becoming more divided. There was a "sense that overwhelming problems were building up. ... The riots, culminating in 1969, expressed African American rage at racial isolation, housing, and job segregation, overcrowding in slum neighborhoods, and troubled relations with police and city government. Their chief immediate impact, however, was to accelerate white flight from the city and to damage the neighborhoods where the rioters lived."[141]

"I was out in the streets protesting the conditions along with everyone else," Louis said, referring to the unrest and demonstrations in Hartford in the 1960s.[142]

"When Martin Luther King, Jr., was assassinated, there were riots. We tried to march to city hall, but they blocked the roads and locked us in. Where is it that we could go to protest?" Louis asked. "This is still a major concern in my life.

"Businesses were destroyed: furniture, clothing, and grocery stores and pharmacies. The businesses didn't belong to the people who lived there. They were making money off of us. Those businesses never came back. You can still see the scars today.

"At one point, I was adopted by the Black Panthers. I was being chased by a bunch of Spanish kids, and we were running down the street past where the Panthers had an office. They saw us coming and stepped between me and the group of them. I think they intervened because it wasn't fair, one kid up against a bunch of kids. They protected me, kept me from getting beat up.

"In tenth grade, the school told me they were going to hold me back a year. I couldn't take the idea of three more years of school, and I had a child on the way. I quit school when I was seventeen. I worked at a car wash for a few years. Eventually I enrolled in a program at CRT [Community Renewal Team] and started cooking.

"How did I turn out?" Louis asked, then answered his question. "I'm not rich. Not poor. I love life. But I've also got fear.

"My mother was a caregiver for a white woman who lived in Avon [an affluent suburb of Hartford]. She did it a few days a week for a couple of years, and I drove her back and forth. I can't count the number of times I was stopped by the police. The cops knew who I was, and they stopped me anyway. It happened often enough that I was ready for it. Prepared for it. And still afraid of it. It's happened in New Britain, too. I got pulled over by two white cops.

"My daughter ran out of gas one night in New Britain. She had just gotten off the highway, and it was a dark stretch of road. She called me, and I got over there as fast as I could. You don't want to get stopped in a place that isn't well-lit.

"I don't want to go camping or hiking. I don't want to go skiing. I don't want to be by myself where there are no witnesses. The fear is real.

"When I was growing up, and we went back to Kentucky or West Virginia to visit family, we could all be sitting around having a good time. Then a white person shows up at the door. Everyone stopped talking. You had to stand at attention. You might not know what they wanted, but you had to give them all the respect. Those memories affect my fear today.

"About ten years ago, my wife, Carmen, and I bought a house in the suburbs. Five bedrooms. Enough for our kids and grandchildren to visit. We found out we weren't welcomed in the neighborhood. They were afraid of what we were going to do to them. The lady across the street peeked out the window any time we went out. The next-door neighbor complained that we drove on their yard. They came to the door and yelled at us. They complained when we had family over; they said we made too much noise. When they had parties, they made noise and threw their beer bottles over the fence onto our property. I told my kids not to throw them back. We bagged the bottles up and left the bag on their side of the fence.

"There was no peace," Louis said. "The message I hear is that it's my culture that has to change. I refuse to give any more than I've already given."

Louis relaxed when he shifted to talking about his children. "I love my kids. I wouldn't trade them for anything in the world. I do wish, though, that I waited until I was ready so that I could have given them everything they deserve."

Louis has ten children, including Carmen's four. Two of Carmen's daughters waitressed at a Ruby Tuesday's restaurant where Louis was the chef. They liked Louis and pestered him until he took their mother on a date. "As they say"—Louis laughed—"the rest is history." Carmen is his third wife; they've been together for more than twelve years. "Her girls are like daughters to me," Louis said.

"My first wife left me. She left the kids, too. The kids blamed me for her leaving. She got hooked on drugs, and I was unfaithful. I was using drugs then, too.

"I decided not to leave my kids. I chose to stay. I regret their anger, though. They were angry at me for working all the time to support us. They were angry because I wasn't home more. They were angry at my unsavory alliances and angry at my womanizing. My kids witnessed a lot of things, and for them to turn out okay makes me proud of them. They are the most loving and caring kids. We talk on the phone or see each other every day. My sons have followed me into the profession of cooking. My son Keith won't make a decision without checking with me first. He calls me up and asks, 'What do you think of this, Dad?'

"I had one of those 'Aha!' moments when my mother died," Louis said. "It's been fifteen years. She had a DNR [Do Not Resuscitate order], and I didn't know what that was. I couldn't bear it when she died, and I insisted that the doctor bring her back. I carried on so much that she opened her eyes and told me to let her go.

"I saw that Mama was happy where she had gone. Why did I have to do that to her?" Louis asked.

"It made me realize that Jesus has been with me my entire life, saving me. Even when I didn't know it or ask for it, he's been saving me.

"Why do I come to the Friday Gathering? I want more out of church. Where is the church in all that is going on today? I want more than going to service on Sundays and paying my tithe. I want to be on the street where people are having the hardest time. I want to be a part of something, but the churches don't want to work together. They want to hold on to their authority.

"Everybody is blaming someone else for their troubles," Louis continued. "They blame the police or the government. They blame the teachers and the parents. They blame the kids, but nobody is blaming themselves for what's not working today. The church has a responsibility to care for its community. There was a time when the church and the community were the same thing. You can't just tell them you love them; you have to live it with them. When they're in pain, you have to share that, too. I want to give witness to the saving grace of Jesus. Every Monday night, you can find me in the North End of Hartford, on the street, standing with the people and sharing life."

***

Like Gladys and Louis, sisters Cheryl and Sharon learned about the Friday Gathering because their congregation, St. Matthew Lutheran Church in Avon, had a relationship with Grace. The congregation contributed financially to Grace's outreach ministry and regularly brought homemade casseroles to serve on Fridays. When Pastor Julie was installed at St. Matthew, she encouraged members to volunteer at the Gathering. Families with young children and teens from the youth group came on the fourth Friday each month. They had their portraits taken and added to the wall in the dining room and got to know the diners. Pastor Julie and Associate Pastor Brian alternated with Pastor Rick to lead the prayer circle. Cheryl and Sharon responded to Pastor Julie's summons. Later they brought their grandchildren, and Fridays at Grace became a habit.

Cheryl, born in 1956, and Sharon, born in 1964, have always lived in Connecticut's Farmington Valley and grew up at St. Matthew. Their grandmother was active in the congregation and had served as the church secretary. Their mother was baptized at St. Matthew. Cheryl, Sharon, and their siblings were baptized at St. Matthew, too. Like the congregation's founders from the late 1800s, Cheryl and Sharon are descendants of German immigrants and identify as white.

"I've led a very privileged life," Sharon said. "At first I wanted to volunteer with the Friday Gathering as a way to give back. Volunteering at a soup kitchen was on my bucket list of things to do. The pandemic made me appreciate even more how fortunate I've been."

"One year at Thanksgiving," Cheryl explained, "my husband and I went to New Hampshire to celebrate the holiday with my mother and stepfather. My stepfather regularly volunteered with a group that delivered meals to shut-ins. His dedication opened the way for us to spend the day together as family, packaging meals to be delivered. It felt good to do something worthwhile for others. It was one of the best holidays we enjoyed together. Although we only did it that one Thanksgiving, it planted the seed in me that we would do this work again, together as a family."

"Our mother raised us to not judge others," Sharon said. "She had a summer job driving a school bus, transporting kids from the inner city to attend camps in the countryside. Most of the students on her routes were Black and brown. She loved those kids and talked about them at home.

"Sometimes I think she loved her students more than us. At the end of summer, she had her picture taken with them, and she was the only white person in the photograph. I think she took a kind of pride in it, that these were people she cared about. She showed us the pictures and could tell us something about each child."

"Growing up, our stepfather would say some outlandish things, but Mom would never let him get away with it. She had the last word, and she taught us about treating people with dignity," Cheryl said.

"One time, our mother took us to Auer Farm in Bloomfield," Sharon said. "She showed us chicken eggs that were the usual white and brown colors and chicken eggs with shells that were blue and green. She used nature to teach us that the color on the outside has nothing to do with what's inside. A chicken egg is a chicken egg, and the color of the shell doesn't change what's inside. It's the same with people. Color on the outside has nothing to do with what's on the inside.

"I don't understand the prejudice and inequality that exists in our society," Sharon continued. "I have friends who are lesbian and gay, and I accept them as they are. At Nar-Anon, I learned that JOY means Judge Only Yourself. Letting go of judging others is how we learn to love them as they are."

"When we first started coming to the Friday Gathering," Cheryl said, "we stood behind the tables filled with food and helped serve the meal to diners passing by. We enjoyed the camaraderie and interaction with the diners and other volunteers. We came to know who was vegetarian, who disliked this or that, and who wanted extra helpings.

"We noticed other traits, too, that make one person distinguishable from another. One man, Harry, took on the unofficial role of dining room monitor," Cheryl said. "He liked to direct traffic, make announcements, and tell people to mind their manners. We noticed that Eddie always said something to make us laugh. A middle-aged lady was usually first in line for seconds and very specific about what she wanted and in what amounts. Another woman who had a baby would come occasionally. She was taken in hand by Pastor Julie, who always managed to send her away much calmer and with a prayer. Diners would make cracks about Sharon's Boston Red

Sox cap, taking sides for or against the team.

"As we gained more familiarity with how Fridays run, we were asked to cut and plate the cakes and pies and serve them," Cheryl said. "As often as we could, we brought our grandchildren with us. My grandson looked forward to serving desserts, but the first night he came, there were no desserts to serve. Ever since, he asks, 'Do you think they'll have desserts this time?' This is how I know he looks forward to going with me."

"One night," Sharon said, "I sat down to eat dinner, and a man at the table made an indelible impression on me. He wanted me to understand that he hadn't always been 'this way.' He explained that one of his children, an eighteen-month-old baby, was killed by a tractor-trailer right in front of him. He had never been able to get past his grief. He went deeper and deeper into alcohol until he lost everything."

"Getting to know some of the diners and their experiences," Cheryl said, "has been an eye-opener. I've known people with drug addictions and alcoholism. Of all the levels of addiction I've known people to experience, the Friday Gathering has shown me just how much more difficult it could get for them. I've learned about homelessness. The Friday Gathering has made me grateful to know that when people are suffering, there are places where they can get a meal and be treated kindly."

"I came to understand," Sharon continued, "that everyone in the dining room has a story—breaking their minds or their hearts, but not their soul—that makes them unique. The diners are diverse, and they opened our hearts and gave us an appreciation for a variety of situations and points of view we hadn't considered before.

"All of this came to a halt when COVID-19 forced us to stop serving meals in person. Initially, our day jobs were on hold, and we didn't know when we'd go back to work. We chose to stay involved with the Friday Gathering. We've been privileged to be able to volunteer every week since the pandemic started. Having a team that is used to working together helps keep it safe and consistent for volunteers and diners.

"Now, we come every week to package meals to-go," Sharon said. "We need to be there. We miss not seeing the diners and the other volunteers and bringing our families to experience the fellowship. On the other hand, we have gotten to know and respect even more those who are working alongside us, whether they are orchestrating, cooking, packaging, or distributing. We feel like a small but vital piece of something important that unites all of us."

"Working at the Friday Gathering, before and during COVID-19, has changed us in that we have become more appreciative and more grateful for all the things we take for granted," the sisters said.

"The Friday Gathering has taught me how to accept somebody else doing something nice for me," Cheryl said. "Because I experience joy when I give, I know that others have joy when they give to me. It could be a compliment or a smile. I'm learning how to receive and not overlook kindnesses extended to me.

"I miss serving the diners. It's fine to package meals to-go during the pandemic, but what I miss is the personal contact. I miss being able to offer choice. With a prepackaged meal, you get what you get. We can't adjust portions so that someone who skips the potatoes can have extra vegetables or vice versa. I didn't understand before how much offering choice was part of my joy."

Sharon held up her wrist and asked, "Did you notice my tattoo?" It was a tiny mark, a semicolon, on the inside of her wrist. "It's placed there so that it's easy for me to see," she said.[143]

Sharon learned about the tattoo and its meaning when a friend was suffering from addiction and contemplating suicide. "The semicolon means that the story isn't over," she said. "Today is not the end of the story, and the semicolon means that there is more to come. Just because today is a bad day doesn't mean that there isn't hope or that tomorrow won't be better. The semicolon reminds me to stay strong."

"We owe it to the diners," Cheryl said, "and we owe it to their stories that, when we see a person holding a sign on the street, we are able to see much more and know that we are part of a support system that cares for them. Their story doesn't end there, either."

***

"Where is it that we could go to protest?" Louis asked.

Telling our stories is an act of protest. Speaking up—and rejecting being voiceless—is liberating. The words may be painful and voicing them can't change the past, but speaking up means that we don't carry the burdens of suffering and injustice alone. This is what C. S. Lewis referred to when he wrote that those who keep silence hurt more. Rebecca Solnit, writer and activist, wrote in *The Guardian:* "Words break through unspeakability, what was tolerated by a society sometimes becomes intolerable. Those not impacted can fail to see or feel the impact of segregation or police brutality or domestic violence; stories bring home the trouble and make it unavoidable."[144]

Some of the details in Gladys's and Louis's stories were familiar to me: Jim Crow and segregation, bombings in Mississippi, voter registration drives, excessive traffic stops of Black drivers, harassment of minority homeowners, the violence of gunning down civil rights leaders, and the long history of oppression. Hearing these stories from people I know, people who lived the experiences and then talked about how their lives and the lives of their families were affected, people who are not beaten down despite the continuing vileness, puts a spotlight on the injustices that are unevenly distributed between us. Their stories make me a witness to the wrongdoing and accountable for what comes next.

13

The Grief of Things as They Are

If you have come to help me you are wasting your time. But if you have come because your liberation is bound up with mine, then let us work together.

—Aboriginal activists group Queensland, 1970s, attributed to Lilla Watson

It was chilly when I arrived at Grace. I didn't know what was on the menu but was sure I smelled pea soup. In the church parking lot, a woman I didn't recognize was walking toward me. "Can you smell it?" I asked. "It smells like pea soup!"

She stopped, breathed in the air, and smiled. "Yes," she nodded.

"We serve a free dinner today and the doors open at 3:30. You're welcome to join us," I said.

When I got to the kitchen, Chef Louis was there. Before I could ask, he announced, "We're having pea soup today."

People who attend the Friday Gathering come from many walks of life. The invitation to participate is open-ended, and it embraces volunteers and donors, as well as people who are seeking a meal, companionship, or community. This range of motivations led me to ask: *Whose needs does the Friday Gathering serve?*

***

Samantha started volunteering at the Friday Gathering in the fall of 2019 when she was a sophomore in high school. "I was inspired to get involved in my community," she said. "I'm a Hartford resident and often felt dwarfed by the problems that appear far beyond my control, specifically the poverty that lay just beyond the warmth of my home and the security of the block where I live. I looked at the Urban Alliance website for volunteer opportunities and saw a listing for the Friday Gathering, less than a mile from my home.[145] Volunteering with Grace, I knew, would offer me the opportunity to make a difference beyond simply giving a bag of chips here and a dollar there."

Samantha and her twin sister were born in 2004 in Hartford, and she identifies as white. "I grew up in Hartford; however, I have never attended Hartford Public Schools. I went to a Montessori school and then transferred to Farmington Public Schools through Hartford's Open Choice program. When my moms separated and one of them moved to West Hartford, I transferred to one of the high schools there. Now I split my time between Hartford and West Hartford.

"I've had classmates and friends make stigmatizing comments about Hartford. I didn't take them as insults directed at me but as their impressions of the city and the school system in general. The gist of the comments is that students in West Hartford are smarter and that Hartford is a poor, even dangerous, place. Friends have told me they don't want to come to my Hartford house at night for fear of getting shot. I try not to take offense or become angry, knowing that they are coming from a place of both ignorance and privilege. I attempt to explain the differences in funding and resources and that this is not indicative of superiority or inferiority but of inequity and a flawed education system. I tell my friends that it is unfair and inaccurate to make sweeping statements about Hartford as somewhere that is violent.

"I counter their negative sentiments with my love for my neighborhood," Samantha said. "My block is beautiful, with gardens and interesting architecture. Restaurants like Tisane's and Mo's are within walking distance. And, of course, the Friday Night Gathering and all of the amazing people I'm able to interact with are part of my Hartford community.

"Friday night dinners are one of the best parts of my week," Samantha said. "Every week, I share with my friends and family the night's highlights. I get to socialize with people I ordinarily wouldn't have the opportunity to interact with. I get to learn about the experiences of others that are completely different from my own. It's changed the way I look at my life. I have become more appreciative of certain luxuries that, in the past, I took for granted. For example, I can go shopping at a secondhand clothing store with my girlfriends for the fun of finding something unexpected, while for someone else, secondhand clothing is their only choice, and they are more careful with how they spend their money. I've become more aware of the hardships of others. I've become more comfortable around people who are different from me, people who are more religious than I am or who have a different economic situation than my own.

"So many of the people I have met here are the most kind, funny, and interesting people I have ever known. Diners don't simply come for the food, keep to themselves, and leave. Rather, they greet each other and the volunteers by name. They tell jokes and laugh, they talk about their week, and the conversations are lively. One night, I told Vonda that I was afraid of mice. She told me she used to be terrified of them as well. She said that when an infestation developed in her apartment building, 'I began taking care of them myself.' She laughed and added, 'Now, they're afraid of me!' Her story drew us closer, and I look for Vonda on Fridays when I arrive.

"On my first day of volunteering," Samantha said, "I couldn't figure out how to enter the building. I tried the door, but it was locked. There was no one around to ask for help except a woman walking down the sidewalk and a man lying on a bench by the door. I asked the woman first because I felt more comfortable approaching a woman, but she didn't know how to get in either. I was a little nervous to ask the man. I couldn't tell if he was resting or if something else was going on with him. I asked him anyway.

"He was so kind. He showed me where to press the button to open the door. Later, when I was serving food for the first time, I saw him in line. I thanked him again for helping me, and he said, 'I helped you then, and you are helping me now.' I learned that his name was Alfred and that he was homeless and slept outdoors."

***

Ancient Greek philosophers recognized that there are a variety of ways to express love, and they used different words to distinguish between them. *Éros* represents romantic love and the passion of sexual desire. *Philía* denotes the affection that is expressed in friendship. The Greeks assigned words to the love of self, the love of guests or hospitality, and the love between parents and offspring. *Agápē* describes a love that is selfless and unconditional. For Christians, it is the greatest form of love. It expresses God's love for humankind, which is shown through acts of compassion and altruism. In English, *agápē* is often translated as charity.[146] We show charity when we treat others with empathy and kindness.

In our modern era, charity as a description of how we act toward others has been superseded by the notion that charity is a business organized for the public good. Whereas in the past a parent might have instructed a child to be charitable toward a classmate or elder, the meaning of charity nowadays is seldom connected to how we interact with the people around us. Instead, charity has come to be associated with nonprofit institutions that collect and redistribute assets. People who are connected via the giving and receiving of charity are often strangers and unknown to one another.

Charitable programs like soup kitchens and the Friday Gathering offer an array of services. They provide short-term relief for people who are suffering while also functioning like matchmakers, linking donors with recipients. Viewing charities like soup kitchens as one component of a large system exposes the competing interests that such programs must negotiate to satisfy their donors while serving clients. It calls into question the extent to which donors are invested in the social systems that drive the need for food programs.

In 2019, thirty-five faith-based groups organized to form the Greater Hartford Interfaith Action Alliance.[147] Their mission is to act collectively for social justice and address the root causes of poverty and inequity. Friday Gathering volunteers, including Samantha, Darrell, Nancy, Louisa, Pastor Rick, chefs Emma and Gladys, Barb, Cephus, and me are part of Grace's delegation. In 2021, GHIAA successfully campaigned for Clean Slate legislation, which erased the criminal records of an estimated 300,000 Connecticut residents with misdemeanor and lower-level felony convictions who subsequently remained crime-free.[148] Clean Slate erases the stigma associated with criminal records and improves people's opportunities for employment and advancement. It has a ripple effect, too, on their families' quality of life.

GHIAA also successfully campaigned for legislation to end welfare liens. Connecticut expected recipients of public assistance programs—or their heirs—to repay that assistance, placing liens on real property.[149] Repayment could be demanded when a recipient's home was refinanced or sold, when they received a legal settlement (for example, for personal injury) or an inheritance, or if they died and left property to their heirs.[150] The repeal of welfare liens affected 1,300 people who, at that time, owed the State of Connecticut an estimated $18 million. Helping people hold on to the equity they earn after getting off welfare goes much deeper to relieve poverty than handouts. Matt Ritter, Speaker of the Connecticut House of Representatives, compared the recovery of public assistance to a "poverty tax," saying, "We treat it like a debt and not the temporary hand up it's meant to be."[151]

GHIAA actions delivered other results, including supporting parents in Hartford's North End in renovating the Martin Luther King, Jr. Elementary School instead of permanently closing it; removing three slumlords and overhauling the city's housing code; and reforming and funding Hartford's Civilian Police Review Board. These actions affect our neighbors' access to education, safe housing, and protection against unjust policing.

Samantha reflected on her experiences with the Friday Gathering and GHIAA and said, "While problems—widespread across our state—oftentimes appear unbeatable, GHIAA helped me find tangible ways that I could combat issues such as poverty and racism. I felt a greater sense of strength, community, and ability to inflict serious change. GHIAA demands change instead of waiting around for change to happen on its own. I'm drawn to that feeling of intensity and the urgency that it brings."

At the Friday Gathering, we have come to know the names, faces, and stories of people who cannot lift themselves out of poverty with repeated servings of our charity. As much as "choice" is built into how we serve, the Friday Gathering cannot offer the choice to escape poverty. The Gathering created the setting to know our neighbors, and their stories became our stories, too. To be their allies, Samantha and I and others were called to pursue social justice. If privilege and a sense of entitlement from believing I have worked hard for everything I have made me oblivious to the inequities in our society, those blinders have come off.

More than a century ago, Jane Addams, an activist and reformer who cofounded Chicago's Hull House—one of the best-known settlement houses in the United States—spoke to the convergence of charity and social justice.[152] Settlement houses were located in impoverished urban neighborhoods. Middle-class settlement workers lived among the people they served and provided daycare, education, and cultural activities.[153] Although Addams promoted the values of white culture and Hull House did not serve Black residents or their culture, her reflection on charity and justice helps us appreciate the benefits and shortcomings of each.[154]

In an essay, Addams noted that some settlement workers were stirred by empathy and a desire to alleviate their neighbors' suffering. Addams called them the Charitable. Other workers were motivated to fix the systems that impacted the neighborhood. Addams called them the Radicals. They lobbied the city government to improve working conditions, prohibit child labor, upgrade sanitation services, expand access to education, and build parks, playgrounds, and libraries.[155]

Addams spoke about the tension between the Charitable and the Radicals. Each believed their approach was better than the other's. Acts of charity focus on the individual and alleviate their immediate misery. Social reform—the objective of the Radicals—addresses the flaws in systems that lead to inequities, and its effects are seldom immediate. At Hull House, where the Charitable and the Radicals crossed paths, Addams asserted that the work of each benefited from an understanding of the other's experiences. She observed that the Charitable were compelled to look beyond poverty and crime and contemplate the social systems that governed the daily lives of the people they served. The Radicals were compelled to confront the ideals of their social doctrines through their close associations with people who were disenfranchised. The interactions of these groups deepened their awareness of the suffering around them and its causes.

People have immediate needs—for food, shelter, and more—and acts of charity often focus on them. But satisfying those pressing needs is not enough to alleviate suffering. Many people cannot imagine what it is like to lose their homes, become disabled, or be afraid of the police until they have had such problems. Only when we can separate the suffering from the causes of the suffering—and suspend judgment—can we imagine or have empathy for what it is like to live persistently with these circumstances.

Life has its adversities—being born in a war-torn country, bearing a parent's death when one is a child, bearing the death of one's own child, dealing with floods and natural disasters, coping with disabilities and illnesses. There are twists of fate unrelated to any individual's wrongdoing. Life is not fair. Addams called this the "grief of things as they are" and said that to survive, the Charitable and Radicals have realized that what we need in this world is compassion to relieve immediate suffering and social justice to remedy systemic flaws. None of us is immune to unexpected accidents and misfortune; the day may come when we find ourselves grateful for mercy but ultimately dependent on justice.[156]

Serving at the Friday Gathering led volunteers and me to turn to activism, fortified with the experiences of people we know. Our liberation is bound to our neighbors' liberation. They are not faceless, anonymous people. Stereotypes have lost their potency. To remain silent, to retreat, to turn my attention elsewhere is to allow my privilege to separate and insulate me from my neighbor.

"Listening to stories that are different from my own has expanded my worldview," Samantha said. "I've grown up privileged. My parents are white. They're college-educated, and they have good jobs. They own their homes." She recalled the experiences of two Black high school students who also volunteer at the Friday Gathering.

"Just last week," Samantha said, "Leah was expressing to me her frustration that [her daughter] A'Niya had been asked to speak about racism at an assembly at her high school." Leah and A'Niya live in the Asylum Hill neighborhood, and A'Niya attends a public school in a predominantly upper-middle-class suburb of Hartford.

"The school leaders shirked their duty," Samantha continued. "They failed to get at the root of the problem of racism, and they thought to put A'Niya on the spot in front of her peers. Leah told me, 'They need to examine themselves, including when they left A'Niya off an email list for one of her college AP [Advanced Placement] courses.'

"I've started to see the impact on Jasmine and her family, too," Samantha said. "Jasmine's mother works long hours to make ends meet, and it takes a toll on all of the family. Jasmine attends the same high school as I do and is taking some of the same college AP classes that I did. Seeing firsthand the hurtful impact that racism in school can have on people I care about widened my perspective and made me start to question some of my own school's practices, especially in regard to how minority students are treated or the access they are allowed to higher-level courses. It's something I have never experienced because of my race."

***

Soup kitchens and the Friday Gathering serve more than people who are hungry and volunteers who want to give back. Soup kitchens are but one element in a system that is steered by other constituencies. Considering who the greater system serves requires exploring its sources of wealth and power.

The Friday Gathering depends on a network of food donations. It is a clearinghouse for surplus food donated by food banks and others. Mark Winne, a community food activist and the executive director of the Hartford Food System from 1979 to 2003, described the network as a mutually dependent relationship. "The institution of food banking evolved as one of co-dependency between food donor and food recipient," he said, explaining it as a series of needs. "The food bank needs food to give to its clients, and food donors—food manufacturers, restaurants, retailers, individuals, farmers—must dispose of food they can't use or sell."[157]

Feeding America describes itself as "the nation's largest domestic hunger-relief organization—a powerful and efficient network of 200 food banks across the country."[158] In 2021, they reported that 108 billion pounds of food—nearly 40 percent of all food in America—is wasted each year. Causes of food waste include crops left in the field because of low prices; problems with manufacturing and transportation; food not meeting retailers' aesthetic requirements; and uneaten food at home, restaurants, and stores. In 2020, Feeding America "rescued" four billion pounds of groceries.[159]

The disparity between the abundance that is discarded and the persistence of hunger in America is not new. It came to light during the Great Depression when dairies poured unsaleable milk down the sewers, apples rotted in orchards, oranges were soaked with kerosene to prevent their consumption, and surpluses piled up on railroad sidings.[160] These images recurred during the first months of the COVID-19 pandemic. "Dumped milk, smashed eggs, plowed vegetables: food waste of the pandemic," read a headline in *The New York Times*.[161] These practices reflect a history of community needs competing with economic prosperity.

A 2018 report by the US Department of Agriculture stated that the agricultural economy drives food assistance programs.[162] The most prominent federal program, the Supplemental Nutrition Assistance Program (formerly called food stamps), was established to address the needs of low-income people who do not have the means to purchase food for themselves. The report states:

> Although the current Supplemental Nutrition Assistance Program (SNAP) is nutrition assistance for the poor, policymakers considering changes to the program must also consider the competing interests of a diverse (and politically influential) set of stakeholders that includes farmers, food retailers, and food manufacturers in addition to SNAP participants and other U.S. taxpayers. ... While all three stakeholders are supported by the Food Stamp Program/SNAP,

policymakers face tradeoffs over balancing the competing interests.

There is no doubt: A vibrant society depends on a healthy agricultural system. In 2004, a report prepared by the Congressional Hunger Center outlined the history of the lack of food in the United States. It noted that the effects of long-term hunger became apparent during World War II, when an estimated 40 percent of draftees were rejected due to malnutrition. The authors state, "Hunger was no longer seen through just the national moral prism of concern for the poor as in the nineteenth century or as a way to avoid social strife and revolution as in the 1930s; now hunger was a national security problem."[163]

Janet Poppendieck, professor emeritus of sociology at Hunter College and a senior faculty fellow at the CUNY Urban Food Policy Institute, has researched the history of the federal government's approach to food assistance. She described the system that evolved with mandates and budgets set by Congress and swayed by the public's fluctuating outlook on welfare, capitalism, and agricultural policy. She asked, "Why was the nation left with a farm policy based on limiting production and raising the price of food instead of one based on finding the means to distribute the available abundance?"[164] Soup kitchens and food pantries have stepped in to fill the gap between community needs and government assistance, but they cannot solve the problem that leaves many people unable to afford to feed themselves.

In this context, charities are complicit in preserving the status quo. The public will be satisfied that they have done their duty as long as there are food banks to distribute the waste and soup kitchens to absorb the costs of separating unspoiled food, disposing of rotten food, and transporting, refrigerating, and storing what the corporations will claim as charitable deductions. The public will bear the costs of tax write-offs for profit-making corporations and the costs of government agencies to administer food assistance programs and then throw up their hands, claiming it is never enough. Social justice, not charity, disrupts the status quo.

Karen Washington is a food activist and community gardener in the Bronx. She is critical of charity that only dispenses food. She asserts that nonprofit status does not mean that someone is not profiting. In a May 2021 interview with *The Guardian*, Washington said:

> Non-profit food banks and food entities are mostly white-led and [operating] mostly in communities of color. So as long as we're poor and hungry, they keep making money. It's such a rip-off and I want them out of my communities. These entities came in promising to help us, but 15 years later and nothing has changed because they're pimping us to get money. I don't know how they put their head on a pillow. Handing out food isn't enough, it just makes people working in pantries and soup kitchens feel good about themselves.[165]

The poor and hungry need acts of mercy and compassion. But neighborhood meal programs like the Friday Gathering exist within a social structure that created the demand for them. How differently a soup kitchen might operate if it were motivated to put itself out of business by addressing our neighbors' predicaments at its roots.

14

Something We Must Create

The beauty of antiracism is that you don't have to pretend to be free of racism to be an antiracist. Antiracism is the commitment to fight racism wherever you find it, including in yourself.

—Ijeoma Oluo

During the pandemic, the doors opened at 3:15 for folks coming to the prayer circle. I checked temperatures and face masks at the door and asked neighbors to use the hand sanitizer. One week, two women waited in line while I checked in the person ahead of them. When I turned back to check in the first woman, Tony—who had been coming on Fridays for years—was standing in her place. He had cut ahead of both women.

"Hi, Tony. Are you here for the prayer circle?" I asked.

Tony hopped back and forth from one leg to the other and avoided looking me in the eye. "Yeah," he said, trying to push past me.

"Tony," I said, "these women were here first. Please wait your turn." I motioned for Tony to move to the back of the line.

Tony stood behind the second woman while I checked the first one in. When I turned back to greet the second woman, Tony had cut in front again.

"Tony, there's plenty of time. This woman was here first, and I'm going to check her in next."

Tony grumbled and muttered under his breath.

The woman said, "That's okay, let him go ahead."

"This just takes a few seconds, and you were here first," I said. "It's okay for Tony to wait his turn."

As the second woman headed off to the prayer circle, I asked Tony, "What was that about? You're early, and there are only four of you here."

He said, "A white man never lets Black people get in front of him."

"Not here, Tony," I said. "That attitude does not work here."

I had known Tony for years and was unaware of—or oblivious to—his racist beliefs and actions. *Had he done or said anything like this before and I hadn't noticed? Why did the woman say Tony could go ahead of her when I was advocating for her? Did she experience this kind of aggression regularly? Did they know each other, and would Tony retaliate later?*

I told a few people about the exchange, but there was no system in place for Friday Gathering volunteers to process it together. *What assumptions did I have about Tony or other diners that could block me from seeing other discriminatory acts?* Bystanders who witness an incident and our response to it will draw their own conclusions about our character. Victims who accept their victimization as inevitable may not expect any response at all.

***

Racism. Is it present—overtly or covertly—at the Friday Gathering? The question is the proverbial elephant in the room because, at Grace and as a society, we are still learning to talk with each other about it and uncover and respond to our biases without loathing ourselves or blaming others. Whole books are devoted to the history and impact of racism, the adversity and misery it has and continues to cause, and what it will take to dismantle it. This chapter can only open a discussion, because to keep silent would be negligent and irresponsible.

At the heart of racism and its cousins—classism, sexism, ableism, and heterosexism, to name a few—is privilege.[166] Some people in a community have advantages—privilege—they did not earn simply because of their identities, such as skin color, class, religion, gender, ability, or zip code. This endows them with a degree of status not granted to people with different identities. This inequity in the community causes suffering and oppression to persons denied those unearned privileges and is a burden they did not earn. Privilege is expressed when a school system overlooks its students who reside in another town or when diners stand to bless the meal with a prayer in English and refuse to stay standing when the prayer is said in Spanish. Privilege is exercised when a way of doing things is justified with the statement, "Because that's the way we've always done it." Privilege is housed in power plays, which are grounded in a group's culture and status.

Conversations about racism, power, and privilege are difficult. They expose our worldviews and the degree to which we honor each other's humanity. They push us out of our comfort zone, which can be exciting, scary, and painful. Engaging in this dialogue is important work. As with physical exercise, we grow when we repeatedly work these muscles, and sometimes it hurts. As a person of privilege—a label that I claim—when I recognize my own unearned power and privilege, I begin to understand that what I take for granted is not the reality of many others. When I stop defending my ego, I am freed to align myself with those who are denied such unearned power and privilege. I embrace this work so that justice will prevail.

Classism is also a burden many neighbors bear, and it often coexists alongside racism. Our neighbors endure hardships that arise from cursory judgments about poverty, illiteracy, addiction, incarceration, and mental health. "I have nothing in common with them," a member of Grace told me, explaining their lack of interest in the Friday Gathering. It was a statement based on assumptions, not experience. If I cannot identify with my neighbor, how can I join in their struggle for justice?

Is racism present at the Friday Gathering? We have to ask because white Christian denominations, to which Grace belongs, have a long history of practicing racism and helped create the dominant white culture that prevails today.

The history of the United States is bound up in the Christian beliefs of early European immigrants that sanctioned—even blessed—the conquest of native people and the enslavement of those from Africa. European Christians proclaimed America to be the new promised land and they were its chosen people. This mindset was codified in the original US Constitution that explicitly excluded Indigenous people as citizens and counted an enslaved Black individual as only three-fifths of a person. It persisted into the twentieth century through acts, laws, and regulations which, by denying equal access, gave preferential treatment to white people.[167]

Today, a culture of white supremacy endures and imposes unfair treatment on marginalized racial groups. It is evident in residential segregation, discriminatory hiring practices, schools' dependence on local property taxes, bias in the criminal justice system, and the disruption, pollution, and health effects from routing expressways through Black communities. The rules and procedures that created these inequitable systems are complex, and the term "systemic racism" encompasses the political, legal, and economic practices that maintain them.

Terms like "white supremacy" and "systemic racism" are emotionally charged and many white people deny that problems exist or argue that they are good people who have not committed any wrongdoing. I wrestled with this, too, until I realized that acknowledging white supremacy and systemic racism are not about assigning blame. Instead, they call attention to the problems so that we can confront them. Just as the "author's note" at the beginning of this book addressed naming identities—Black, white, Latino, Indigenous, Asian—we must move past the discomfort of naming problems and rise to the challenge of seeking justice. As Jane Addams wrote, fortunes change and we may find ourselves at the mercy of justice, too. Dominant white culture persists in the unearned distribution of power and privilege across institutions, including the white church.

To begin to uncover how this belief system influences our rituals and practices today, we have to ask: Whose voices carry weight? Do they serve the dominant culture or the underclass? One exists at the expense of the other. An equitable, just society demands that we repair the structures we belong to because we are the system. Even Grace, despite its service to the community, is not exempt from this work. Writing from the experience of being a Black pastor in the Lutheran church, a Protestant Christian denomination of which Grace is a member, Rev. Kenneth Wheeler said, "To be accepted as a person of color in the Evangelical Lutheran Church in America meant that you had to conform to the standards of whiteness; those who refused to conform would always find themselves isolated or pigeonholed."[168]

Drew G. I. Hart is a Black Christian theologian who writes about racism and the church. He challenges Black Christians to examine their responses to racism:

> While there is certainly a rich tradition of Afro-Christian faith that has resisted the domestication of Jesus for generations, we cannot assume that every black Christian is necessarily joining God in divine transformation and resisting white supremacy through active justice and peacemaking. Whether white, black, Native American, Hispanic, Middle Eastern, or Asian, we all get caught up in the currents of our white-dominated society and internalize its messages.[169]

I don't believe there is a neutral ground where Grace, the Friday Gathering, or I can escape this conversation. Although we are a diverse group, we do not function apart from white-dominant culture. The only way to separate ourselves from systems that use privilege against the oppressed is to undo the privilege and create equity. We are either part of the solution or part of the problem. Jemar Tisby, a *New York Times* bestselling author who writes about the Black experience, unequivocally states: "Justice takes sides."[170]

There is no soothing ourselves by talking about how far we have come in reversing the effects of racism. We cannot confuse what we, the privileged, have worked hard for and the obstacles we have overcome with what it means to be oppressed. There are still many for whom working hard results in less, or nothing at all.

Howard Thurman's *Jesus and the Disinherited* offers one lens to consider how the members of Grace and the Friday Gathering can respond to the oppressed people in our community. Thurman, whose grandmother was enslaved, was a theologian and a mentor to Dr. Martin Luther King, Jr. Thurman's contrast between the lowly Jesus and what became the wealthy and mighty Christian church is a jarring indictment for those who do not identify with the oppressed. "That it [Christianity] became, through the intervening years, a religion of the powerful and dominant, sometimes used as an instrument of oppression, must not tempt us into believing that it was thus in the mind and life of Jesus."[171]

Thurman described Jesus as a person who identified with the downtrodden, those who today are labeled as marginalized or disenfranchised, and reminds us that Jesus was materially poor and homeless. His family were migrants when they fled to Egypt to escape Roman tyranny. Jesus identified with those persecuted by their religious leaders, the ones who elevated religious doctrine over charity. He showed compassion for the people society pushed aside and judged unclean: lepers, the impoverished, the lame, prostitutes, and tax collectors. He visited their homes, took his meals with them, talked with them, and was in physical contact with them; he was not afraid to touch them. His actions upended the social structure of the time.

Although Thurman focused on the oppression of Black people, he wrote that each generation has its "cast-down people."[172] In the foreword to the book, Vincent Harding, an African American historian and professor of religion, named the cast-down of *their* era: "the homeless, the working and jobless poor, the substance abused and abusers, the alienated, misguided, and essentially abandoned young people."[173] Well into the twenty-first century, the downtrodden also include immigrants and refugees; Muslims, Jews, and others victimized for their religious beliefs; the wrongfully incarcerated and those released from prison; the disabled and mentally ill; victims of human trafficking; and people who identify as LGBTQIA+.[174] Harding wrote that the oppressed

> are rarely within hearing or seeing range of the company of Jesus' proclaimed followers. The keepers of the faith of the master often find it very difficult, and very dangerous, to follow him into the hard places inhabited by the disinherited of America. And those wall-bruised people [Harding describes the oppressed as people with their backs against the wall] find no space for their presence in the places where the official followers are comfortably at worship.[175]

It's not that it is often actually "very difficult, and very dangerous" to enter the places "inhabited by the disinherited," but that Christians—keepers of the faith—*find* it that way. We have been socialized into thinking about and seeing the outcast as threats to us physically and to our way of life. When I moved to Hartford, I was urged to be careful about where I walked and to avoid places where I might come in contact with people experiencing homelessness, drug addiction, or mental illness. *Were these veiled racist descriptions?* The hundreds of portraits that fill the dining room walls at Grace attest to a different way of being. The Friday Gathering as a place and time for a diverse community to come within hearing and seeing range of each other represents so much more than serving dinner, if we choose to make it so.

Samantha said one of her motivations for coming to the Friday Gathering was to be with people she otherwise would not have had the opportunity to socialize with. Her experiences there have helped her become aware of the systems that impact her and the people she interacts with—classmates at school among them—and not always equitably. Samantha's perspective distinctly contrasts with her friends' fears about safety in Hartford and the view that Hartford's students are less intelligent than West Hartford's. Samantha's outlook is shaped by her experiences.

Thurman called the church's teachings a "betrayal," because of the focus on "heaven, forgiveness, love, and the like."[176] The emphasis on inner spirituality and otherworldliness diminished—drowned out—the companion call for justice. He asserted that church was where the privileged and the oppressed should come together, and "the relations of the individual to his God should take priority over conditions of class, race, power, status, wealth, or the like." Thurman said the church should provide "normal experiences of fellowship," adding, "This cannot be discovered in a vacuum or in a series of artificial or hypothetical relationships. It has to be in real situations, natural, free."[177]

Hart identifies a set of practices we can follow to break the cycle of oppression, including what he calls "sharing life together." He speaks to the value of proximity, of getting physically close to each other, akin to Thurman's fellowship.

> What I am gesturing toward isn't the idea of merely attending the same church service as people from another racial group. It's something much grander than that. The practice of sharing life together has everything to do with no longer allowing the racial hierarchy to pattern our social lives, manage our geographical movements. ... Sharing life together means intimately identifying with people who carry the stigma of varying racial meanings in

their actual bodies. Most practically, this can be expressed in regularly sharing life together around a table. ... The table—and I specifically mean sharing meals together—offers an opportunity to practice hospitality and intimacy that renounce racial hierarchy and racialized social patterns.[178]

Sharing meals is not the same as standing on one side of the serving table and asking diners, "Would you like green beans or broccoli?" It is not a "one and done" event. Hart speaks about "regularly" getting around the table. Sharing life together means cultivating a deep familiarity that stirs us to feel connected.

Although Hart focuses on racism, he speaks to all systems of hierarchy that privilege one group at the expense of another. He invites the diners, members of Grace, and Friday Gathering volunteers to make it a practice to sit down together at the table. To take nourishment from the same pot. To engage in conversation. To learn each other's stories.

Who we ask for help—and who we accept it from—is another gauge of our relationships with our neighbors. It reflects who and what we esteem. If we cannot imagine asking our church neighbor or diner for help, it means we cannot imagine anything they could add to our lives. That is a problem. The direction in which help flows reflects how power is distributed. If help only flows in one direction—such as feeding the hungry—then the spirit of sharing life is cheapened.

Grace has been an ethnically diverse congregation for decades, and the Friday Gathering is, too. We have moved closer, occupying the same space, worshiping together, and preparing and eating dinner side by side. Pushing back at us is the rest of the week and in whose company we spend our days. We must still face that Grace and the Friday Gathering operate in a society that continues to privilege people based on their identities.

"My observation," Hart explained, "is that most multiethnic churches are normed by white, dominant-culture sensibilities, even when diversity is being reflected on the stage. And it is a real struggle for communities to break from that stronghold."[179]

What can we do? There is work we must pursue individually and organizationally. At both levels, we can commit to self-examination and be open to embracing change, even change in leadership.

Holding Grace and the Friday Gathering accountable for its formal and informal power systems is critical work. For years, organizations large and small, for-profit and not-for-profit, have promoted increasing diversity and becoming more inclusive. There is a sentiment that if we could engage with more minorities, everything would be fine. But the white dominant culture—with its standards and procedures—prevails, and success within an organization often depends on conformity, even for minorities. It is not the absence of diversity that is the problem but the change that diversity brings. Until we—the ones with power—change and create an environment where all members are full participants, we cannot be inclusive. Anything less is tokenization.

Change begins with self-examination, pursuing diverse perspectives, and being willing to see ourselves from others' points of view. We yearn for authentic relationships, which require having the courage to speak truthfully and expecting the same from others. When we hold ourselves and others accountable, self-examination leads to making systemic changes. Then resources and assets will be reallocated because a reshuffling of priorities will demand it.

Self-examination and talking about conflict and competing interests deserve attention at every meeting of an organization because changing behaviors and norms is more than just a single task on an agenda. Each new level of self-awareness leads to a deeper understanding of what it means to be equitable. It challenges where power resides, including the prerequisites for membership. If monetary contributions are expected, how do they devalue other ways of contributing? If communication depends on electronic media—social media, smartphones, texting, emails—how does that affect people without internet access or electronic devices? Challenge the assumption that members must be literate in English in order to fully participate. If an organization's property and assets are exempt from local taxes, assess the drain that creates on the neighborhood and make amends. Self-examination is meaningless unless it's followed by change.

Being receptive to others' worldviews and experiences has strengthened my connections to the people around me. Surrendering the need to be right, allowing contradictory perspectives to coexist, and challenging my biases and privilege has opened the door to more meaningful and satisfying relationships.

***

Even when our actions are upright, they may still cause pain. With self-examination, we have the opportunity to repair relationships.

I was working at a concession stand on an unusually busy day. The woman I was waiting on said she needed more time to consider her options. She agreed to move to the rear of the counter so I could help the next person. After that customer was finished, I went to the rear counter and finished helping the first customer.

When I returned to the front, the next customer in line was furious with me. She asked for a complaint card and later wrote a letter about her experience. She was Latina, she explained, and said I had snubbed her. We later got together to talk about her experience.

She said, "This happens to me all the time. I will be waiting in line, and when it's my turn, the clerk turns around—they don't even say hello—and talks to someone else. I can hear the conversation. It's not even about work. What am I supposed to think?" This situation had occurred often enough to be more than a coincidence. On the day she met me, she'd had enough.

She was unaware that the woman I had helped at the back of the counter—a white woman—had been in line before her. When I left to help the customer in the back, I didn't explain that I would be back or clarify that the other customer had been there first. I didn't acknowledge her, or the time she had already spent waiting. She felt invisible, unimportant, and insulted.

I appreciated her candor and that she put herself out so I could put myself in her shoes. As a clerk, I owed her and all customers common courtesy, and I apologized. I wanted to believe that I would have been just as rude to any white customer that day and that my behavior wasn't motivated by bias. But it was impossible to know for certain. I hoped that processing the incident and empathizing with the customer would prevent me from overlooking the people right in front of me again.

Some people questioned why I invested so much effort in this customer. They didn't agree that I had snubbed her. After all, it was a busy day. But I have another perspective. I had no relationship with the woman, and there was no reason she owed me the benefit of the doubt. The expectation that she should be the one to "let it go" because it was a busy day put the burden on her. I didn't want to snub her again by minimizing her experience.

The woman said she felt she was ignored because she was Latina. Who gets to decide what is biased or racially motivated and what isn't? If a person can't truly know another's motives, and if an act is not as blatant as Tony's, can it still be labeled racist? Innuendo, ambiguity, veiled threats, and obscure language conceal motives that can be felt and discerned the same as blatant hostilities. Even good intentions can be demeaning and insulting. Each of us carries our past experiences with us; they create a lens through which we make sense of new experiences.

***

One Saturday afternoon in late August about forty-five people from the neighborhood met in the parking lot at Grace. We were there to celebrate new pollinator gardens planted around Asylum Hill in the spring. First we fanned out to pick up litter on nearby streets. Afterward we enjoyed a box supper while listening to musicians and presentations about solar panels and hydroponic gardening.

I arrived late, after most people had left to claim their block and collect litter. I saw Carmelita, an African American woman I had gotten to know at the Friday Gathering. I was her sponsor when she joined Grace's congregation. No one had yet claimed the street in front of the church, so we grabbed a garbage bag and set off together. We talked about her nieces. Carmelita helps her sister, Rhonda, raise her daughters. The oldest is a teenager and was starting high school. We chatted about how different life is for teenagers today compared to when we grew up and the challenges they face.

A white man whom neither of us knew asked if he could join us, and we said yes. He told us his sister had lived in Carmelita's building and had died a few weeks earlier. Carmelita remembered her. He was visiting from Philadelphia to collect her things and close up the apartment. As we continued to chat, the man said, "You two must be friends."

Instantly, Carmelita replied, "She used to talk too much. It's better now, and she's okay."

Carmelita was referring to the E-Talks program, a weekly discussion group that I help lead. My role is to facilitate the conversation so that everyone has an opportunity to contribute. When the discussion stalls, I recap what others have said and pose new questions to open the conversation up again. After the program one week, Carmelita told me, "You talk too much."

I care about Carmelita, and I care about our relationship. Her criticism stung. But it would sting even more if people stopped coming to E-Talks because I "talk too much."

"What do you mean?" I asked, and encouraged her to help me see what was happening from her perspective.

She said she was offended when I summarized what other people said. It seemed that I didn't believe others expressed themselves well enough, that I could say things better. And she thought I was taking credit for other people's ideas.

As a white woman, whether I claim it or not, I wield a degree of power because I am perceived as part of the dominant culture. I am privileged even if I don't claim it, because that is the society I reside in. If I care about my relationships, I need to grasp that we sometimes have different ideas about power and how it is exercised. When I speak up at E-Talks, my good intentions may not matter.

Carmelita made it possible for us to share our different perspectives, and we each came away with a broader outlook and respect for the other. I took to heart that sometimes I talk too much and need to step back.

I talked with a few friends about Carmelita's feedback, and they dismissed it. They said that facilitators are supposed to recap and ask questions. When Carmelita said I "talk too much" six months later, I appreciated even more her willingness to confront me the first time. She salvaged our relationship when I was unaware it was at risk.

Exercising empathy takes effort. Dr. Martin Luther King, Jr., called attention to this when he wrote:

> Like life, racial understanding is not something that we find but something that we must create. What we find when we enter these mortal plains is existence; but existence is the raw material out of which all life must be created. A productive and happy life is not something that you find; it is something that you make. And so the ability of Negroes and whites to work together, to understand each other, will not be found ready-made; it must be created by the fact of contact.[180]

"Fact of contact." All three men—Howard Thurman, Drew Hart, and Dr. King—urge us to share life together. In the moments of contact, differences surface, and how we resolve them pushes us toward growth, or not. This is the essence of the Friday Gathering, sharing life together and creating the fact of contact.

Occasionally there are clashes. I don't know if they are racially motivated. Some incidents are about power, one person bossing another, telling them what they can or cannot do. The tone of voice or choice of words can provoke an argument. Sometimes quarrels erupt because people are tired, worn out, or misconstrue a situation. Regardless, these moments test the strength of our relationships.

Occasionally a diner feels shortchanged, that they were served less food or offered fewer choices than someone else. Some weeks there are more volunteers and we can cater to specific needs, and when we cannot, a diner may feel slighted. It is challenging to determine whether to interrupt meal preparation to respond to a request or stick to the routine so we can be ready on time. Some diners and volunteers receive additional allowances because their situation is more precarious, or the relationship is stronger, or they are pushier, or they are delivering to neighbors who cannot get to Grace. A diner who feels slighted may shout, "You play favorites!" or "You're racist!" We are left in limbo because we lack a practice to reflect and process the circumstances we face and our responses.

"We are building community," the host announces. Community depends on relationships, and relationships depend on trust. Meaningful relationships are challenging, and perceptions about race and power add to their complexity. We must be brave enough to fight racism in ourselves and to move beyond the comfortable places where it is easy to be Christian.[181]

15

From Seeds of Desire

A tree as great as a man's embrace springs from a small shoot.

—Lao Tsu, *Tao Te Ching,* trans. Gia-fu Feng and Jane English

The Friday Gathering spawned new ways of being in community. These sprouts or offshoots were inspired by neighbors' aspirations and willingness to lead. Encouraging them to pursue their ideas strengthened the community and opened more ways for us to be in contact with one another. Some activities developed and evolved while others were short-lived. What mattered was that the community was free to experiment.

***

When diners were asked what they would like to do for fun, some suggested a dance. They formed a committee and hosted two dances in 2013. A DJ was hired, the dining hall was decorated, a disco ball was hung from the ceiling, and a table was set up with soft drinks and snacks.

Diners and members of the congregation came: Albert, Hilda, Lamont,

Arnell, Todd, Richie, Jesus, Lorraine, and others. A few brought their children and grandchildren. "I remember how much the little kids enjoyed the attention," Todd said. "They enjoyed the adults enjoying them and the music. Everybody had fun."

***

Janet's Closet sprang from the desire to create a free clothing bank. Leah and Lorraine volunteered to run it. Leah brought lunch cooked with the African flavors of her birth country, and the volunteers ate lunch together.

"It felt natural to me," Lorraine said. "It's part of who I am. I love people and helping others. I was born with this gift, and I was raised by strong God-loving parents, especially my mom. Even when we didn't have much, what we did have was doubly blessed." Over the years, Joycelyn, Claudia, Lee, Tracy, and others took turns running Janet's Closet.

***

Another seed sprouted when Darrell and Nancy established the Karis Emergency Shelter, the name *karis* referring to the Greek word meaning grace. The need to formalize their residence as an emergency shelter became apparent when a family with a young child was experiencing homelessness. To qualify for assisted housing, the family required a reference from a shelter. But shelters wouldn't accept them because of the mother's past behavior. Darrell and Nancy created a brochure, defined a code of conduct, and required that clients be screened by Grace's pastoral staff. The Karis Emergency Shelter has provided a safe, temporary home for many, helping them transition to more permanent housing or simply providing a safe place to stay for the night.

***

Open Doors was inspired by Kevin, who was homeless at the time. Louisa recalled, "On Labor Day, Kevin and I were talking when he said, 'You don't know what it's like to have a place to be on a holiday.' The way he said 'a place to be' really hit me. It was about belonging, being welcomed, being loved. Kevin said that normally on a holiday, he would find a tree, curl up under it, and get through the day. We talked more, and the idea to open Grace's doors on holidays took root. Kevin said he would help. He could cook."

Public spaces like libraries and senior centers close for federal holidays. Soup kitchens may take a holiday, too. As well as people experiencing homelessness, many neighbors live alone and depend on public places to meet and socialize. The anticipation of a holiday and the isolation it brings can take a toll, especially on the vulnerable, who have few if any alternatives. Holidays are tough for them.

***

Another seed, E-Talks, sprouted in January 2020. The title is short for Everyone Talks and refers to TED Talks—short, informative videos presented by people passionate about their subject matter. Louisa sensed that some diners had an intellectual curiosity and an appetite for meaningful conversations. E-Talks was designed to nurture both.

"Louisa is one of those people who's always on the lookout for ways to make things better in the neighborhood, usually by making connections between people with a need for opportunities, and opportunities looking for people," Bernie wrote in the Asylum Hill newsletter. "She also noticed that while many of the people she runs into in the neighborhood are reasonably thoughtful, they often just end up talking about one another. ... She devised a plan to help them talk about something a little more challenging, like TED Talks."[182]

The program ran for ten weeks until the pandemic set in. In the summer of 2021, it was relaunched. Carmelita was one of the neighbors who returned.

"I like being around new things, new ideas," she said. "I want to do something different instead of the same thing over and over. Coming to E-Talks is like taking a trip and seeing something new. I want to learn about what's going on in the world and hear other people's ideas. Socializing with other people is good for me. I've made new friends."

***

A convergence of circumstances planted the seeds for what became Fresh Start Pallet Products®: neighbors stopping to chat when Louisa was working in the garden; a high concentration of apartment buildings with no outdoor spaces; neighbors issued citations for loitering on the sidewalk by Grace; and no place to sit outdoors.

"The thought of building benches came from hearing angry people on Friday nights at dinner," Louisa said. "It was summer, and the weather was beautiful. Diners said they would be standing around outside, talking with their friends, and the police would show up and give them citations for loitering.

"I didn't have a budget or money to purchase benches and was thinking about how to make them for free. I found a design for building them from wooden pallets. I asked Lee if he knew someone who could build a bench, and it all clicked. Lee said he was a retired carpenter and would love to build something again. What's more, there was a stack of discarded pallets at his apartment building down the street. We took off in my little station wagon and hauled the pallets back to Grace. The idea of repurposing the wood and turning it into something useful was appealing, too."

During the summer of 2013, Lee designed the benches and Kevin helped build them. The benches were painted blue to match the color of the church doors and placed in the backyard garden around a table also built from pallets. A canopy for shade was added later.

In the spring of 2014, "the garden became a hangout," Louisa said. It was included in the Hartford Blooms tour—an annual event to showcase private and public gardens across the city. "It won a HUG [Hartford Urban Gardens] award," Louisa added. "Jesus and I were invited to a gala where we accepted the recognition."

That year, Pastor Rick was installed at Grace. "The Friday Gathering acquainted him with many of the challenges people in our neighborhood face," Louisa said. "When spring rolled around in 2015 and the benches, table, and canopy went up, another seed of inspiration sprouted. The not-so-new pastor asked questions about the pallet-made furniture. He asked Lee and Jesus to build a custom table for a special model sailing ship he didn't have a proper way to display. They set up shop in the garden and built a very beautiful table. Jesus made a little bit of money. The seed sprouted a little more. Our new pastor, with more than thirty years of professional experience, asked if a business building furniture out of pallets could help rebuild lives.

"Pastor Rick asked Lee if he would work with some of the men and build more benches. See if we could sell them," Louisa said. Lee offered to teach woodworking, and Richie, Jesus, and Todd joined his workshop. The men were paid a small stipend from the sale of the benches.

"We had a relationship with the Charter Oak Cultural Center," Louisa said. "Their gala was coming up, and they asked if we would donate a bench to the fundraiser. I would paint it with a custom design. The bench sold at their auction, and they collected orders for more. Then a few more orders came in, most for custom-painted benches.

"Around that time, the Town & County Club, just a few buildings down from Grace, wanted to connect with the neighborhood. They put a call out to churches in the area and asked them to come to their meetings and present on their initiatives. Pastor Rick went. The connections he made there were impactful and still are.

"Addison, a member of the congregation and a professional musician, asked Pastor Rick if he could help. He introduced Pastor Rick to his friend, a retiree who led the development department for a large charitable hospital. They organized a fundraiser event, and Addison played piano for it. In the span of six weeks, they raised about $17,000."

In 2019, Fresh Start Pallet Products® became an independent 501(c)(3) nonprofit organization.[183] "Building furniture, rebuilding lives" became their slogan. Fresh Start moved into its own dedicated manufacturing space and by 2020 had an operating budget approaching $400,000.

Rich began volunteering with Fresh Start in 2016. He and his wife, Barb, had been living in the Asylum Hill neighborhood since 1996.

"I was recently retired," Rich said, "after twenty years of traveling back and forth to Eastern Europe and East Africa, frequently staying for several months at a time. I was totally disconnected from Hartford. It's far too easy to lose touch with friends by lack of contact for such a long time, so I found I had few friends to bum around with. I took about four months exploring the different nonprofit groups and programs going on in the neighborhood. I was looking for something challenging, a place to sink my teeth into where I could volunteer. A friend suggested that I meet Rick, the pastor at Grace. I volunteered for a while at the Friday Gathering—I even suggested to Barb that she check it out—and then Rick introduced me to Fresh Start.

"My experience working internationally with Mosaic fit well with Rick's aspirations for Fresh Start," Rich said. "In Romania, Kenya, and Tanzania, I worked with small, local groups to start social businesses that would support people with intellectual and developmental disabilities. Around the world, people take pride in themselves when they have meaningful work."

The "social business" concept developed from the work of Muhammad Yunus, who believes that poverty strips people of all human dignity. He developed a new business model based on the principle of balancing an enterprise's social goals—solving social problems—with its financial goals.[184] For this work, he was awarded the Nobel Peace Prize in 2006. Applied to Fresh Start, the objective to address employability development is balanced with the need to create a financially viable business.

"For me, Fresh Start is all about social justice," Rich said. "It was designed to be a training program for people who need a fresh start; people who had faced homelessness, addiction, incarceration, or were refugees."

Fresh Start partners with social service agencies to address the needs of the whole person. Wheeler Clinic and InterCommunity Inc. are two providers that offer medical, mental health, and addiction recovery services.

"Part of our work is to prepare employees for the workforce beyond Fresh Start. We help them navigate making the transition to be able to meet employers' expectations. There are cultural norms that must be met to be successful. Sometimes, unfortunately, an individual's choices are not in their best interests, and they leave the program.

"In August 2021, we launched the Fresh Start Academy. It's funded by the state and federal government and is designed to help people overcome barriers to employment. Students receive four hours of training a day, five days a week for three months, and they're paid through a stipend from a grant. In addition to carpentry skills, they're coached on the qualities that employers require: showing up on time, disciplining yourself, and teamwork.

"Fresh Start appears to be a business; however, since it was founded as a social business it has two bottom lines," Rich said. "First is building social capital in each individual. Second is building a business that strives for sustainability without a return to its investors. We have to manufacture a quality product while investing in our employees. I don't want people to make a purchase out of pity. The business won't be sustainable if purchases are primarily motivated by charity and viewed as donations. Businesses that are heavily dependent on donors are susceptible to donor fatigue. We want to reduce our dependence on sponsorship. This is what it means to give back to the community.

"Fresh Start was highly subsidized when it began," Rich said. "We needed to raise $3 for every dollar of product sold. Each year, we have reduced that ratio in order to meet our sustainability goals. Funders and individual donors have helped us purchase the equipment we need to run a professional shop and employ a master craftsman to teach and mentor both those in the academy and core workers on the shop floor. The board is 'all in' as volunteers and major investors.

"All board members make financial contributions and support the enterprise with their time," Rich explained. "They're called on to deliver product, pick up materials and supplies, and staff booths at shows like the annual Flower & Garden Show at the Connecticut Convention Center and the spring and fall Open Studio events. They maintain the website, provide human resources support, write grants, and cultivate more partners. Most valuable to many of us is the time spent on the shop floor, mentoring apprentices, learning about their challenges, and cheering their successes. Board members and volunteers contribute about 10,000 hours each year. This is what 'all in' means.

"People amaze us with how resilient they are and what they can come back from. Fresh Start can provide them with one of the cornerstones of what they need—employment—to live independent and fulfilling lives. Valid work is what we offer. It's inspirational to see what some of these people have done with their lives."

Quoting Yunus, Rich said, "'Poverty is the absence of all human rights. The frustrations, hostility and anger generated by abject poverty cannot sustain peace in any society.'[185] I like to think that Fresh Start is chipping away at that kind of poverty, right here, in my own neighborhood."

***

The Friday Gathering spawned other offshoots. A weekly Bible study met at the apartment building where Albert, Hilda, and Paul lived. Children's programs and community groups that needed a place to meet were welcomed at Grace. The relationship with the Charter Oak Cultural Center led to neighbors receiving stipends for maintaining small vegetable gardens and attending the Beat of the Street education program, which awarded its graduates with free laptops and free tuition at Goodwin University. Louisa, Woody, Roy, Sonny, Leah, Richie, and Lorraine were BOTS graduates.

Like the Friday Gathering, the offshoots bring people into "the fact of contact" that Martin Luther King, Jr., wrote about, where neighbors share life: building furniture, discussing TED Talks, gathering on holidays, hosting a dance, sharing a cup of coffee while visiting the clothes bank, or giving temporary housing. Coming together to solve problems and explore new interests increased neighbors' connections to one another and the community.

16

What Community Looks Like

For whenever and wherever there is a storyteller, there will also be a storyhearer. In the communal act of telling and listening, listening and telling, the sense of belonging begins.

—Ernest Kurtz and Katherine Ketcham, *The Spirituality of Imperfection*

The repeated insistence, week after week, that we are building community made me wonder: *Is there evidence that the Friday Gathering contributes to the greater community beyond the church walls or the Friday supper hour?* Mister Rogers, the creator and host of the PBS children's series, said, "There is something of yourself that you leave at every meeting with another person."[186] What do diners and volunteers leave with one another that they bring to the surrounding community? In April 2021, I got a glimpse of the possibilities.

Asylum Hill residents were gathered outdoors on a warm sunny Sunday afternoon, a few blocks from Grace. They filled the parking lot in a small shopping plaza and the adjacent side street that was closed to traffic for the event. A drum corps played to kick off the festivities. Their percussive rhythms echoed off the buildings and could be heard blocks away. It united the crowd and drew the attention of people passing by.

Residents were there to celebrate a new mural, funded by a Love Your Block grant from the city.[187] Louisa was awarded the grant and she painted the mural, twenty feet high and sixty feet wide, on the side of the shopping plaza. She engaged neighbors to paint the guardrails, storefronts, and sidewalks in front of the plaza, and to plant perennials in the concrete boxes around the parking lot. Giant letters across the top of the mural spelled out: "In Asylum Hill. Black Lives Do Matter. We welcome refugees & immigrants."

Large swaths of yellows, greens, oranges, reds, and blue formed the backdrop. Layered on top were trees that stretched from the bottom to the top of the building. The spaces between the trees were filled with inspirational quotes. Albert Bell had lived in the building across the street, and he could have seen the mural from his window. A corner of the wall paid tribute to him. It read, "Speak truth to power. The future depends on it."[188]

It was a neighborhood event, and Friday Gathering diners were there: Shirley and Barb; Cephus, a kitchen volunteer; Rachelle and her eight-year-old daughter; Bernie and his wife; Pastor Rick, his wife, and their adult son; and Vera, a member of Grace who volunteers on Fridays. Grace's organist came and documented the party with his camera. Margaret, a member of Grace who lives in Hartford's West End, came, too. She knows Samantha and her parents, who were also there. Leaders from the Asylum Hill Neighborhood Association came, along with the city's director of the Office of Community Engagement. The block was teeming with diners, friends from the suburbs, and residents from Asylum Hill and other Hartford neighborhoods. Their energy was joyful, friendly, and upbeat.

Lynn—the neighbor who first collected stories—emceed the event. She introduced Louisa, and the crowd applauded her. Carol, a white woman who used to live in the neighborhood, presented Louisa with a corsage made of flowers that matched the colors in the mural. The gesture was touching and Louisa whispered, "I can't remember the last time I wore a corsage."

Louisa invited three diners to sing, and Lynn announced them one by one. She introduced Sonny as the Italian Prince. "If Bobby Vinton could be the Polish Prince, then I can be the Italian Prince," he said. He performed "You'll Never Walk Alone," which he had planned to sing at his church until the pandemic put his performance on hold. His friend Edison came just to hear him sing.

Next, A'Niya sang "The Rose." She had sung at church and for the Gathering, but she considered this her first solo performance. You could have heard a pin drop when she began. The crowd leaned in and gave her their attention. A bystander said that A'Niya had a wonderful future ahead of her.

Sophie went last. Pastor Rick once loaned her his Aretha Franklin CDs so she could practice her singing. She performed "Give More Love" and challenged the crowd: "If you believe in Hartford, if you believe that change is possible, put your hands together and clap along." She kept urging them on until everyone joined in the clapping.

Of course, there was food. Louisa ordered pizza and Lorraine helped her set it up. Louisa invited youth from Our Piece of the Pie—an organization that serves young people who have been impacted by child welfare injustices—to volunteer.[189] They set up tables and chairs, and helped serve the pizza. Later they helped clean up, too.

Diners socialized with neighbors who don't come to the Friday Gathering. Members of Grace were introduced to diners and their neighbors. Lorraine, who once lived in the neighborhood, visited with her old friends. Samantha introduced her parents to diners she'd come to know, including A'Niya and her mother. Barb saw a former student from her literacy class, an immigrant from Ethiopia, who was with her daughter. The next day Barb texted, "I got caught up in my delight of seeing Laia and all other thoughts vanished for a few minutes."

Barry was there, and we had a chance to catch up. A Black man born in 1964, Barry stopped coming to the Friday Gathering when he became homeless. He said the distance was too far, but he later explained that he needed to protect the area where he slept at night. Barry had an identical twin brother who died of COVID-19 the summer before, and when we met in the park that summer, he reminisced about their childhood. Now Barry had a new apartment. "It's just around the corner," he said, smiling and pointing over his shoulder. "Life is good again."

***

Edith came to the party, too. She sneaked up behind me, put her arms around my waist, and hugged me from behind. I grasped her arms, and we clung to each other until she was ready to let go. "I helped paint the guardrails," she said. She raised her arms above her head and did a little jig. We laughed and hugged again.

Months before the pandemic, Edith had shared her story with me. She is a Black woman, born in 1960. She grew up in the Stowe Village housing project and graduated from Weaver High School. "The most important thing I do is volunteer at the House of Bread. I'm there every day except Thursday, 8:30 in the morning till 1 p.m. I love it! I see everybody there—Roy, Edison, Sonny." Her voice trailed off as she looked around the dining hall and the photos on the walls. "I'm related to half the people in this room," she said.

"Who?" I asked.

Edith pointed to Tracy, Arnell's girlfriend. "We're cousins. We grew up together."

Then she pointed to Shirley. "She calls me her 'child.'"

Shirley overheard Edith and headed our way. She put her arm around Edith and said, "You're my child."

Edith was the "baby" in the family; she had two older sisters and a brother. When she was nine, her mother passed away in a house fire. "My older sisters raised me," Edith said. Then she added with a mischievous grin, "They all spoiled me. And they still do!

"My mother was my best role model. She helped everybody, and I try to be like her. Whatever I can do to help somebody, I'm available. My mother passed, but my father is still here. When he needs me, he calls, and I'm there for him. He has a vegetable garden in Bloomfield. I go up there and help him in the garden.

"I still love my mommy. You write that down," she said.

Edith and I had gotten to know each other years before at the Friday Gathering. One evening she confided that she was scheduled for a colonoscopy, and she was scared. "Don't tell anyone," she made me promise. We counted down the weeks together. She made plans to stay with one of her sisters. The doctor found a large polyp and scheduled another appointment to remove it. Edith was still scared, but she was dealing with it. She finally got the good news: there was no cancer, and she made a full recovery.

One winter, Edith fell on an icy sidewalk while walking to the Gathering and injured her ankle. She came to dinner anyway, but during the evening, her ankle swelled up. She used a chair to elevate her leg and said she wanted to stay for prayers. The woman leading the service that night placed her hands on Edith's shoulders and began praying aloud. Edith stiffened and tried to push the woman away, but her protests were ignored. Edith sat hunched over and cried until it ended. Afterward, I drove Edith home, and she said, "I don't want to go through anything like that again," referring to the unsolicited touching. Edith didn't return to the Friday Gathering for at least a month.

Just before the pandemic lockdown, Edith arrived at the Gathering on a wintry afternoon. "I saved a woman's life!" she said. "I was walking to Grace when I saw a woman in front of me crossing the street. At the same time, I saw a car speeding toward us. I rushed ahead and pushed the woman out of the way. That car would have hit her.

"You don't have to take my word for it," Edith continued. "There was a policeman sitting in his car, and he saw the whole thing happen. He's the one who said I saved that woman's life. He said the city would give me an award. He said I'm a hero."

That evening at dinner, Pastor Rick celebrated Edith's heroism, giving thanks for her and the life she had saved. When the applause for Edith receded, Pastor Rick remarked that acts of heroism are all around us. He paused and his gaze took in all of the seated diners. Then, he urged them to look around, to pay attention to the "Ediths among us," and to tell their heroic stories.

***

In 2013, the Harwood Institute for Public Innovation engaged the Asylum Hill community to discuss ideas that could strengthen the neighborhood. Their final report called attention to the power of story.

> The stories people tell to themselves and to one another shape how we see ourselves, our community and what is possible. Neighborhoods that seek to strengthen themselves inevitably face a competition between an ingrained negative narrative and a new emerging narrative of possibility.[190]

The Friday Gathering provided neighbors with a sorely needed space to come together regularly and share life. We were in contact with each other around the dinner table and in sharing the tasks to prepare the meal and serve it. We began to share stories. Through the repetition of a weekly gathering, intimacy and trust were nurtured.

The Friday Gathering taught us about hospitality. We confronted who would be served, and which needs would be served, too. The movement toward a spirit of unconditional hospitality guided us to share decision-making—power—and to endure with grace the chaotic outbursts that inevitably erupt. This new spirit nourished offshoots that we couldn't have predicted, like Janet's Closet, E-Talks, and Fresh Start Pallet Products. We didn't simply accommodate each other's differences. We began to appreciate that we depend on these differences to make our community whole.

Storytelling and story hearing make the Friday Gathering more than a soup kitchen. The relationships that formed, because of the story sharing and the "fact of contact" for which Martin Luther King, Jr., advocated, changed us into a community where the need to belong can be satisfied. Vivek Murthy, the former surgeon general, makes the point that valuing our differences and the collaborative effort it takes to make the community strong is what binds us together.

> The simple reality is that we no longer have the luxury of thinking and acting tribally. Not only is it becoming harder to isolate ourselves from members of different cultures, but isolation costs us in terms of perspective and experience, which are ever more valuable resources in our global society. ... We may have to make some sacrifices to be part of a community, and that's good. Giving and serving others doesn't just strengthen our communities; it enriches our lives and strengthens our own bonds to the community and our sense of value and purpose.[191]

In many stories, there comes a pivotal moment when things shift, and the trajectory that the characters were following changes direction. That moment could slide past without any notice or impact. But it is magical—blessed, some would say—when the moment arrives and we are inspired and seize it. One of those moments occurred when Bernie's photographs began to fill the walls of the dining hall. It changed the narrative about how neighbors viewed themselves and each other. Diners who had preferred to remain distant were excited to point out their portraits and those of their friends. The collection of portraits was a portrait itself, of community. It inspired a desire, even a need, to know each other more fully.

All along the way—putting up 8" x 10" photographs and taking down mug shots, empowering diners to experiment with offshoots, welcoming gifts of every description, accepting every offer to volunteer, listening to stories without judging, and giving diners control over their narratives—trust was tested. The reward—profound relationships that extend beyond the walls of the church building—is satisfying.

We each decide what is meaningful to us and what is not. Our decisions shape the stories we tell about ourselves and the ones we pay attention to that others tell. As listeners, we become the vessels for each other's memories and witnesses to their lives. In sharing stories, we discover belonging and a new way to imagine the future. There is risk that a story will change us, that we cannot go back to who we were, when it opens up new ways of seeing ourselves and each other.

Epilogue

We have a choice. We can embrace our humanness, which means embracing
our broken natures and the compassion that remains our best hope for healing.
Or we can deny our brokenness, forswear compassion, and, as a result, deny
our own humanity.

Bryan Stevenson, *Just Mercy: A Story of Justice and Redemption*

I began reading stories aloud at the Friday Gathering in the fall of 2019,
when the COVID-19 pandemic was still a few months away. As more diners
agreed to let me share their stories, my own remained private. I wanted to
reciprocate the trust that diners had invested in me but didn't want to take
the spotlight when diners were willing to occupy it. Before I could share my
story, we went into lockdown.

The pandemic put a pause in storytelling but it didn't stop the story
sharing. Diners and I met in the park or in the church garden. These spaces
gave us privacy, and we often lingered for two or more hours at a time. The
interview format that guided the early storytelling gave way to
conversation. We laughed about the pranks that diners had pulled in their
youths, and at their cleverness and their innocence. The laughter opened us
up to sharing some of our longings and heartbreaks, too.

Diners were sometimes curious about my life, but our conversations revolved mostly around their experiences and how they made sense of their place in the world. Kenny was different. He started our get-togethers by demanding that I answer his questions first. He was curious about what motivated me to collect stories, why I wanted to spend so much time with "people like us," as he put it, and what was in it for me. We talked until he was satisfied that he had gotten at my truth, sometimes for as long as an hour, before we turned to his story. Finally, after the Friday Gathering resumed in-person dining, I shared my story with diners.

***

I am a white woman of German ancestry, born in 1955 in St. Louis, Missouri. Before I turned a year old, my parents and I moved to Monroe, Connecticut, where my sister and two brothers were born. At the time, Monroe was a small, rural community of 4,000 people. Our neighborhood was remote enough that we could ride our bikes and play kickball in the street. On weekends, my sister and I packed a lunch and took off on long bicycle rides. We lived within walking distance of a bus line that made it possible for me in my early teens to volunteer at St. Vincent's Hospital in Bridgeport. It was a childhood that juggled innocence and freedom with the threat of the Cuban missile crisis; the assassinations of the Kennedys, Martin Luther King, Jr., and other civil rights leaders; and the Vietnam War. Except for the air-raid drills that we practiced at school, the threats seemed far away. At home, my father's increasing dependence on whiskey was overlooked.

I was six years old when my parents and a few neighbors started a mission Lutheran church in Monroe. My father played hymns for worship services and did the maintenance work on the pastors' cars. On Sundays, I helped him set up chairs for church and Sunday school and then put them all away when services were over. When I was older, I taught Sunday school, was an advisor to the youth group, served on the church council, and played piano for worship services. I was immersed in church. Pastor Charlie Schwarz mentored me, and years after I joined Grace, I learned that Grace is where he grew up. I've often wondered if it was his spirit that drew me there.

My dad's parents moved from Pennsylvania to live with us when I was eight. They were bankrupt and living with little food and no heat, and my father was their only child. In the evenings, I listened to my father work with his parents to distribute their social security checks until all their debts were paid. My father, who was a veteran of World War II, had high standards and expected all of us to do our duty, fulfilling our obligations at home, school, and church.

"I got my first buzz from alcohol when I was nine years old," my brother Timmy said. He is five years younger than me and the youngest of my siblings. He was the pawn in the fights between my parents. While my father's alcoholism was excused because he went to work every day, he considered Timmy's dependence on alcohol, and later drugs, shameful. He said Timmy was an embarrassment to him and that he'd disown him if he and my mother divorced. The yelling and the threats took a toll on all of us. It was Timmy who took the worst of the physical abuse. Timmy told me that he couldn't understand why the neighbors, who could surely hear what was going on, did nothing to help.

Like Paul, who said that a good book is an escape and you can imagine yourself to be anything, I had a big appetite for reading. I devoured every Nancy Drew mystery that I could get my hands on. But my real passion is for true stories. In 1967 when I was twelve, I read Helen Doss's *The Family Nobody Wanted,* and it changed my life. The book is about a couple who adopted twelve children of mixed backgrounds, including Mexican, Native American, Filipino, Asian, and European, who were unwanted because of their ethnicity or disability. The book addressed the racism that the family faced and the ethical issues associated with transracial adoption, matters that would someday challenge me, too.[192] In sixth grade, I announced to my friends that when I was grown, I would adopt children whose circumstances made it difficult to match them with families. This vow became the lens that defined the choices I made as I grew into adulthood. Like the family in the book, I believe that love, not bloodlines, makes a family.

In my early thirties, I adopted three children from Costa Rica, as a single mother. When I had shared my dream of adopting with men I dated, they said, "I won't raise another man's seed." It forced me to choose between marriage and adoption.

I built a career so that I could support a family on my own. I worked first in the pharmaceutical industry, then as an environmental engineer, fields that were heavily male dominated. I was called butch or accused of sleeping my way to the top. I was told that I wasn't eligible for a pay raise that my peers received because men were the breadwinners. There was sexual harassment and sexual assault, and I learned to persevere. I also learned what it feels like to be intimidated and alone.

When I started the adoption process, I faced more discrimination. Again my sexuality was questioned because I was unmarried; single parents were required to pass a psychological evaluation that married couples didn't need to complete. A friend I'd known since childhood refused to write a character reference because, she said, statistics showed that children raised by single mothers are likely to live in poverty, and she couldn't condone that. A few said it was sinful to be a single mother because God intended for children to have two parents. When I adopted my first daughter, immigration officials in Costa Rica questioned whether I was homosexual and delayed our trip home. A few months later, when I returned for the twins, immigration officials asked if I was a prostitute because they couldn't imagine how a single woman could support a family of four. The delays cost us dearly. There were hotel and meal expenses that I couldn't afford as well as the time I had set aside for us to transition before I went back to work and the children went to daycare. It was one thing to treat me like this and another to further stress children who were too young to understand what was happening to them.

As a parent of children who had been abused and neglected, I confronted sexual exploitation, mental health matters, and the impact of separating biological families. It was assumed that the children were conceived illegitimately, and people told me that they were damaged goods and would be nothing but trouble. Strangers questioned the children about why they didn't look like me; the questions were never directed at me even when I was present. Friends told them how lucky they were that I adopted them. What child is born wanting to be adopted? What is lucky about being born into a family where you aren't cherished? Adoption was my dream, not theirs. I am proud of the adults they have become and the families they now parent.

Three years after the adoptions, I reconnected with a college friend and we married. We tried to make it work, but we were mismatched. Raising children, let alone adopted children, was not his dream. As the children grew into teenagers, they needed more attention to help them make sense of their circumstances, and my husband withdrew from us. On our seventh anniversary, we agreed to go our separate ways.

In 2006, I changed careers and moved to Hartford. I was ready for a makeover. The kids were out of the nest and living their lives, I was grieving the sudden death of my best friend, and I was fresh out of graduate school with a degree in education and adult learning. I had my dream job of working in a museum and didn't want to commute a hundred miles a day, so I moved to Hartford. I was excited to embrace city living: walking to work and walking the neighborhoods, immersing myself in different cultures, and making new friends. In Hartford, the fullness of my life's experiences opened me up to the richness of my new community.

I joined Grace in 2008 and the listening committee that was just being formed. My older daughter and her children came with me to the first Christmas Eve dinner in 2010. My seven-year-old grandson's face was featured on the front page of the *Hartford Courant* on Christmas Day. When the Friday Gathering was launched a few weeks later, just like Lamont, I kept coming back until it became a habit.

***

How did I respond to Kenny's questions? First, there is no financial benefit to me. Our story sharing has always been about building community. Any proceeds will be directed to the neighborhood.

But Kenny's questions went deeper. Why stories, why with these people, and what's in it for me? All in all, the answers are the same. Stories get at the essence of being human. It is in the give-and-take of story sharing where I feel most alive.

Helping my children make sense of their lives drew me to the power of storytelling. Receiving each other's stories is some of the most important work that we do as human beings. The significance of this was underscored for me by Daniel Dennett, a philosopher and cognitive scientist at Tufts University.[193] Dennett wrote that as much as it is the nature of spiders to spin webs, it is the nature of humans to spin stories. The stories we tell ourselves and each other are how we develop our sense of who we are and our place in the world.

On the surface, we—the diners and me—had been sharing stories for years. On Friday nights, we chatted during dinner and shared our concerns at the prayer circle. We worshiped together on Sundays, met up in the park during the week, visited when someone was in the hospital, and toured the art museum together. In sharing life, we grew comfortable with each other.

Recording stories was a different matter. These stories were not a simple recounting of the time we spent together. They probed our innermost being and opened us up to exploring what makes us tick. They considered what experiences and relationships have shaped who we are now. We knew that these stories would be shared publicly, at dinner, and later in print. But in the moment, the telling and listening created intimacy between us and affirmed our humanity.

Storytellers need a story listener, someone who will be engaged without prejudging or interrupting. When no one pays attention to our stories, we feel isolated, alone, and painfully disconnected from the people around us. A short exchange with a colleague at Christmastime stirred all those feelings in me. She asked about my holiday. I hesitated because I had spent it alone, without any family. While I thought about how to respond, she said, "Just say it was good," and walked away before I could answer. When we find the people who will receive our stories, we also find belonging.

In the mutual act of telling and listening, I found belonging among the diners. I am comfortable being myself with them. We don't need to impress each other. I can express disappointment when my family doesn't live up to my Norman Rockwell image, and neighbors empathize without belittling me or the people I love. When diners ask how I'm doing and I evade their questions, they insist that I be real with them. They rejoice with me when I take a vacation or go fishing with my grandchildren, and they reach out when I'm tired or stressed. I'm happy to celebrate what satisfies them, too, and to empathize with their struggles.

As I've shared stories about the diners and the Friday Gathering with others, every so often I'm asked, "How has it changed you?" Apart from my relationships and gratitude for our community, my shifting perspective on hospitality makes me look at life differently now. How we express hospitality signals how we value each other and how we assess our relationships.

When the Friday Gathering began, I expected that we—the hosts—would be warm and welcoming, and friendly and courteous. And we were. We smiled, greeted people as they arrived, and learned their names. We were interested in what would put diners at ease. We offered coffee, snacks, music, and time to socialize. Menus featured fresh foods, balanced nutrition, and ethnic variety. Diners were invited to commemorate significant milestones with the community.

But I noticed that how people perceive "warm and welcoming" varies, depending on cultural norms, the depth of trust, and sociability. Etiquette is an example of cultural norms. In Western societies, etiquette is a "conditional" type of hospitality where each party fulfills a role, either the gracious and thoughtful host or the grateful and thoughtful guest. There are norms about what services a good host will offer and norms about what liberties a good guest will—or won't—take. In America's dominant culture, the host sets the boundaries and a proper guest abides by them. There is power in setting boundaries and power in breaching them. When host and guest fulfill their roles accordingly, there is order, predictability, and harmony. Practicing conditional hospitality preserves the status quo.

Alternatively, communities that value diversity and cultivate a sense of belonging gravitate toward "unconditional" hospitality. The hosts are generous, kind, and respectful without expecting that it will be reciprocated. Unconditional hospitality is like *agápē* love, unearned and not based on merit. Unconditional hospitality is a practice—a choice—that is not concerned with the self or with thoughts of being repaid. It benevolently endures interruptions, differences, and inconveniences.[194]

Unconditional hospitality is the antidote for when life gets messy—which it inevitably does—when a diverse group of people come together. The clashes are familiar: egos are threatened, authority is questioned, and words are misunderstood. Emergencies arise, deliveries are late, and equipment fails. We each bring different aptitudes, talents, and states of physical and emotional well-being to the group. At any given moment, hospitality may be tested and our true natures revealed.

Embracing unconditional hospitality taught me how to practice social justice. Although serving dinner doesn't relieve the poverty that so many of our neighbors experience, practicing unconditional hospitality is how we honor their dignity and see them as whole and contributing members of the community. It relieves us of the burdens of being right, being in charge, and planning for every contingency. The spirit of unconditional hospitality compels us to see more than what merely eyes can see. It shapes the quality of our relationships. It is a radical prescription for loving.

The Friday Gathering became my doorway into the city and its many cultures. But it was the story sharing that was transformative. We learn about ourselves when we listen to others' stories, and that learning changes us. Story sharing opened me up to new ways of seeing and thinking about the world. The stories—told and received with dignity—allowed trust to flourish between the diners and me, a trust that is a measure of the bond between us. I am immeasurably grateful that we are part of each other's lives.

Afterword

Although the Friday Gathering continued to serve hot, home-cooked, nutritious meals during the pandemic, the twenty-eight-month pause in sitting down together affected our relationships. After the dining room reopened in July 2022, it was months before more than a few people came regularly. It took time to fathom the effects that social distancing and isolation had levied upon our neighborhood and the Friday Gathering community.

By summer 2021, a year into the pandemic, we acknowledged a shift in attendance. Although the number of meals served was relatively constant, many neighbors we had come to know had stopped attending. I kept in touch with several of them and saw others on my walks around the city. Some had found new meal programs that suited them better and others found new communities to replace what they missed at the Friday Gathering. By the time in-person dining resumed, they had become attached to their new friends. In addition, a few diners had passed away. It wasn't just us, the volunteers, who missed all of them. Their absence was also felt by the diners who remained. The sense of community that had been present before had frayed.

Early on in the pandemic, a tremendous strain was placed on the food supply chain. Producers suffered labor shortages, people shifted to eating at home, and many shelves in grocery stores were barren. Some soup kitchens and pantries closed, and food insecurity increased, especially among low-income people. Foodshare encouraged their clients who remained open to distribute as much food as possible. Grace was recruited for Foodshare's "retail rescue" program and received pantry items and fresh produce that stores needed to remove from their inventories. In addition to the hot meal, we began serving milk, yogurt, tuna fish, cereal, peanut butter, crackers, and similar staples.

It's impossible to know whether offering these items attracted new diners, but it has changed the expectations of the people who come on Fridays. As inflation increased, more people mentioned how difficult it was to make ends meet, and they were grateful for the food we distributed. Even as inflation has started to ease, food insecurity persists in our neighborhood.

Since in-person dining resumed, the Friday Gathering committee and Grace have wrestled with whether to stop offering take-out meals and food staples so we can focus on dining together, or find ways to offer even more. We feel the burdens and challenges that new diners express to us. Our relationships with them are thin; we seldom learn their names, let alone have time to share stories. Offering handouts without getting to know our neighbors and our neighbors coming to know us has shrunk the depth of connection within the Friday Gathering community.

There have been other changes, too. The leadership role that Louisa filled has been taken up by a staff person, and Louisa is now on her own to pursue new projects to beautify the neighborhood. Two chefs turned eighty years old and two more are a few years shy of it. The staffing of Janet's Closet changed, and clothing is no longer available in the hallway on Friday nights. Pastor Rick and his family, although now doing well, have gone through harrowing health ordeals.

It's tempting to conclude that the pandemic forced change upon us. But as the Friday Gathering enters its fourteenth year, it is facing transformation just like any organization would. The first generation of leaders that inspired the Gathering is now complemented with second and third generations of volunteers who bring their own visions and motivations to the program. Although there is sometimes mourning for the people and camaraderie we once experienced, there is also energy and enthusiasm for new ways Grace is called to be in the neighborhood. And there is gratitude that so many people find their way to Grace: to enjoy a meal, chip away at their loneliness, find a way to be useful, and matter to people who matter to them.

Acknowledgments

Gratitude unlocks the fullness of life. It turns what we have into enough, and more.… It can turn a meal into a feast, a house into a home, a stranger into a friend.

—Melody Beattie

Mere words cannot express my immense gratitude to all the people—past and present—who shape the Friday Gathering and make it possible for us to share life, and to all the people who helped me tell these stories. Your trust and generosity made this journey possible.

The seeds for community building were planted in the congregation at Grace Lutheran Church, and I am indebted to them, Pastor Eva, and Pastor Rick for staying the course when they might have chosen to remain isolated, move to the suburbs, or close the church.

Those seeds were nurtured by Gail Morgan Lindstrom, who boldly decided that Grace would host a Christmas Eve dinner for the neighborhood. Gail sponsored me when I joined Grace in 2008 and has been a steady source of spiritual encouragement ever since.

The seeds Gail nurtured fit together with Darrell's and Nancy's commitment to serve dinner every Friday for a year, an action that grew out of the discernment with Pastor Eva and the listening committee. Thank you for your leap of faith.

Thank you to the chefs—Nancy, Louisa, Evelyn, Hilda, Gladys, Louis, Joycelyn, and others; the kitchen helpers; and the musicians. Thank you for turning a meal into a feast.

Bernie's portraits made it possible for us to linger on the faces of our neighbors and to see more fully. It ignited the yearning to authentically know each other. Pastor Rick, Louisa, and Lynn responded to that urge. Thank you for inspiring me to pursue it.

I am deeply grateful to all the people who shared stories. To the early storytellers and the ones whose stories are not in the book, you gave courage to the next wave of storytellers: Neil, Orlando, Danny, Sparky, Nick, Maria, Reinaldo, Igor, Raymond, Roxie, Jackson, and refugees for whom it isn't safe to share their names. To all of you, thank you for the privilege of being your story hearer.

Some storytellers passed away before their narratives were completed. I'm grateful to their family members and friends who contributed remembrances, especially: Leonard, Roy's brother; Judy, Janet's twin sister; and Albert's grandson. Gladys's daughter, Judith, wrote her master's thesis on the legacy of her grandfather, C. C. Bryant, and she generously confirmed the details of their family history as they are presented here.

Thank you, PK Allen. Before there was a book, you encouraged me to write. Thank you, Fengbeiling Wang, for drawing pictures to explain the elements of a story. Thank you, Barb, Leslie Hammond, Ginny Anton, Darrell, Pastor Rick, Gary Vollinger, and Ron McLean, for the conversations that helped me to articulate what I didn't yet have the words to express. Thank you, Ken Johnson, Yvonne Matthews, Michelle McFarland, and Martha-Rea Nelson, for loving Hartford and sharing it with me. Thank you, Joe Eshleman and Hartford Public Library, for helping me with the research and citations. Thank you, Louisa, for your friendship and for showing me how to love our neighbors. Thank you, Lois Arsenault, Ed Brookman, Sondra Chrusciel, Carol Connors, Peter Hinks, Peggy Parisi, and Judy Veach, for reading drafts and encouraging me when doubt crept in.

I am deeply grateful to Dr. Nancy Naples, Board of Trustees Distinguished Professor of Sociology and Women's, Gender, and Sexuality Studies at the University of Connecticut. Your endorsement at the inception of the project meant the world to me and sustained me. Thank you for championing this project before I was convinced of it myself, and for insisting that sharing these stories with a wide audience matters.

I am deeply grateful, too, to Cynthia Rockwell, the former managing editor of the Wesleyan University Magazine, for teaching me to write and sharing all your worldly wisdom. You created a safe space where I could explore what I experienced and learned from the diners and their stories, and guided me to the place where I could write about it. Thank you for seeing past my rough edges.

Nancy and Cynthia steered me to the work of anthropologist Ruth Behar and *The Vulnerable Observer: Anthropology That Breaks Your Heart.* Behar argues that the observer—the recorder of other people's stories—is shaped by their own emotions and experiences. Nancy and Cynthia encouraged me to tap into this reservoir of empathy. Although I did not want to detract from the diners, I wrote about a few of my experiences. Those reflections made it possible to explore some of the nuances and complexities of our social interactions. Thank you for helping me find my voice and the confidence to express it.

My friend Heidi Buatti was my sounding board from the beginning. No one read more words, more iterations, or more revisions than Heidi. Writing is a solitary venture, and there were many days when I was discouraged, lonely, and frustrated. Heidi always knew what to say to get me back on track. Thank you for walking this journey with me.

Thank you, too, to the professional writers and editors who, at critical moments, lent their expertise to the project. Thank you, Marc Fitch, for providing in-depth critiques and mentoring. Your perspective pushed me to dig deeper and be a better writer. Thank you, Linda Tucker, for affirming that these stories resonate beyond our city. Thank you, Leslie Kriesel, for believing in this project and polishing the manuscript. Thank you, Dr. Melissa-Sue John and the staff at Lauren Simone Publishing House, for fulfilling the dream of sharing these stories. Along with Nancy Naples and Cynthia Rockwell, the collaborative spirit that each of you extended to me and the storytellers means the world to me.

Finally, to my children, Pilar, Elizabeth, and Michael, thank you from the bottom of my heart. You are my dreams come true, and my life is richer beyond imagination because you are in it.

Notes

Author's Note

1. Ibram X. Kendi, *How to Be an Antiracist* (New York: One World, 2019), 37–8.

2. Drew G. I. Hart, *Trouble I've Seen: Changing the Way the Church Views Racism* (Harrisonburg, VA: Herald Press, 2016), 21.

Introduction

3. "U.S. Census Bureau QuickFacts: Connecticut, Per capita income in past 12 months (in 2022 dollars), 2018-2022," accessed January 1, 2024, https://www.census.gov/quickfacts/fact/table/avontowncapitalplanningr...owncapitolplanningregionconnecticut,hartfordcityconnecticut/I NC910222.

4. Jacob Sweet, "The Loneliness Pandemic: The Psychology and Social Costs of Isolation in Everyday Life," *Harvard Magazine*, January-February 2021, https://www.harvardmagazine.com/2020/12/feature-the-loneliness-pandemic.

5. John T. Cacioppo and William Patrick, *Loneliness: Human Nature and the Need for Social Connection* (New York: Norton, 2008), 30.

6. Cacioppo and Patrick, *Loneliness*, 5.

7. Vivek H. Murthy, MD, *Together: The Healing Power of Human Connection in a Sometimes Lonely World* (New York: HarperCollins, 2020), 51.

8. Murthy, *Together*, 23.

Chapter 1: What They Thought They Knew

9. Drawn from church records including commemoratives written for the congregation's 75th anniversary, November 1969 and "Amazing Grace: Yesterday, Today, Tomorrow," *Centennial*, October 2, 1994.

10. "In U.S., Decline of Christianity Continues at Rapid Pace," PEW Research Center, October 17, 2019, https://www.pewforum.org/2019/10/17/in-u-s-decline-of-christianity-continues-at-rapid-pace/; Jeffrey M. Jones, "U.S. Church Membership Falls Below Majority for First Time," *Gallup*, March 29, 2021, https://news.gallup.com/poll/341963/church-membership-falls-below-majority-first-time.aspx; Nicole Radziszewski, "The Shrinking Church: Congregations Look for Solutions as They Face Declines in Membership, Attendance," *Living Lutheran*, January 7, 2013, https://www.livinglutheran.org/2013/01/shrinking-church/; Stated in the 75th anniversary (November 1969) commemorative: "The year 1957 marked the high point in membership with 713 confirmed and 918 baptized members."

11. Quoted statements are responses recorded during the survey.

12. Susan Campbell, *Frog Hollow: Stories from an American Neighborhood* (Middletown, CT: Wesleyan University Press, 2019), ix.

13. Mara Lee, "At Grace Lutheran Church, A Big Helping of Fellowship on Christmas Eve," *Hartford Courant*, December 25, 2010.

Chapter 2: Delving into Our Neighborhood and Challenging Perceptions

14. "History of Early Hartford," Society of the Descendants of the Founders of Hartford, accessed March 5, 2024, https://www.foundersofhartford.org/historic-hartford/history-of-early-hartford/; Susan Campbell, *Frog Hollow: Stories from an American Neighborhood* (Middletown, CT: Wesleyan University Press, 2019), 10–36; Ellsworth S. Grant and Marion H. Grant, *The City of Hartford 1784–1984: An Illustrated History* (Hartford: Connecticut Historical Society, 1986), 47–53; Louise B. Simmons, *Organizing in Hard Times* (Philadelphia: Temple University Press, 1994), 6–8; Andrew Walsh, "Hartford: A Global History," *in Confronting Urban Legacy: Rediscovering Hartford and New England's Forgotten Cities*, eds. Xiangming Chen and Nick Bacon (Lanham, MD: Lexington Books, 2013), 21–45.

15. "American School for the Deaf," Hartford on the Brain, Trinity College Commons, accessed May 19, 2021, https://commons.trincoll.edu/hartfordbrain/2021/12/08/american-school-for-the-deaf/.

16. Ken Johnson, Executive Director of the Northside Institutions Neighborhood Alliance, Inc. (NINA), generously contributed to the descriptions of buildings and architecture; see https://ninahartford.org.

17. Gregory E. Andrews and David F. Ransom, *Structures and Styles: Guided Tours of Hartford Architecture* (Hartford: Connecticut Historical Society, 1988), 143–149.

18. The Goodwin Castle "reception room" was preserved and can be viewed at the Wadsworth Atheneum Museum of Art.

19. "Grace Lutheran Church to Launch $75,000 Drive for New Building," *The Hartford Times*, April 27, 1946.

20. "Grace Lutheran Church, Hartford (1951)," Historic Buildings of Connecticut, accessed June 9, 2020, https://historicbuildingsct.com/grace-lutheran-church-1951/.

21. "History of Asylum Hill," Asylum Hill Neighborhood Association, accessed January 4, 2022, https://www.asylumhill.org/history-of-asylum-hill.html.

22. "Final Asylum Hill Strategic Plan 2022 – 2031," Asylum Hill Neighborhood Association, March 7, 2022, 7, https://www.asylumhill.org/uploads/1/2/9/7/129735110/ahna-strategic_plan_final-03-7-22.pdf.

23. Rev. Sarah McLean, report to the Asylum Hill Christian Community, May 1991, in the archives of Grace Lutheran Church. The Asylum Hill Christian Community, a collaboration among six churches, was "an ecumenical organization with multiple purposes responding to the multiplicity of needs and issues raised in the complex neighborhood which is Asylum Hill."

24. Grace Lutheran 75th Anniversary commemorative, November 1969.

25. "History," NINA: Revitalizing Asylum Hill, accessed March 23, 2022, https://ninahartford.org/about/Nina/.

26. "History of Asylum Hill," accessed March 23, 2022, https://www.asylumhill.org/history-of-asylum-hill.html.

27. Kelly Davilla, Coral Wonderly, and Mark Abraham, "Hartford Neighborhood Changes 2010 to 2020," DataHaven, March 5, 2022, https://ctdatahaven.org/hartford-neighborhood-changes-2010-2020; "QuickFacts: Hartford City, Connecticut," United States Census Bureau, November 5, 2022, https://www.census.gov/quickfacts/fact/table/hartfordcityconnecticut/PST045222#PST045222; "Population of North East, Hartford, Connecticut (Neighborhood)," Statistical Atlas, March 5, 2022, https://statisticalatlas.com/neighborhood/Connecticut/Hartford/North-East/Population.

28. "Final Asylum Hill Strategic Plan," 10; "QuickFacts: Hartford City, Connecticut," United States Census Bureau, accessed November 5, 2022, https://www.census.gov/quickfacts/fact/table/hartfordcityconnecticut/PST045222#PST045222; "QuickFacts Connecticut," United States Census Bureau, accessed November 5, 2022, https://www.census.gov/quickfacts/CT.

29. "Final Asylum Hill Strategic Plan," 10.

30. "Final Asylum Hill Strategic Plan," 29.

31. Simmons, *Organizing*, 3; Walsh, "Hartford: A Global History," 35.

32. Walsh, "Hartford: A Global History," 36.

33. "Case: Sheff V. O'Neill," Legal Defense Fund, accessed March 10, 2022, https://www.naacpldf.org/case-issue/sheff-v-oneill/; "Sheff v. O'Neill," Center for Children's Advocacy, accessed March 10, 2022, https://cca-ct.org/sheff/.

34. Simmons, *Organizing*, 35–36.

35. "Refugee Resettlement in Connecticut," Refugee Council USA, accessed March 10, 2022, https://rcusa.org/wp-content/uploads/2019/01/2019ConnecticutRCUSA.pdf.

36. McLean, report to the Asylum Hill Christian Community.

37. Median household income is a five year estimate as of 2021. Asylum Hill census tracts are 5031.01 and 5031.02, and the Downtown census tract is 5021, per "2020 Census – Census Tract Reference Map: Hartford County, CT," United States Census Bureau, modified 2021-02-08, https://www2.census.gov/geo/maps/DC2020/PL20/st09_ct/censustract_maps/c09003_hartford/DC20CT_C09003.pdf; Median household income by census tract: "S1901 Income in the past 12 months (in 2021 inflation-adjusted dollars)," United States Census Bureau, accessed March 7, 2023, https://data.census.gov/table?g=1400000US09003502100&tid=ACSST5Y2021.S1901.

38. "QuickFacts Hartford City, Connecticut," United States Census Bureau, accessed February 25, 2023, https://www.census.gov/quickfacts/fact/table/hartfordcityconnecticut/PST045222#PST045222; "QuickFacts Connecticut; United States," United States Census Bureau, accessed March 4, 2023, https://www.census.gov/quickfacts/fact/table/CT,US/PST045221.

39. Chase Sackett, "Neighborhoods and Violent Crime," U.S. Department of Housing and Urban Development, Summer 2016, https://www.huduser.gov/portal/periodicals/em/summer16/highlight2.html.

40. Regina Austin, "'The Shame of it All': Stigma and the Political Disenfranchisement of Formerly Convicted and Incarcerated Persons," *All Faculty Scholarship* (2004), 615, https://scholarship.law.upenn.edu/faculty_scholarship/615.

41. Bernard Weiner, "On Sin Versus Sickness: A Theory of Perceived Responsibility and Social Motivation," *The American Psychologist* 48 (September 1993), https://www.researchgate.net/publication/14984194_On_Sin_Versus_Sickness_A_Theory_of_Perceived_Responsibility_and_Social_Motivation; Bernard Weiner, Danny Osborne, and Udo Rudolph, "An Attributional Analysis of Reactions to Poverty: The Political Ideology of

the Giver and the Perceived Morality of the Receiver," *Personality and Social Psychology Review* 15, no. 2 (November 2011): 199–213, https://www.researchgate.net/publication/47644820_An_Attributional_Analysis_of_Reactions_to_Poverty_The_Political_Ideology_of_the_Giver_and_the_Perceived_Morality_of_the_Receiver/link/02e7e51826257e1bcb000000/download.

42. Matthew Desmond, *Evicted: Poverty and Profit in the American* City (New York: Broadway Books, 2016), 240.

43. Desmond, *Evicted*, 241.

44. Chimamanda Ngozi Adichie, "The Danger of a Single Story," filmed July 2009, Oxford, England, video, 12:45, https://www.ted.com/talks/chimamanda_ngozi_adichie_the_danger_of_a_single_story/.

45. "Social Eating Connects Communities," University of Oxford News and Events, March 16, 2017, https://www.ox.ac.uk/news/2017-03-16-social-eating-connects-communities; David Myers, "The Social Significance of a Shared Meal," Macmillan Learning, April 12, 2019, https://community.macmillanlearning.com/t5/talk-psych-blog/the-social-significance-of-a-shared-meal/ba-p/5761.

46. McLean, report to the Asylum Hill Christian Community.

Chapter 3: Sharing Meals, Sharing Gifts, and Sharing Stories

47. Virginia Woolf, *A Room of One's Own* (New York: Harcourt Brace, 1989), 18.

48. Foodshare suspended cost-sharing in early 2020 at the start of the COVID-19 pandemic; see https://www.ctfoodshare.org.

49. Bernie Michel, "Portraits of Divinity in a Soup Kitchen," Sri Sathya Sai International Organization – USA, accessed March 21, 2022, https://sathyasai.us/slia/region01/portraits-in-a-soup-kitchen.

50. "Paul Tillich (1886-1965)," ed. Derek Michaud, Boston Collaborative Encyclopedia of Western Theology, accessed May 22, 2022, https://people.bu.edu/wwildman/bce/tillich.htm.

51. Pastor Eva, email correspondence, August 17, 2021.

Chapter 4: Building Trust

52. From William Mather Lewis, "Abiding Values," *Vital Speeches of the Day* I (1935).

53. Lynn Johnson, "The Gatherings of Grace: The Beloved Community at Grace Evangelical Lutheran Church, Hartford, Connecticut," [unpublished] 2016-2017.

54. Leslie Jamison, *The Empathy Exams* (Minneapolis: Graywolf Press, 2014), 23.

55. Jamison, *The Empathy Exams*, 23.

56. "Malcolm Gladwell—How to Be Truly Empathetic," December 23, 2019, YouTube, video, 0:26, https://www.youtube.com/watch?v=z6AlEfbE4RU.

57. "The Lion And The Hunter," accessed September 23, 2022, http://thelionandthehunter.org/about-this-project/.

58. Tammy Erickson, "My Father's Greatest Gift: Multiple Truths," *Harvard Business Review*, June 15, 2010, https://hbr.org/2010/06/multiple-versions-of-truth-my.

59. Pastor Rick, email correspondence, April 19, 2022.

Chapter 5: Our Truest Dignity

60. Alvin Powell, "For Disabled, Jobs Light Their Way," *Hartford Courant*, April 7, 1983.

61. Susan Campbell, "The Other Side of Mental Illness: The Prejudices," *Hartford Courant*, November 2, 1992.

62. "Volunteer of the Month," Asylum Hill Neighborhood Association, July 2018.

63. "Oral History of a Migration from Jamaica," *Hartford Courant*, July 5, 1995, updated December 6, 2018; https://www.courant.com/news/connecticut/hc-xpm-1995-07-05-9507040066-story.html.

64. Tom Keyser, "A Tribute to a Victim of Gun Violence Ground Near Where 6-Year-Old Was Slain To Be Named 'Tiffany Square,'" *Baltimore Sun*, August 23, 1991, https://www.baltimoresun.com/news/bs-xpm-1991-08-23-1991235178-story.html.

65. "Food, Shelter, Housing and Education with Compassion, Dignity and Respect," The House of Bread, accessed January 16, 2022, https://www.hobread.org/?p=63.

66. Proverbs 3:27-28 (NRSV).

67. Pastor Rick, email correspondence, October 16, 2020.

Chapter 6: Honoring the Struggle

68. Psalm 121:8 (NRSV).

69. Renamed in 2021 the Hartford International University for Religion and Peace; see https://www.hartfordinternational.edu/about/our-recent-name-change.

70. Pastor Rick, "Saying Goodbye," Grace Notes, December 2017–January 2018, 4.

71. "Albert E. Bell," Find a Grave® Memorials, accessed January 24, 2022, https://www.findagrave.com/memorial/198874897/albert-e-bell.

72. Joseph I. Lieberman, email correspondence, January 17, 2020.

73. Mary Otto and Constance Neyer, "Sand Struggles with Realities," *Hartford Courant*, March 7, 1993; Mike McGarry, "Remembering Albert Bell," *The Hartford News*, January 4–11, 2018, 2.

74. Personal correspondence, November 25, 2021.

75. "The Passing of Albert Bell," *The Hartford News*, January 4–11, 2018, 4.

76. "The Passing of Albert Bell," 4.

77. Pastor Rick, "Saying Goodbye," 4.

78. McGarry, "Remembering Albert Bell," 2.

79. Personal correspondence, November 25, 2021.

80. McGarry, "Remembering Albert Bell," 2.

81. Pastor Rick, "Saying Goodbye," 4.

Chapter 7: For the Enjoyment of Others

82. Michael L. Millenson, "For Tiny Infants, Too Much Oxygen Can Mean Blindness. Too Little Means Death," Health & Science, *The Washington Post*, November 16, 2015, https://www.washingtonpost.com/national/health-science/for-tiny-infants-too-much-oxygen-can-mean-blindness-too-little-death/2015/11/16/40128dba-691a-11e5-9ef3-fde182507cac_story.html.

83. "Volunteer of the Month," Asylum Hill Neighborhood Association, February 2019.

84. "Janet Dudek," Obituary, *Hartford Courant*, January 23, 2019.

85. Martin Luther King, Jr., "What Is Your Life's Blueprint?" filmed October 26, 1967 at Barratt Junior High School, Philadelphia, PA, video, 10:49, https://www.youtube.com/watch?v=ZmtOGXreTOU.

86. Oliver Sacks, *Musicophilia* (New York: Knopf, 2007), 245.

87. Sacks, *Musicophilia*, 246.

88. Cathy Malchiodi, "Please Don't Take My Collective Effervescence Away: Synchrony and Entrainment Are Key Rhythmic Factors in Health and Well-Being," *Psychology Today*, August 1, 2021, https://www.psychologytoday.com/us/blog/arts-and-health/202108/please-don-t-take-my-collective-effervescence-away; Adam Grant, "There's a Specific Kind of Joy We've Been Missing," Sunday Opinion, New York Times, July 10, 2021, https://www.nytimes.com/2021/07/10/opinion/Sunday/covid-group-emotions-happiness.html.

Chapter 8: Keeping the Doors Open During the Pandemic

89. Jacqueline Novogratz, *"The Opposite of Poverty,"* Acumen: ideas, accessed March 10, 2022, https://acumenideas.com/the-opposite-of-poverty-8534d6fa7102.

90. The New Britain State Teachers College became Central Connecticut State College in 1959 and acquired university status in 1983; see https://centralconnecticut.stateuniversity.com.

91. Christine Palm, "Urban Oasis," *Hartford Courant*, December 12, 2004.

92. "Group to Honor 'Movers & Shakers,'" *Hartford Courant*, May 31, 2005.

93. Marietta Vazquez, "Calling COVID-19 the 'Wuhan Virus' or 'China Virus' is Inaccurate and Xenophobic," Yale School of Medicine, March 12, 2020, https://medicine.yale.edu/news-article/23074/.

94. Darrell, email correspondence, March 28, 2022.

Chapter 9: I Can Do It Myself

95. Nancy O. Albert, "A Tale of Two Cities: The Rise & Fall of Public Housing," *Connecticut Explored*, Winter 2003, https://www.ctexplored.org/a-tale-of-two-cities-the-rise-fall-of-public-housing/; Bellevue Square was a 1941 500-unit public housing project.

96. "What is Job Corps?" U.S. Department of Labor: Employment and Training Administration, accessed March 21, 2022, https://www.dol.gov/agencies/eta/jobcorps.

97. Emily Dickinson, "There Is No Frigate Like a Book," Poetry Foundation, accessed March 6, 2022, https://www.poetryfoundation.org/poems/52199/there-is-no-frigate-like-a-book-1286.

98. "Amniotic Band Syndrome," Boston Children's Hospital, accessed December 14, 2021, https://www.childrenshospital.org/conditions-and-treatments/conditions/a/amniotic-band-syndrome.

99. The polio vaccine became available in 1955. "History of Polio: Outbreaks and Vaccine Timeline," Mayo Foundation for Medical Education and Research, accessed December 14, 2021, https://www.mayoclinic.org/coronavirus-covid-19/history-disease-outbreaks-vaccine-timeline/polio.

100. "Widows' Homes (1865)," Historic Buildings of Connecticut, accessed December 14, 2021, https://historicbuildingsct.com/widows-homes-1865/.

101. Maya Angelou, "Caged Bird," Poetry Foundation, accessed February 10, 2023, https://www.poetryfoundation.org/poems/48989/caged-bird.

102. Amber O'Neal Johnston, *A Place to Belong: Celebrating Diversity and Kinship in the Home* (New York: Penguin, 2022), 2.

103. Claudia Mazzucco, "Claudia Mazzucco: Living with the Effects of Autism," The Art of Autism, April 13, 2015, https://the-art-of-autism.com/claudia-mazzucco-living-with-the-effects-of-auti.

104. Claudia, email correspondence August 7, 2021.

105. Mazzucco, "Living with the Effects of Autism."

106. Claudia Mazzucco, "Lost in Autism, Found by Golf," *Golf Digest* 64, no. 7 (July 2013), https://www.golfdigest.com/story/golf-saved-my-life-claudia-mazzucco.

107. Mazzucco, "Lost in Autism."

108. The Sisters of Mercy are an international community of Roman Catholic women who advocate for people in need; see https://www.sistersofmercy.org.

109. Mazzucco, "Living with the Effects of Autism."

110. Claudia Mazzucco, "Autism in the Time of COVID-19," Cortical Chauvinism, June 8, 2020, https://corticalchauvinism.com/2020/06/08/autism-in-the-time-of-covid-19/.

111. Mazzucco, "Autism in the Time of COVID-19."

112. "In Hartford Seminary Library, Immigrant Finds Haven to Overcome Challenges," *Hartford Courant*, May 16, 2016.

113. Claudia, email correspondence, August 7, 2021.

114. Bradley S. Klein, "Claudia," *The Golfer's Journal* 16 (June 2021): 79–80.

115. Mazzucco, "Living with the Effects of Autism."

Chapter 10: Belonging to Each Other

116. Words and Music by Bob Montgomery.

117. "Born with the veil," or "en caul," refers to a fetus born with the amniotic sac intact. Carroll Y. Rich, "Born with the Veil: Black Folklore in Louisiana," *The Journal of American Folklore* 89, no. 353 (1976): 328.

118. Jeffrey R. Backstrand and Stephen Schensul, "Co-Evolution in an Outlying Ethnic Community: The Puerto Ricans of Hartford, Connecticut," *Urban Anthropology* 11, no. 1 (1982): 16.

119. Backstrand and Schensul, "Co-Evolution in an Outlying Ethnic Community," 16.

120. Susan Campbell, *Frog Hollow: Stories from an American Neighborhood* (Middletown, CT: Wesleyan University Press, 2019), 110.

121. "Another Shoddy Chapter in Public Housing," *Hartford Courant*, January 3, 1953.

122. Maritza Fernandez, "Hartford, Connecticut Riot (1969)," Blackpast.org, March 1, 2018, https://www.blackpast.org/african-american-history/hartford-connecticut-riot-1969/; "Not Guilty, Says Black Caucus—Violence Was Already There," *Hartford Courant*, September 21, 1967.

123. "Evaluation of the Urban Initiatives Anti-Crime Program, Hartford, CT, Case Study," Prepared for U.S. Department of Housing and Urban Development, Office of Policy Development and Research, 1984, 5, https://www.huduser.gov/Publications/pdf/HUD-004060.pdf.

124. The Harwood Institute for Public Innovation in partnership with United Way of Central and Northeastern Connecticut, "Creating a Safer, More Connected Asylum Hill: How to Accelerate and Deepen Meaningful Conversations and Collaborative Efforts," September 2013, 11.

125. The Harwood Institute, 7.

Chapter 11: Home Is Where One Starts From

126. *The Green Mile*, directed by Frank Darabont (1999; Burbank, CA: Warner Bros. and Universal Pictures), "Graham Greene: Arlen Bitterbuck," IMDb, https://www.imdb.com/title/tt0120689/characters/nm0001295.

127. "History," Boys Town, accessed March 23, 2022, https://www.boystown.org/about.

Chapter 12: Changing What We Cannot Accept

128. "Medgar Evers," NAACP, accessed March 23, 2022, https://naacp.org/find-resources/history-explained/civil-rights-leaders/medgar-evers.

129. "Robert Parris Moses," The Martin Luther King, Jr. Research and Education Institute, Stanford, CA, accessed March 23, 2022, https://kinginstitute.stanford.edu/encyclopedia/moses-robert-parris.

130. "C.C. Bryant," Digital SNCC Gateway, accessed March 23, 2022, https://sncdigital.org/people/c-c-bryant/; Ted Ownby, "C.C. Bryant (1917-2007) Activist," Mississippi Encyclopedia, https://mississippiencyclopedia.org/entries/cc-bryant/.

131. Judith E. Barlow Roberts, "C.C. Bryant: A Race Man Is What They Called Him" (master's thesis, University of Mississippi, 2012), https://egrove.olemiss.edu/etd/248.

132. "Thurgood Marshall," NAACP, accessed March 23, 2022, https://naacp.org/find-resources/history-explained/civil-rights-leaders/thurgood-marshall.

133. Kelly A. Spring, "Ruby Hurley (1908-1980)," National Women's History Museum, 2017, https://www.womenshistory.org/education-resources/biographies/ruby-hurley.

134. "Who Was Julius Rosenwald?" Julius Rosenwald & Rosenwald Schools National Historic Park Campaign, https://www.rosenwaldpark.org/julius-rosenwald; Lory Hough, "Forgotten Schools Remembered," *Harvard Ed. Magazine*, Fall 2009, https://issuu.com/harvardeducation/docs/ed_fall_09; Daniel Aaronson and Bhashkar Mazumder, "The Impact of Rosenwald Schools on Black Achievement," Federal Reserve Bank of Chicago, October 2009, https://files.eric.ed.gov/fulltext/ED509827.pdf.

135. Stephanie Deutsch, "Rosenwald Fellows and the Journey to Brown v. Board of Education," National Trust for Historic Preservation, August 11, 2020, https://savingplaces.org/stories/rosenwald-fellows-and-the-journey-to-brown-v-board-of-education#.YV76nS2cZ-U.

136. Amy Schmidt, "McComb Civil Rights Movement," Mississippi Encyclopedia, accessed March 23, 2022, https://mississippiencyclopedia.org/entries/mccomb-civil-rights-movement/; "Civil Rights Incidents in McComb," Civil Rights Movement Archive, https://www.crmvet.org/info/mccomb1964.pdf; Robert S. McElvaine, "'Operation Mississippi Freedom': When State-Sponsored Terrorism was American," Origins: Current Events in Historical Perspective, The Ohio State University, June 2005, https://origins.osu.edu/history-news/operation-mississippi-freedom-when-state-sponsored-terrorism-was-american?language_content_entity=en.

137. "Memo: re Three Bombings in McComb, Miss," and "Affidavit of C.C. Bryant," Civil Rights Movement Documents, McComb & Pike County MS, 1961-66, accessed March 23, 2022, https://www.crmvet.org/docs/pikedocs.htm.

138. Barlow Roberts, "C.C. Bryant, A Race Man," 68–69.

139. Andrew Walsh, "Hartford: A Global History," in *Confronting Urban Legacy: Rediscovering Hartford and New England's Forgotten Cities*, eds. Xiangming Chen and Nick Bacon (New York: Lexington Books, 2013), 35.

140. Fiona Vernal and James Kolb, "How Hartford's North End Became an African American Community," *Connecticut Explored*, Fall 2022, https://www.ctexplored.org/how-hartfords-north-end-became-an-african-american-community/; Nancy O. Albert, "A Tale of Two Cities: The Rise & Fall of Public Housing," *Connecticut Explored*, Winter 2003, https://www.ctexplored.org/a-tale-of-two-cities-the-rise-fall-of-public-housing/.

141. Walsh, "Hartford: A Global History," 38.

142. Vanessa de la Torre, "Hartford Photo Exhibit Stirs Memories of '60s Riots," Connecticut Public Radio, March 1, 2019, https://www.ctpublic.org/arts-and-culture/2019-03-01/hartford-photo-exhibit-stirs-memories-of-60s-riots.

143. *Dictionary.com*, s.v. "semicolon tattoo," accessed March 23, 2022, https://www.dictionary.com/e/pop-culture/semicolon-tattoo/.

144. Rebecca Solnit, "Silence and Powerlessness Go Hand in Hand—Women's Voices Must be Heard," *The Guardian*, March 8, 2017, https://www.theguardian.com/commentisfree/2017/mar/08/silence-powerlessness-womens-voices-rebecca-solnit.

Chapter 13: The Grief of Things as They Are

145. Urban Alliance is a nonprofit that supports churches and other organization in their efforts to serve their communities; see https://www.urbanalliance.com.

146. *Encyclopedia Britannica Online*, s.v. "charity," September 13, 2016, https://www.britannica.com/topic/charity-Christian-concept; *New World Encyclopedia*, s.v. "agape," accessed August 3, 2021, https://www.newworldencyclopedia.org/entry/Agape.

147. The Greater Hartford Interfaith Action Alliance engages diverse faith-based and allied organizations in organizing actions for social justice; see https://cljct.org/ghiaa/.

148. "Clean Slate," CONECT: Congregations Organized for a New Connecticut, accessed September 11, 2021, http://www.weconect.org/clean-slate-2/; Tom Hopkins, "Clean Slate: Connecticut's New Pathway to Automatic Pardons," Inside Investigator, October 2, 2022, https://insideinvestigator.org/clean-slate-connecticuts-new-path-to-automatic-pardons/.

149. Jennifer Proto, "State Liens on Real Property of Public Assistance Recipients," Office of Legislative Research, February 20, 2020, https://www.cga.ct.gov/2020/rpt/pdf/2020-R-0051.pdf.

150. "Welfare Liens," Center for Leadership & Justice, accessed March 9, 2024, https://cljct.org/welfare-liens/.

151. Keith M. Phaneuf, "House Democratic leaders want to repeal CT's 'poverty tax,'" *CT Mirror*, January 27, 2021, https://ctmirror.org/2021/01/27/house-democratic-leaders-want-to-repeal-cts-poverty-tax/.

152. Jane Addams, "Charity and Social Justice," *The North American Review* 192, no. 656 (1910): 68–81.

153. Louise Carroll Wade, "Settlement Houses," *Encyclopedia of Chicago*, accessed September 11, 2021, http://www.encyclopedia.chicagohistory.org/pages/1135.html.

154. Rima Lunin Schultz,"Hull-House and 'Jim Crow,'" in *Hull House Songs: The Music of Protest and Hope in Jane Addams's Chicago*, ed. Eleanor Smith. Series: Studies in Critical Social Sciences, Volume 131 (Leiden: Brill, 2018), https://brill.com/view/book/9789004384057/BP000009.xml; Charles Hounmenou, "Black Settlement Houses and Oppositional Consciousness," *Journal of Black Studies* 43, no. 6 (September 2012): 646–666, https://www.jstor.org/stable/23414663; John E. Hansan, "Settlement Houses: An Introduction," VCU Libraries Social Welfare History Project, accessed August 3, 2021, https://socialwelfare.library.vcu.edu/settlement-houses/settlement-houses/.

155. Addams, "Charity and Social Justice," 68–81.

156. Addams, "Charity and Social Justice," 68.

157. Mark Winne, *Closing the Food Gap: Resetting the Table in the Land of Plenty* (Boston: Beacon Press, 2008), 70.

158. "Our History," Feeding America, accessed July 18, 2021, https://www.feedingamerica.org/about-us/our-history.

159. "How We Fight Food Waste in the US," Feeding America, accessed July 27, 2021, https://www.feedingamerica.org/our-work/our-approach/reduce-food-waste.

160. Janet Poppendieck, *Breadlines Knee-Deep in Wheat* (New Brunswick, NJ: Rutgers University Press, 1986), xiii.

161. David Yaffe-Bellany and Michael Corkery, "Dumped Milk, Smashed Eggs, Plowed Vegetables: Food Waste of the Pandemic," *New York Times*, April 11, 2020, https://www.nytimes.com/2020/04/11/business/coronavirus-destroying-food.html.

162. Victor Oliveira, Mark Prell, Laura Tiehen, and David Smallwood, "Design Issues in USDA's Supplemental Nutrition Assistance Program: Looking Ahead by Looking Back," U.S. Department of Agriculture Economic Research Service, Economic Research Report Number 243 (ERR-243), January 2018, 51, https://www.ers.usda.gov/webdocs/publications/86924/err-243.pdf?v=0.

163. Doug O'Brien et al., "Hunger in America: The Definitions, Scope, Causes, History and Status of the Problem of Hunger in the United States," Congressional Hunger Center, 2004, https://www.hungercenter.org/publications/hunger-in-america-the-definitions-scope-causes-history-and-status-of-the-problem-of-hunger-in-the-united-states/.

164. Poppendieck, *Breadlines Knee-Deep in Wheat*, xvi.

165. Nina Lakhani, "'The Food System is Racist': An Activist Used a Garden to Tackle Inequities," *The Guardian*, May 25, 2021, https://www.theguardian.com/environment/2021/may/25/karen-washington-garden-of-happiness-us-food-system.

Chapter 14: Something We Must Create

166. "Social Privilege: The Flipside of Oppression," Studio Theatre, accessed March 4, 2021, https://www.studiotheatre.org/plays/play-detail/2016-2017-straight-white-men/social-privilege; Peggy McIntosh, "White Privilege: Unpacking the Invisible Knapsack," The National Seed Project, accessed March 4, 2021, https://nationalseedproject.org/Key-SEED-Texts/white-privilege-unpacking-the-invisible-knapsack.

167. Robert P. Jones, *The Hidden Roots of White Supremacy and the Path to a Shared American Future* (New York: Simon and Schuster, 2023), 19–20.

168. Rev. Kenneth W. Wheeler, US: *The Resurrection of American Terror* (Los Angeles: Precocity Press, 2023), 173.

169. Drew G. I. Hart, *Trouble I've Seen: Changing the Way the Church Views Racism* (Harrisonburg, VA: Herald Press, 2016), 19–20.

170. Jemar Tisby, "Justice Takes Sides: Why Neutrality Is Arrogance and Action Is Required," *Footnotes by Jemar Tisby*, September 20, 2023, https://jemartisby.substack.com/p/justice-takes-sides.

171. Howard Thurman, *Jesus and the Disinherited* (Boston: Beacon, 1976), 18.

172. Thurman, *Jesus and the Disinherited*, 18.

173. Thurman, *Jesus and the Disinherited*, xiv.

174. Willie Garrett, "Marginalized Populations," Minnesota Psychological Association, accessed March 4, 2021, https://www.mnpsych.org/index.php?option=com_dailyplanetblog&view=entry&category=division%20news&id=71:marginalized-populations; J. M. Sevelius et al., "Research with Marginalized Communities: Challenges to Continuity During the COVID-19 Pandemic," *AIDS and Behavior* 24 (May 16, 2020): https://doi.org/10.1007/s10461-020-02920-3.

175. Thurman, *Jesus and the Disinherited*, xiv.

176. Thurman, *Jesus and the Disinherited*, 19.

177. Thurman, *Jesus and the Disinherited*, 88.

178. Hart, *Trouble I've Seen*, 168–69.

179. Hart, *Trouble I've Seen*, 177.

180. Martin Luther King, Jr., *Where Do We Go from Here: Chaos or Community?* (Boston: Beacon, 2010), 28.

181. Rachel Lapp, "Vincent Harding: King for the 21st Century Calls Us to Walk with Jesus," Goshen College, January 21, 2005, https://www.goshen.edu/news/2005/01/21/vincent-harding-king-for-the-21st-century-calls-us-to-walk-with-jesus-2.

Chapter 15 From Seeds of Desire

182. "Volunteer of the Month—E. Talks at Grace," Asylum Hill Neighborhood Association, March 2020.

183. See https://www.freshstartpalletproducts.org.

184. "Muhammad Yunus Biographical," The Nobel Prize, accessed December 21, 2021, https://www.nobelprize.org/prizes/peace/2006/yunus/biographical/.

185. "Muhammad Yunus Nobel Lecture," The Nobel Prize, accessed December 21, 2021, https://www.nobelprize.org/prizes/peace/2006/yunus/lecture/.

Chapter 16: What Community Looks Like

186. Diana Bruk, "12 Beautiful Life Lessons Mr. Rogers Taught Us," *Good Housekeeping*, December 5, 2014, https://www.goodhousekeeping.com/life/inspirational-stories/a22776/life-lessons-mrrogers/.

187. "Love Your Block Hartford," The City of Hartford, accessed August 29, 2021, https://www.hartford.gov/Government/Departments/Mayors-Office/Mayor-Initiatives/LYB-Hartford#section-1.

188. "Speak Truth to Power: A Quaker Search for an Alternative to Violence," Prepared for the American Friends Service Committee, March 2, 1955, accessed August 29, 2021, https://afsc.org/sites/default/files/documents/21955%20Speak%20Truth%20To%20Power%20-%20Publication.pdf.

189. "About," Our Piece of the Pie – Hartford, accessed August 21, 2021, https://opp.org/about/.

190. The Harwood Institute for Public Innovation in partnership with United Way of Central and Northeastern Connecticut, "Creating a Safer, More Connected Asylum Hill: How to Accelerate and Deepen Meaningful Conversations and Collaborative Efforts," September 2013, 14.

191. Vivek H. Murthy, MD, *Together: The Healing Power of Human Connection in a Sometimes Lonely World* (New York: HarperCollins, 2020), 96.

Epilogue

192. "*The Family Nobody Wanted, 1954,*" The Adoption History Process, updated February 24, 2012, https://pages.uoregon.edu/adoption/topics/familynobodywanted.htm.

193. Daniel C. Dennett, "The Origin of Selves," *Cogito* 3: 163–73, accessed January 18, 2020, https://ase.tufts.edu/cogstud/dennett/papers/originss.htm.

194. Mark W. Westmoreland, "Interruptions: Derrida and Hospitality," *Kritike* 2, no. 1 (June 2008): 1–10, http://www.kritike.org/journal/issue_3/westmoreland_june2008.pdf.

About the Author

Susan Carey relocated to Hartford, Connecticut, eager to embrace city living and a vibrant multicultural community. She explored its neighborhoods on foot, absorbing their history, cuisine, and music. But it was at her church's weekly community supper where she came to know her neighbors. She is a life-long Lutheran and from an early age was drawn to social justice.

Made in United States
North Haven, CT
11 August 2024

55943723R00161